TIME'S FOOL

Glyn Maxwell was born in 1962 in Hertfordshire. He studied
English at Oxford and poetry at Boston University. Among the
honours he has received are the Somerset Maugham Prize,
the E. M. Forster Prize, which he was awarded in 1997 by the
American Academy of Arts and Letters. Maxwell now lives with
his wife and their daughter in New York City.

Poetry by Glyn Maxwell

GLYN MAXWELL

Time's Fool

A Tale in Verse

PICADOR

First published 2000 by Houghton Mifflin Company
First published in Great Britain 2001 by Picador
an imprint of Pan Macmillan Ltd
Pan Macmillan, 20 New Wharf Road, London N1 9RR
Basingstoke and Oxford
Associated companies throughout the world
www.panmacmillan.com

ISBN 0 330 48544 X

A CIP catalogue record for this book is available
from the British Library.

Phototypeset by Intype London Ltd
Printed and bound in Great Britain by
Mackays of Chatham plc, Chatham, Kent

for Geraldine

and

for Alfreda

'Jüngster Tag!
Wann brichst du an in meine Nacht?'
WAGNER, *Der Fliegende Hollander*

'To speak is to be forever on the road.'
MANDELSTAM

Chapters

Time's Fool

1 *The Chance in Hell*

CHRISTMAS EVE, 1984. Edmund Lea has ridden the same Ghost Train for fourteen years and believes he is in Hell. When the Train stops in the middle of nowhere, he discovers in the next carriage a Poet, whom he takes for a Redeeming Angel. He tells the Poet how seven years earlier, the Train arrived back at his home town, Hartisle, on Christmas Eve 1977 . . .

He had not aged, but the world had not waited. Only Clare, the girl he loved, recognized him, but she was now a wife and mother. His family were not at home. A ferocious blizzard drove him back to the station, where a 12-year-old boy and his little sister accompanied him on to a train. When he woke next day he was alone again, in endless fields . . .

I

When the train stopped I started and woke up.
Was nowhere like before, no change in that.
Nothing new in trundling to a stop

where nothing seemed to call for one. The light
was winter afternoon, with 'afternoon'
a term for darkness. In the cold and wet

were trees beside the line, grey evergreen
unknown by name. And not a soul to hail,
I said again and with a smile so thin

it died before its life. And not a soul,
I called. The sky was murk, its memory
of sunshine like my memory of school,

of sunshine in the morning. Next to me
my hands were inching off the dirty felt
towards each other, meeting gingerly,

lovers twining, brothers known and held,
then strangers upright like the poor in prayer.
My eyelids met in secret, my eyes filled

with vision, then reopened on nowhere.
I craned against the glass to see ahead
and did see lights along the way so far,

but into nothing known, and I sat forward,
hands set on my knees, and, weighed down
with swallowing, I scanned them. What I said

when I was ready I had voiced alone
so many times. I said: 'This is the day
of freedom. If the day will prove me wrong

the day will never come and I'm away
forever.' This I said, these were the words
I had. I said my name was Edmund Lea,

to stitch a little wing on my few words
so they could fly. Then I was on my feet,
glancing out again at the rainy woods

and the rain beyond the window scribbling it.
I made my way to the Men's. An hour had come
I'd waited for like an island for a boat

that never comes, like a boatman for a home
he doesn't have, and where did I have to be?
– I giggled as I wiped – in the white room.

'The day will never come and I'm away,'
I called into the flush, 'for all of Time.
I hope I'm home. My name is Edmund Lea,

I stand before you every day the same,
I stand before the emptiness, I lean,
I kneel to it, I beg to be brought home.'

I curled into a fold of prayer, my frame
I curled into that kind of form. The lights
came on along the carriage one by one

as if to bid me to regain my wits,
and I rose and shuffled back in a dull shame
at my poor prayer towards the numbered seats.

And there he was, there's where I found him,
slouched across two places, a young man
and fast asleep or so it – oddly – seemed,

so suddenly he'd come. I hadn't seen,
I calculated, any soul at all
in sixteen days, since from the slowing train

I saw one man with buckets by a well.
No one I ever saw again, and no one
ever on this train. It was not the Hell

you know about. No one seen again,
no one in here, and no one speaking this,
the English language. This was not a tongue

they spoke in Hell. Theirs was a gibberish
devoid of rhyme or reason. But this one,
perhaps a student, in his early twenties,

appeared here when we stopped a while in rain.
And his empty book fell open as he snored,
and the pages leafed themselves until they came

decisively to a page that bore the word
Poems, bore the English word for poems,
Poems, and I weakened then and cried.

I didn't even wake him with these moans
of bliss. They were the train, perhaps he thought,
grilling itself for stopping here. My hands

were shuddering to the page to be a part
of English, of these *Poems*, though I could see
he'd written nothing in it, or not yet—

the devils in me told me in my glee
Blow me, it's all coincidence, and Poems
means in his world 'Help!' or 'Edmund Lea,

*I've come to nail a lid on all your dreams
of seeing home again!'* And then my fingers
reached the page and stuck there like names.

This woke him, and his book fell down between us.
He picked it up and sat up opposite,
still waking up, and held it to him, precious

it seemed for something blank. Oh, I doubted
it meant to him a mite of what it meant
to me to happen on one English word.

I wondered how to let him know. I sent
a wave of this his way but he just stared,
his volume held like something lost and found

and me held in his sight like one who'd dared.
The window was now mirror, now the lamps
had brought the day inside; outside the world

was frozen rain and mist, and a brief glimpse
of gathered lights, green lights, a string of green
a necklace for my mirror image. Dreams,

they were to me: to see through real rain
real points of light at last. Nothing I'd seen
for years was lit by human hand. 'O man,'

so my reflection whispered: 'Us, between
us two we might, we might – begin to talk,
between ourselves, in English, on this train,

perhaps?' His image threw me such a look
I had to turn to see him in real life.
Surprise had drained away and he could speak:

'Getting a little shut-eye. I get off
at the next, therefore we've stopped. If I don't sleep
I'm going to scream, you see.' It seemed enough

to him, he took his coat and bunched it up
to make a pillow. 'What is, may I say,'
I ventured, 'this, in English, this stop?'

I heard him breathe in secret 'Go away,'
so keen was I to hear. Not knowing that,
he growled, 'It's not one, is it? It's nowhere.'

'Is it Hartisle?' I asked him. 'Is it what?'
'Is it Hartisle?' I said, the beloved name
foundering in the ocean like a rowboat,

'it's my home town,' which sank it all the same,
'I'm headed there.' 'It better not be, mate,'
my friend the Poet said, 'or it ain't my train.

It better be bloody Welwyn. Isn't it?'
He stood and peered along. He wasn't sure.
But I was trembling with the weight of what

I knew had come. 'It's Hartisle, I'm here,'
I couldn't help but say, 'I'm going home . . .'
'This is a joke,' he said. 'That extra beer,

that extra beer, always the frigging same.
Wrong frigging platform at Kings sodding Cross
and no one but one's bleeding self to blame,

if you'll excuse my phrasing. I don't need this
on Christmas bloody Eve.' 'Yes, Christmas Eve!'
I cried out, 'and I'm home!' 'It bloody is,'

the Poet confirmed, 'and, would you believe,
I'm on my way to Cambridge with a guy
who wants a chat.' 'No, I'll be getting off

at Hartisle,' I was so sweet to say, 'that's my,
my native town, my stop, and it comes soon.
I know it's next.' 'Well, double-cream hooray,'

he went, 'here's to a well-spent afternoon.
Should have been Christmas shopping. Bugger that,'
he started to search his pockets: 'You're going home,

I'm going nowhere, got no cigarettes,
nothing to drink, no girlfriend, but hey,
Merry Christmas, native, light the lights,

feed the world, for this day is the day
of all days I have opted for a ride
into the Great Unknown. I've flown away

along the other line into the cloud
that waits for us on Platform Nine, that haunts
la bière encore. So it's so long, old world,

good afternoon, alternative existence . . .'
He found a broken cigarette, a lighter
he shook aflame. He smoked for a few moments,

looking down. 'Will you have a pint of bitter?'
I heard him ask himself, 'yes, thank you, man,'
he answered. 'Life would certainly get better

if I spent the afternoon on the slow train
to Neverland in lieu of Christmas shopping,
or seeing friends, who needs them? No one, Glen,'

he soothed himself. 'Where have we fucking stopped?'
he shouted at me: 'Why, by the way, is no one
on this train? Is it all boarded up,

the dark side of mid-Herts? Is it not open?
Has it closed down? Where are we?' He was unwell,
I saw, with his empty book, he was angry, Glen.

If I could have avoided what I had to tell
I gladly would have, but my day had dawned,
my voice had meaning: 'Look. We are in Hell.'

So my reflection said. I saw beyond
his shoulder the dark wind and the wild trees
waving to the sky, and a grey wound

of sky was where the darkness was least,
an opening or a closing where a hole
was yellow almost with a feel of west,

while the train groaned beneath us on the rail
and didn't go. His smoke had crossed the floor,
and voyaged through my hands. I'd been in Hell

for fourteen years. I rose to meet his stare
and held it, speaking: 'This day, I believe,
I shall be briefly freed, because this hour

I've recognised my language, in yourself.
I've counted to this day and now it's come.
For I was damned to this on Christmas Eve

and don't know why, how long, or in whose name.'
Glen turned his stare unchanging to the glass,
then turned it down. He sat there for a time,

then suddenly relaxed and with a voice
from somewhere low and sad he asked my name.
 – 'I'm all ears, Edmund Lea. Don't have much choice,

tonight in Hades, do I? Take your time,
this train's not one for forward motion, plainly,
and look, I have a thoroughly empty volume

low on verse and yearning for a story.'
He opened up his book and dug around
his pockets, muttering foully for a biro

until I gave him mine: 'It's new, my friend,
it never empties.' 'Hell as office work,'
he cackled, 'always knew it, note that down . . .

fact. So, Edmund, an . . . original bloke,
met on the wrong train, twenty-fourth December
1984, check almanac

for signs of this. Avoid same in future.
Only joking, Edmund. At . . . say four.
Weather foul. Hardly an *aide-memoire* . . .

So, let's start. How long have you been aware
of this unfortunate circumstance?' The Poet
sat there grinning with his matted hair,

his army coat, his boots. His eyes were red
from sleeping or not sleeping, and his skin
was pale as paper. Everything he said

amused him, he so wanted to begin,
to take his mind off missing out on home,
so I tried to tell it properly, for Glen,

who wanted it for what? For some poem
he may or may not write. As I began
I prayed with my poor hands that by the time

he wrote it I'd be free, and a grown man,
restored to home, with Clare, in my home town,
Hartisle, and the two of us alone.

'Talk me through it, Edmund,' said Glen,
'it's all I've got for Christmas.' Open wide,
his book was empty and the whitest thing

we had. The rain was getting worse outside,
as if the light could fight it, and had tried.

II

'You and your book are the only things this scene
has added to a scene I'll trace around,
a scene of seven years ago, that's seven

dead, I mean, spot on. I have a mind
to keep them in, the days, a number's fixed
politely in its seat until the end

arrives, and then aloud I count the next
and out it goes. Thirty days hath April,
I'm well aware, I count leap years. My facts

are crisp as yours, I swotted in that school.
I'm not insane but expelled, went elsewhere,
Glen, I was taken elsewhere. What you might call

the dark side of our county, in care,
if of a distant sort. I've found you, Glen,
this afternoon in 1984,

but picture me in 1977,
when I was twenty-four. Now I'm thirty-one.
I take you to be less – what do you mean

I look like I'm at school, do I look so young?
It's living a missing life. We all live one,
really, but by evening you belong,

no? When the day goes dark and the lights go on,
no? TV to watch, your mum and dad
dressed to go out, so you ring and arrange a plan

for later, LP covers on the bed,
a girl's relived remark. Mum calling you
down for a noisy tea. There are times ahead,

good times, dull times, but a night to get to
anyway. And it's never quiet, I bet,
till morning, Glen. Morning I never come to,

am never listed present. My days start
by dying, though they take as long as yours.
My light is always leaving, always part

of what it was. Where was I? Seven years.
Fourteen years, but that's so long ago
it's down a well. Fourteen of your years

makes you a child, and me? Well, I don't know.
A thing did happen that I don't see yet.
It lives forgotten, some experience so

unwilling to come forth it's like a root,
but this proliferating deadly plant
you may shake by the leaf. For it is not

like other forms of life. Now is the present,
Glen, unwrap it, see? Now when I try it,
when Edmund tears the wrapping with intent,

there's nothing there but paper, and there's not,
by tomorrow, even that. Are we moving?
Not yet. I know its baritone, its note,

my train, and it said *Listen*, then said nothing.
I think it runs on silence, is my new
faith about it. That would mean it's stopping

to hear me out, like you! Oh, I do know
you never meant to, merely took a walk
across a platform in a bitter glow

one Christmas Eve and now you're in the dark.
Believe it if you like. It's hard for me
to term it accident that one who speaks

my language sits at last this suddenly
beside me and on Christmas Eve, his book
open to the sky! Look at that sky,

it's moving now. It rested for a look
inside our little lighted window crack.
Full throttle now to Hell's profoundest nook

to say *He's still alive and he's on track*,
his day has come ... Your eyes too are down there,
I see by redness and a peckish look,

and how they have to either shut or stare,
neither bringing peace. You will deny
everything. You will say you were not here,

but gently, I can see, not in a lie,
believing what you think. For seven years
I travelled on the train, until a day

when suddenly the window turned to this,
the world I know: I spoke as if alive,
as if my words could matter in the ears

of anyone. This place is Chadwick Grove,
the outskirts of, though that's a place that's all
outskirt. No one ever says what of.

You'll see a hill come up. Behind the hill
some lights I think are Stortwood, or, who knows,
Chadwick proper. Then there'll come a tunnel

we used to say was haunted with the souls
of a crash in 1930. You'll excuse me
if I don't believe this any more. Those tales

are little winding relics. Any story
ending is a story. You look lost,
Glen, but I think you said it all already:

you're on the other line now. Having missed
the line you know too well to know, you ride
for the first time a line you never missed.

For me, your entire life is a dark side.
Soon the tunnel, home in a bare mile.
I'll know the names of streets by then, I'm afraid,

and tire you like a tour-guide. Hartisle,
gem of the east-south-east, city of dreams?
Dump of them, then. Home once in a while.

I left it though, that home, the other homes.
Home is the ride, Glen, on the scarlet train
with the black roof – but this description seems

to trouble you. You double-check, my friend,
you're on the ride, just visiting in Hell.
I had as short a visit, though, in Heaven

the year this all began. Or so I feel
when I can feel at all. You'd call it Heaven
to think alike and hold hands with a girl,

the name of Clare, like me that Christmas Eve . . .
Not knowing her's no reason to say no,
Glen, or not seeing her to disbelieve,

for you could see her in a mile or so
and murmur at the sight – but who can help
the laughter when it's at the throat? I know

I'm mad in your eyes, but you think we've stopped
for something? In my own eyes you are cracked
to smile and think this randomly dreamed up.

Whatever caused this, I am its effect.
I ride a train in Hell. Hear me. The cause
is a wall with no door, let alone a lock,

a wall. First seven of the fourteen years
I did decide my mind had gone, this train
a loop I sickened with between the ears,

the sky mere mottled surface of the brain,
and death a long-regarded destination.
For seven years I waited for the sun

once to climb the sky, for its direction
once to be reversed; for seven years
it sank towards the dark, by that same suction

tugging me to sleep. For seven years
I looked to see the shape of hereabouts
created in the window; seven years

of various sights invariably remote,
or altered only in my terms for them.
You can't know what it is to see the sight

that is about to pass us. Think of home
denied you for so long! You look out there
towards the window where it ought to come,

you see the looming country: this is where
joy struck me and I filled with new belief –
that I was free, that what had brought me here

was letting me go back. I filled with love
for what a monstrous mercy! I was sure
the snowy sky (which was a frosted mauve

that afternoon, and not this dirty war
of water with the night) was my own eye
stopped and clouded in a restful corner

of some brain hospital, checked with a sigh
by nurses, or my mother or my father
dropping by the ward with presents. Oh I

ticked away in there, I was no bother.
In the prison of a graph I was a line
of slow recurring hills into forever:

they'd always deck my bed-end with a twine
of tinsel for the season. On I came,
past Stortwood and Tows Hill in a high pain

of ecstasy and plummeting in time.
We soon began to slow, with an immense
weakening of sound. The sign of home

resolved into a word that hurtled once,
illegible, then suddenly went by,
then steadily, then slowly, then it inched

and HARTISLE it conceded with a sigh.
The time was 4.19, and the cold place
utterly unchanged. Into my eye

the people came with bags and bikes – the face
of one I thought I knew in a breath of steam
she made and went. How somehow in this daze

I stepped down from the train to the platform
has not survived in memory. I even –
after seven years' procession in a dream –

I even left the station with not one
glance at what I came from, and by now
the years could not have passed, it was insane!

Seven years? Infection. This was how
the poison in me functioned, in jest,
making me think that way, for I well knew

as I walked to the cold ticket-hall it must
at least be the same Christmas! I was slow,
looking back, I was slow, a man of mist,

to think that way, but think of me, think how
my brain was bursting only to explain,
to beat the weight of years back into hours,

to turn each eerie day on the dry plain
or the marsh lands, blue meadows, every sight
I'd stood in in a desperate dream in vain,

only to reawaken in my seat
with absence passing by – to turn the whole
outrageous horror back into some fit,

some coma! So it flickered with this skill,
insisting I recite: *I've had a vision*
no man has ever had, but I fell ill,

remember, and it's over, and it's heaven
walking by the shop-signs: by the Boots,
the Smiths, Kentucky Fried and is it Craven's?

Yes, Jemima's Flowershop, and the seats
we lay on when they wouldn't let us in
at George's or the Oak, those dizzy nights

with cider in the cold of the still town.
I should have said by now I'd had a sense
of one behind me when I stumbled down

ecstatic to the platform, heard the sounds
of one alongside as I climbed the stairs,
but set them by, so flooded was my mind

with thoughts of seeing home again, and Clare.
But now as I went out into the brace
and chill of twilight I was well aware

of two, not one, behind me. Hooded boys,
I thought at first, but seeing the smaller child
squat to check some broken thing up close,

I saw she was a girl. In my lost world
nobody rode the train with me. I stared,
and saw them look and move away. I felt

clearly I'd mistaken what I'd heard,
but they stayed in my mind and, as you'll learn,
they stayed in more than that. Now by the broad

High Street I sat down. I said, "So ends
the nightmare." And you smile, but it's the smile
we mortal creatures crack against the wind

that ages us, it hooks back that muscle,
shows the teeth like headstones in a field,
and you've a gap, I notice. You could whistle.

You may as well. For sounding what I felt,
no language is enough. Cold Christmas Eve
in a town I thought I knew, in a whole world

where I belonged, I burned to disbelieve
that seven years had really passed, that I
had truly lost my mind. And I felt saved,

now I remember, though I couldn't cry.
No, I felt saved, and damned if I knew why.'

III

'No, *I* don't think you're nuts,' the Poet sighed,
doodling a pyramid on a half page,
'but then if I thought you were, and well I might,

I suppose I wouldn't say so, man. A sage
is what you are, who knows, a seer of stuff.
Stuffed to the brim with sage and onion. Which

reminds me, *I've* gone missing from *my* life.
No points for guessing what's in Santa's sack
tonight. *Hey Glen, you rip that wrapping off*

and join the happy throng. Well? Tick-tock.
Anything? Not this year, Mum, I'm afraid.
Best wishes, praise the Lord and pass the turkey,

Dad. No, Edmund, you're the Paxo Kid.
You want to meet real lunatics, you come
and doss with me at Oxford.' 'You're at Oxford?'

I wondered, and he shrugged, 'I guess I am,
you know, for my . . . my sins.' And he stared out
till his image caught his eye and grinned at him.

'So go on,' now he said to it, 'about
this town. You're telling me you couldn't tell
those seven years had passed? Oh I've no doubt

they passed, Edmund, sure, that's swallowed whole,
I've seen 'em do it – hell, I've been fifteen,
and eight, I've been newborn, and in this veiled

waiting room being told to fill this in,
block capitals . . . but you're telling me you left,
or vanished in a puff of smoke in, when,

1970, "All You Need Is Love"
presumably, then you come back and it's what,
Pretty Vacant? And that's not enough

to tell you you've been gone a while? No shit.'
I can't have heard that right, as to this day
I've never understood a word of it,

but that's what the Poet said. Then he looked away
and told his image, 'Santa Claus, old mate,
I know I've been no good, but if I may,

I'd like to make a lone request tonight,
perhaps a bed for Edmund and a bowl
of any soup he likes. For me? Forget it,

just dump me here an hour on Dingbat Hill
and call it quits.' I let a silence in,
to nudge his stupor and impose its will,

which soon it did, enveloping the man
until he turned the page and with a nod
was ready to hear more. So we began.

'It was as if a raindrop with a thud
had landed in my mind, but looking up
my eyes would see blue sky without a cloud!

My brain was adamant, would not accept
a sign that what I'd felt, the seven years,
had truly passed. I tottered as I stopped

beside the Monument and peered ahead.
It seemed a street I'd never seen before
was strung with patterned lights. There was a crowd

of carol singers, children standing there,
heads tilted upward for the sky was weird,
a frozen green and glistening the air.

So I shied away along a lane that cleared
ahead towards a warm beloved glow,
the Oak, at long last! Then those kids appeared.

This time the boy came up, "You gonna go,
Superspy?" while his sister, with her limbs
curled around him started singing, "Oh,

Little Tom of Bethlehem . . ." My own arms
waded me towards the Oak, alive
to a freezing smell of town I'd smelt in dreams

till now, and to these citizens, their love
desired of them and given, and the snow
they all had hoped for imminent above!

So hard I tried I could believe by now
a drug had done this, and my ride was that,
a trip, a thing I'd taken God knew how,

and I'd recover. All I found so odd
would be explained by that, all that was new
would form into familiar, to beloved,

given time. I steadied, and the blue/
brown iron pub-sign of the Oak I made
my only focus in a mist of view.

If it existed something else had stayed,
apart from me, to greet me. We were poles
to throw a line between, or trees with shade

to shelter in a while whatever falls.
Still that boy kept up, and the singing elf,
debating like two allocated fools

for a king gone very wrong, and fooled enough.
I had to lose them. He was describing times
he'd "got himself pissed up on Scots and stuff!"

and seeing I didn't turn he called me names,
his heroes, "Superspy! Mr James Bond,
or are you Starsky?" throwing out his arms

as if for mercy. She, further behind,
was slowing down her carol to find words,
then stopped and stamped in vain until he turned,

went back towards her. By extended strides
I made a space between us, glancing back
only the once to see them, two red hoods

conferring by a lamppost. By the Oak
I found myself intruding in a ring
of carol singers, lanterns on sticks,

facing a balding man and his tall tin
he shook and shook, they all shook them, so I
cold-shouldered through the throng and made it in.

This is the place and not the time, was my
immediate thought. The place was hot and full
as every Christmas Eve, or the last three,

the three I'd come to when the gang at school
had gathered there. And now I couldn't move
for lads. The music was unbearable,

brute, distorted, even shouted stuff –
it sounded like some joke, but no one laughed
or cried. Faces were pale and new and rough,

came at you quicker, someone's head was shaved.
A big lad in a cap was Michael Nelson,
I suddenly decided, as he moved

and stared a sec – but I was reforgotten,
to my relief; he hated me, and once
he'd jabbed me in the gut, for no good reason

ever mentioned. I achieved a glimpse
of girls in a little group beyond the darts,
scheming in the glow of the green lamps

I'd never noticed either. Now my path
had reached the ocean. This was the right place
but could not be that Christmas. Now my breath

was rope above a chasm. I felt close
to something that had never known an end,
and yet I thought a blink of my blown eyes

would change the picture back, would set a friend
for every stranger. Every blink was worse,
like pages turning blindly in the wind

without a reader to an unmarked place.
To shut my eyes was to begin to spin,
or run the risk of waking in the space

I always woke in, the unending train.
There was nothing but to gain the ledge and think.
And so I pressed through everything, my brain

lifted high and low like a filled drink
I balanced through the multitude with care.
I saw to my surprise a gap, a chink

between the corner and the closest chair
the girls were using, so I deep-inhaled
as if about to dive, and landed there.

Lamps, as they come on in the long cold
of afternoon – the limited pink light
that dies to amber – dotted my new world

with certain faces I was sure about:
Straton at the jukebox, I could swear,
but his hair cropped; beside the bolted exit

Dodge Mendis, from the band, and Burke, a pair
you'd always see, though Burke had a thin beard
and had gained weight. Dodge had spiky hair

and chains, but he was fatter too. The third
was Moon, and there he was, the Shimmer, tall,
he held a beer-tray high above the crowd

and edged towards them. The maroon-haired girl
who reached the bar and turned was Janet Bow,
who signalled with her hands then gave a yell

towards the girls close by. One in a low
sarcastic tone as if to no one else
said something, and they laughed but Janet Bow

up at the bar was staring in her purse.
The more I watched them there the more I knew:
my eyes reclaiming anyone there was,

and even some so alien and new
given a moment turned familiar
and more, not less, appalling, for I saw

time was askew. I felt I knew how far.
As immaterial to any then
as any stranger, so I shuddered there,

Glen: the way your hand has got that pen
my mind clung on to memory, for now
the ages I'd expected to regain

were gone for real, and this unyielding show
was life itself. "Now there's a man with hair,"
I heard a girl say mildly from below

my standpoint, as if Clare and it was Clare,
it *was* her, by the sad expression her,
by the attention her, just sitting there,

like I'd been gone a moment, for a beer,
and for a second what in this was strange?
That I should reach the Oak and find her here,

and we could meet, resuming without change?
But then I blinked and let the nightmare back,
in other voices and an outer range

of lads somebody'd nudged to have a look,
till only Clare of all of them was still,
her hair swept up unclasping at her neck,

her eyes all dark about with crayon, pale
her throat where now she wore a studded collar,
pink the style of lips, in a gloss style.

She took a drink of someone else's lager,
then rose away from them. She took her cig,
her nearly empty pack, her folded leather

coat I'd never seen her in, her bag,
and came towards me like she had no choice
for now. They watched her leaving, she was mad,

they knew she was, they didn't mind. The noise
was rushing back like water. She reached me,
she set her things below, and in a voice

as close to me as you said, "Edmund Lea?
You're playing him. Or else you're one of two.
Either way, you're here. And obviously

you may be no one, which you're welcome to,
but that may mean the gist of what I say
will tend to pass you by." Her eyes were blue,

they held me in my breath. "You've been away
like nobody. Nobody leaves forever.
They did look everywhere, you know. That day

I saw your father when they tried the river.
He said he used to fish there. But it's years
since anyone particularly wondered

where you doggy-paddled to. Because
we had to press on with – civilization.
I don't think you went anywhere. Or the place

you went was pretty kind to your complexion,
chick. I'm not so sure about the look,
it's in the realm of naff. So it wasn't London,

I take it, that you conquered? Way back
when you were someone we were thinking of,
in olden times, I'd say you were in the nick

for something druggy. Were you? Peace and love
is out as out gets." "But I lost my way,
Clare, I was let go, you won't believe

the price I've paid." "For what?" She looked away.
"Me?" she mouthed, then said: "You used to have,
in olden times, for me . . . *the price you pay* . . .

That's very funny. Fuck it, I can't breathe,
Mister Lea. It's boiling here. Let's leave." '

IV

'Four o'clock,' explained the Poet. 'Hmm.'
He'd caught me catching him in a quick look
at what the time was; now it had to seem

important to him. 'Well, it's really dark,'
he noted, 'and in real life right now
I'd be beside the fire with a gin and coke

and snipping the wrapping paper for – or no,
I tell a lie, I'd be chopping carrots first,
being the useful offspring. Anyhow,

my Christmas shopping would be *feat accomplished*
and we'd be hanging lights.' 'If it's gone four,'
I said, in case he hadn't thought, 'we're almost

home.' '*You're* almost home. I'm in thin air,'
Glen muttered down the cap of my fountain pen:
'Your story's going to end exactly where

you're going to snog the chick, exactly when
you're at it in a snowdrift. Big shame.
I could have done with just a pinch of porn

to get me through this pause in real time.
Or not a pause, a dry. Like God has dried,
it's gone.' I smiled and went along with him,

but he told me anyway: 'Like we've each a part
to play in what is *in itself a play*,
you following? It's complex, and His part

has many lines. One day there comes a day
He dries, and then we wait. It's embarrassing,
stuck on stage. We're not allowed to say

the speech He should have. Finally from the wings
you hear a hiss, and on we go.' The train
then hissed below but he didn't link those things,

and only said: 'You could be right there, man,
sounds like we're moving on. So what went down?
It is your story, isn't it, make a plan,

get her into the bushes, it's your town.'
I understood again with a mild jolt
my lodging here in Hell was to Glen a yarn,

a story, and of course it was. His world
rode on the other line, he was in the mist
where we were now, he was scowling in the cold

to stave it off. 'Come on, spit out the rest,
Ed, this story's got to do the work
of all my Christmas presents, else I'm lost.

Years to come, my family'll look back
at Christmas '84, forgetting every
gift they got, till all they'll recollect

is Glen's extraordinary fireside story . . .
Where'd you hear that, Glen? they'll wonder. *Oh,
I heard it from the Flying Scotsman.* Surely

you've heard of the Flying Scotsman, Edmund?' 'No,
don't think I have.' 'Really? That's a bind.
Forget it, shut me up. So where'd you go,

let me guess, high-tailed it to the Land
That Time Forgot? I'm listening. Your *lurve*,
let me guess – *I still want to be friends*,

that's the one they drop on me. Now I have
eighty female friends, and there's not one
I need in that capacity. Enough,

shoot me, tell the tale.' He found his pen,
reopened his big book on another blank,
licked his lips, and posed as *ready when*.

'Clare said: "It's me or you who needs a drink,
but either way it's desperate." The George
was where it always was, beside a bank

I could have sworn was Lloyds, and did so. "Language,"
she went. The place was just as dark and packed
but our lot never came except at lunch

and nobody would know us. You'd expect
the questions to have come in a cascade
in there, but it was louder still and dark,

and I was hanging on like the half-dead
to a lifeline while a marsh as thick as pitch
was dragging me below. Facing the crowd

around the door she sighed and struck a match,
lit up a cig and looked at me. "No chance,"
she blew the smoke, "this Christmas Eve's a bitch,

frankly, Mister Lea, unless you *want*
to waste an hour waiting, while some smartarse
wonders who on earth you are. I don't.

Want to or wonder. I get gold stars,
the only one who picked you out. Let's split,
or we don't get a drink. We'll go to yours."

Yours. It took all Mallow Street to get it,
yours, I was going home. *Mine* was a place
God knows I yearned to see, you can believe it,

Glen, you're missing yours. But seven years
I'd gone, that's something more. My plans had been
to reach the Oak and get my bearings first,

to find out what had happened here, to glean
how much was lost and how much left for me.
But now I knew what had seemed gone was gone,

and only Clare had bobbed above the sea
to catch a breath and know me by my name.
"So is it only us you never see

in your new world?" she chatted as we came
shivering down Wheaton Hill, not far,
"or do you treat your family just the same?

We used to talk of sightings, once a year
somebody was convinced, but we got tired.
And if you didn't care, we didn't care.

And when I said I heard he lived in Ireland,
Cheryl said, *Who did?* And you were gone
entirely. All that time we thought you'd tried

to make us think of you. We were that wrong.
You really went like nobody does, Lea.
Love of my life, or not, or not for long."

We reached the lane and now came memories
of 1970, Christmas in the fog . . .
She'd placed in a back pocket of her jeans

a map I drew, and in her low-slung bag
a sweater that she'd needed and I lent her
once in Private Study, when the dark

made all the classrooms festive. That December
a desk alongside was the one she picked.
Then term was ending and the sound of her

grew sharp inside and giddying like luck . . .
Glen, I haven't told you that I write,
or that I wrote a poem on the back

of the little map she'd needed and I made,
forgetting that the writing there was mine,
my poem, my first poem though indeed

my last, and lost. *When she was seventeen*,
my brain was bleating in its agony,
in the old days. We were together, Glen,

on Christmas Eve of 1970
when something fell between us, and I swear
it's lost to me. Sometimes at night I see

the extra figure drawing up his chair
to join us in the pub, but not his face,
and someone lights his cigarette, not Clare,

though she arrives ... then seven years ... My house,
brick-cold, unaltered as a home in dream,
was garlanded with little lights. The place

was quiet, we could hear the fizz and hum
of bulbs against a window pane. In there
a little fir stood colouring the room.

I felt for them, and knew. "Nobody's here."
"Are they not? It is still yours then, do you know?
I mean, don't tell me you've got no idea.

It may be ultra-cool to simply go,
but seems to me you didn't give a damn."
"Something, something, seven years ago,"

I slowly started, "Clare, I have been gone
for seven years, from this, from everything,
and I can't tell you why." She let her tongue

around her lips. "Let's knock, and see who's in.
Plenty of time to sober up." The door
was unfamiliar, though the doorbell-ring

did strike me like light coming off a star,
and something made me say, "Pick up the mat,"
for there she found a key I could have put there

yesterday. She tried it and it fit.
Then I was in a hall and in a room,
swaying and with a choice of where to sit,

so I sat down and told her I was *home*.
Then there's a hollow hour or so I swear
the word itself created, as if time

could lose itself in *home*, quite disappear,
because the well went infinitely down.
But I still see us slouching on a stair,

her gloved hand and my cold hand somehow
together and our eyes accustoming,
and watching from the landing window now

the snow at last illimitably falling
over the garden. I recall three rooms:
my parents' at the end of the long landing,

thick-carpeted and tidy just the same,
and Caroline's was cold, she must have gone.
Twenty-six she'd be, and by that time

my guess was she was married to that man
whose name escapes me. Martin. In the gloom
we saw two beds. "They're twin, though, no fun,"

Clare Kendall said to me from in a dream,
and led me to a third alternative,
where they had made a study of my room.

The pun was hers, not mine. "It's Christmas Eve,"
she said: "Whatever ghastliness there was,
guess what, it's time to fuck it and forgive,

and wake up in the morning in your house,
surprise them like the Son, eh? And meantime . . ."
and then Clare kissed my lips and said, "A ghost,

you are, you know, and gone for too much time,
too much time to know me now." I breathed:
"Gone? My mind was gone, now it's come home,

and so have I now. Clare . . ." Her face was bathed
in the pale violet light of the lawn below,
and I was reaching to the ending craved

eternally, so near – "Because you'd know,"
she dipped aside to say, "if you'd not gone,
you'd know if you'd not gone, that I'm, it's so

so crazy, Ed, I'm married, you know, grown,
responsible. In fact I married Nick,
Nick Straton? We had holy union,"

she chuckled to herself, "me and that bloke,
and we still have it, if you call it that,
on the odd Sunday. Press on if you like,

it's quits." I did, a second time and tight,
our tongues attaching and a deeper third,
a twisting into her, a loving fight,

then a time held for ages. I grew hard
and dazzled when my eyes were closed, my nails
descending down her leather coat towards

its hem, then smoothness endless to the frills
of skirt and a short drop to a woollen thigh.
"Also, my ghost, we had a little girl,

Rachel Aretha Rose. And *she* is why
you can't assume you get your wicked way.
Ghost has to get me back at once, or I

myself will be a phantom, courtesy
of my life-affirming husband. Mister Lea,
phone me." "But – tomorrow?" "Boxing Day,

you pagan!" and she talked about her baby,
as if about a film she'd gone to watch
and loved and went again and now went daily,

knew it all, which didn't matter, which
had made it better still. We were in the hall,
then she was crying. We were on the porch,

I told her I was genuinely ill,
as I was sure I was. By the front gate
the snow was thick and squeaked at each footfall

and more was coming, high in the orange light
of street lamps, higher still from the pale brown
brimming sky, and a small snowball fight

we had, and now it snowed as if the town
were soon to be alone. I turned to see
my house step out of sight, and we pressed on,

wincing forward. I was witlessly
planning our life together. Think of me.'

V

The Poet made his hands like empty hands,
like *Why did nothing happen?* but I knew
he thought I was creating these events

for a first time, could do what I wished to.
He would have had her home in bed, his eyes
suggested. 'So she loved you and left you,

is what you're building up to, wild surmise
and major disappointment.' 'That's a term
for what I felt,' I nodded, 'you could use.

Straton's place was actually Clare's home.
I tried to stop her once for a goodnight kiss,
Glen, but now the snow was drifting down

in silence and it heaped its silences
around us as it fell and filled the air.
A mother and a wife were what she was,

the snowfall stuttered as we got to there,
and with the briefest wave at me went Clare
in a thick stumble to a floodlit door.

It opened on her and a second figure
shutting it. Not true her silhouette
had motioned to me, no. I was nowhere.

I thought I knew my way, though. Don't forget
I am a native of it, Glen, but Time
had redeveloped everything, and sprayed

the snow to make it alien. My home
was in a radius of Clare's, but now
the spokes of that had spun, the ways become

unknowable, signs buried in the snow.
I'd stood so long I left behind a ditch,
then chose one of two streets I didn't know.

All streets led slower to the question *Which?*
at every junction. There was no landmark,
no light to look for, there was nothing much

but snow unceasing, plus the muffled creaks
of footsteps made by one afraid to turn,
afraid to find the snow behind him blank,

unprinted. Far away I saw a form
of someone striding at the road's lit end,
but out of earshot, and I couldn't run

with snow knee-high, thigh-high. Somebody's hand
drew curtains at a window, and a face
appeared and disappeared, leaving a candle.

I told myself *There's not a single house
that would not take you in in this extreme*,
but I was set by hook or crook for *yours*,

and hook or crook for waking in my room,
a miracle, a prodigal, this day
of all days! Like the Son, she'd said, he's home,

by hook or crook! I grimaced, let it be,
hook or crook, and hook or crook was all
the action of my breath, till finally

I followed nothing but my own footfall.
I saw them by the stalk of a thin tree,
waiting. They were recognisable

only by a football scarf the boy
had wrapped around his wrist. In the wild light
his team was pink and purple. Close by

they'd made a kind of snowman. "It's Snow White,"
he said, the little boy, as I came in range,
"without no face. The Witch is who done that."

"*Poor* Snow White," I said, "but she can change,
look." And I thought I'd find a scrap to make
a face for her but no. "I made an angel,"

a tiny voice announced to me, "and look,
it's gone." "She dunno why," her brother told me
man-to-man, "She reckons iss magic!"

"Don't," she said, "I said it's missle-tree."
They didn't live there, Glen, it took some time
to learn. In my dazed state I could still see

the two were lost. I mentioned I first met them
that evening on the steps at Hartisle station,
or earlier; had I seen them on the platform,

even on the train? I asked the question,
expecting little back: "Did you arrive
like me, in the red train?" "He's on a mission,

Pelly," said the boy, "he's got a knife
to get him out of stuff." "Are you two cold?
You must be cold." "Too cold? I'm cold enough,

I don't need no more cold. She might be cold,
but I'm not cold, me. You're a murderer."
I looked at him a moment. "Like, you're old,"

he added, "and I know you got your orders,
with fighting like the Evil an' all,
but that don't make you *not* a murderer. Murder's

sometimes all you got. You're professional,
Mr Bond. What that means is he's paid,
Pell, he's Double-O-Seven, free to kill

sometimes, gotta say you're on his side,
Pell. *I'm* on your side." "I'm very pleased,"
I told him, "glad to have you, but I'm afraid

you're on the side of somebody who's lost.
You know Laburnum Lane?" "No, we don't know
nothing these days," and his little sister

pounded Snow White back into the snow.
"We're going down the station," said the boy.
"Got a train to take us, got to go

down Creslet, see our mum." "We went to see
the founting," said the girl. "It goes in colours
what with the water change and all. It's green,

and then it's yellow, and then it's blue, then yellow."
"You *said* yellow," her brother snorted. "It's blue,
then silver." "It ain't silver." "Um, tomorrow,"

I ventured in the argument, "you two,
it's Christmas Day, with presents, and . . . a tree,
right? and holly – where are you walking to?

Where are you trying to get to? Tell me."
"Station," said the boy. "He's Dark Vader,
Pell, he's in disguise." "Can you show me

the way to the railway station?" "That's no bother,
Mr Dark Vader. We was only stopped
cos she was cryin' on about another

bleedin' snowman! Now she smashed it up!"
"I never was," said Pell, "and I'm not Pell,
it's only what you reckon." "Watch your lip,

Pell the Smell, cos he's all free to kill,
Dark Vader, when he's in his Bond disguise.
You never know wiv him, he's professional."

I started walking till to no surprise
they followed me, and walking's not the word:
we stooped into the storm explorer-wise,

it always slanting into us – *absurd*,
it was conceding as it fringed the bone –
and we descended down a shape of road

towards a shape of building. Then, a lone
blackness, sharp in a soft world snow-dimmed,
we saw the cutting of the railway line.

Originating at a distant bend
to south and fading into the far whiteness
north, it glistened in its heated ground,

went through me like an arrow shaft, a minus
everything. And as we passed beyond
the gate and to the platform – MERRY CHRISTMAS

red, live, hissing on the roof – we found
there was a train lit up like it could go:
only one carriage long, and not designed

remotely like my dream-train, but it had no
passengers so far. Pell and her brother
raced ahead and scuffled in the snow

to reach the open door. "You comin', Vader?"
he yelled when he was in. "Oh no, I'm home.
I was only making sure you children had a –

a ride, and now you do. I'm going home."
Though what I really meant was it was time
to find some people, throw myself at them,

plead lunacy, play innocent, play dumb.
The children looked unhappy. In the light
of where they stood I saw for the first time

they were dark kids, brown-skinned. I'd never met
a black kid at our school. There was only Johns,
in the third year. Once by the cricket net

he stared at me. The boy now said, "Oi, Bond,
you gonna 'sterminate us?" Then he pressed
whatever shut the doors: "Too late, THE END,"

he shouted, then was muffled as they closed.
He shouted more, but a wind came up so keen
I had to gasp and grip myself. The doors

reopened. I was looking towards the cabin.
I told the children I would check the times
and crunched along the platform. There was someone

in silhouette; the cab was dark. Three times
I knocked without response. When the wind blew
I doubled up and dug my freezing hands

against my very skin. What I would not do –
go back upon a train – was the only room
available. I gritted the word *No*

as if to salt myself to the platform,
and still the doors would close and open, close
and open, with the children working them.

A gust of wind as if a hail of blows.
Another the next second had me skinned,
then I was skeletal in thinning clothes,

beginning to back away. "No, Mr Bond!"
the girl cried out, "there's enemies!" "He knows,"
the boy insisted, "part of his own plan:

he throws him off the bridge and then he goes,
you know, all dead? The dead man, not Bond.
Bond's okay, he got official orders."

I had to speak and could not, and I turned
in a slow frozen circle to begin
to inch towards the steps. While I could stand

I had to move, while I could move a limb
I had to move away. At the first step
I paused to peer above, into the gloom,

and saw somebody waiting at the top.
I blinked and there he was, when like a claw
thrust under for its prey, with a smart rip

the blizzard took me out into the air
and dragged me to the train. I had no chance,
no pulse, I think I would have died out there,

but it was Hell that shot out its four hands
to help me on. And by the time I murmured
"Saw a face," and took a fearful glance

at the fierce blizzard, we were moving forward,
abandoning my town in the first hours
of Christmas Day. The girl was sleeping. "Vader,"

the boy began, "you comin' back to ours?
Does our mum know that, Vader? Dark Vader.
It's quite okay by me. We're going to hers,

for turkey. That girl Pelly, she's my sister,
and *she* says let's stop here and see the founting.
She means fountain. Not that she ain't clever,

she is, but it's her word for it. And next thing
we dunno where we are!" He said the same,
more or less, again, and then he sang

a line of something: "Chelsea is our name."
Then he was sleeping too. This was the last
hour I could believe myself insane,

or a drug victim, Glen, or that at least
the longest ride was over, though I strained
with all my might to think it. First and best,

that Clare was in my life, would understand
the worst dementias I had suffered. Then,
that home was where I left it, and I found

some solace in imagining again
our decorations on the Christmas pine
in the Lea household. Third, I was their son,

and would amaze them soon. I rode the train,
and seven years of hopes were one last time
sent out across the years. Then I began

to tire, and shook awake, and then the same,
and thought of waking them, but I by then
knew what was coming for me, and it came,

as I was dozing, thinking of a friend
I had in infant school, his name was Hayes,
he thought my name was Edward, it's Ed*mund* –

and then I woke alone, and watched for days
the train's gold shadow on a sea of maize.'

2 *We Did It in Music*

CHRISTMAS EVE, *1984*. The Poet, humouring Edmund, tries to recall the legend of the Flying Dutchman, and advises him to find a girl who will 'pledge eternal love' to him. Edmund takes him at his word. The Train arrives at Hartisle again. Edmund and the Poet re-encounter the little boy and girl, Wasgood and Polly, now nineteen and sixteen.

Edmund finds his local pub replaced by a *brasserie*. He is briefly reunited with his mother and his sister, but his old love, Clare, has left the town. The Poet deserts him. A group of his former friends – now in their thirties – thinks he must be Edmund's nephew, and he pretends he is. A woman falls for him and he gains a pledge of love.

VI

Out there the reflection sat, the empty volume
propped against him, and his pen long lowered
away. He looked at me in my bright room,

as if to make some contact, break a word
beyond the reach of the far more dubious stare
the flesh-and-blood Glen levelled at my shade,

so pained it couldn't meet it. 'Yes, we are,'
I said. He'd doubted we were moving now,
so unattuned he was to how the burr

of the train-engine changed, though I allow
the outer darkness, flattened by the lamps
reflecting us out there in our dual show,

gave little clue of motion. Then a glimpse
of quivered light and he was in the know,
surer than I was. '*Now* we are.' Perhaps

a part of him, perhaps that floated shadow,
had grown so used to listening it needed
words of mine to know a thing. 'Oh, *now*

we are,' he could declare, 'it's been decreed
somewhere on high I *shall* go to the ball,
perhaps a second short of twelve, and Ed,

ain't you a punter with a port of call . . .'
And I record this as it was expressed,
as I remember, though my heart was full,

my eyes illuminated and the rest
alert to the dim land becoming known,
becoming mine. My knowing head I pressed

against the glass and cupped my hands around
to darken all and see it better. Thus
I saw the lights of Stortwood, and the grand

houses on the crest go by, and the bus
that ambles round the Brink Estates arrived,
lit up alongside with a row of faces,

which stopping at red lights was left behind.
Red-coloured lights, red lights, I had to wince
to have them, I was shuddered open, pained

by what I wept to have again this once.
Red and orange! Green . . . I looked at Glen
with that hot greenness tremoring my hands

and wondered what it was to him. He'd gone on
all the while. 'It's not as if you've missed
Apocalypse. You missed the movie, man,

but you can rent them nowadays. You missed
the Falklands, yes, but that one's going to sound
at least as unconvincing as this last

light entertainment. Punk was in, punk went,
we got the fascists in, you know, not fascists,
but. You know. Nightmare. Price of a pint,

what else? Hell, I don't know, it's not as if
you notice when you're there. I've had some times
I found quite fascinating, you know, Love,

Lurve, I wrote a novel, nine – eight poems.
Christ, I sound like you, hey settle back,
it's the Passenger From Hell! And I have dreams,

if you're interested, sarcasm there. Hey look,
it's nothing.' 'It's the tunnel.' 'Is that right,'
he queried, 'thank you, Edmund. In the dark

a moment there I thought I'd also died
and gone your way.' It made us very clear,
symmetrical in blackness on our ride,

I had to look away. 'Though you seem here
I don't think you can share this.' 'Can I not,
Edmund, man? Mind if I shed a tear?

I'm that let down. We've sat in here for what,
half an hour, and I'm resolved already
never to take a train again. I've got

second thoughts. That's thoughts that took me only
seconds: when a fellow-traveller stares,
you shut your flaming eyes. Cos he's a loony,

and *he* may be in Hell, that's his affair,
but you've got time to waste.' He grinned at that.
'Don't mind me, Edmund.' Mind? I didn't care,

he was of all the spectres that would sit
for hours or minutes in those carriage-seats
one of the liveliest, or the least sad,

or the most sarcastic, but the only features
mattering were two: his English words,
his coming now. These were the only matters

touching me. Whatever thing he was,
he didn't know what brought him to that train
that afternoon. He'd gasp to have been *caused*;

I saw that and was loath to ask. The one
surviving query from his wild oration
I asked as we shot out of the rushed tunnel

into the realm I knew: 'The Flying Scotsman,
you called me, Glen. We are about to part.
You hope so, but I know, for it's a function

of being here.' 'What is?' 'To part.' 'That right?
Well then I'll stay and prove you wrong.' 'Please do,
please God, but tell me what you meant by that.'

- 48 -

'Oh I don't know. We did it once in Music,
I didn't listen. Then one night at home
I noticed it was on, it could be homework,

watching TV. Fine, I thought, game on,
we say at Oxon. Oh, and he was this,
this captain, you know, Admiral, big man,

he sailed his boat, his ship. The seven seas,
all that. I got that from a magazine
about it. He was doomed to, like a curse,

because of something earlier it seems
I missed, I was also watching some old soap
so I didn't catch it all. From time to time

it looked like he'd arrived somewhere, he'd stop
and sing for about an hour in lengthy German,
and then what? I don't know. It was when I'd dropped

German. '*ch habe meine Deutsch vergessen,
meine Freund.* Now he'd done something wrong,
I mean, in opera, full-orchestral rotten,

to have to sail that boat, that ship. This gang
who hung with him, I guess you'd call them crew,
were terribly well done, they were disgusting,

I think their costumes got awards. Did view
that show, or half of it.' 'What had he done?'
'I came in late, I don't know, I told you,

I switched on in the middle. It was when
you mentioned seven years that rang a bell,
thinking about it now. It was after then

he came ashore, and then there was this girl.'
'A girl, why?' 'I watched when she was on,
I didn't half. She sang like *eine* Angel

by towering sea-cliffs of polystyrene.
She had to love him.' 'What?' 'The Admiral,
she had to love him, that took a whole scene

for him to say. Mind you, you took a while,
what with your ghostly children. Seven years.
I can't believe you never heard this tale,

especially since you plundered it for yours.'
'And did she love him?' 'Did she? Did she now.
I had to watch the end of something else,

but he was saved, I saw the boat go down,
the ship, it sank with copious use of lasers,
I would assume she loved him. In a gown

she seemed to go to Heaven. That won prizes,
that whole effect. And, thinking as a writer,
yes, I would presume she came up roses.'

'It's how it feels to me,' I heard a mutter
stem from me, 'that that would in some way
redeem him, I could see how that might matter

in the wide scheme, if this was song, or play,
or novel it might have to. For if not,' –
a phrase extracted as a pang from me –

'there'd be no ending to the . . . to the plot.'
'No curtain and no prizes and no cast
party, God forbid, we can't have that.

Which does mean, Edmund, I may be the last
of all your fellow-travellers, now it seems
I've told you all you need. Chalk up a ghost

consummately busted. This dream
is pulling into Realsville. Get the girl,
get the promise, bring it all back home,

end of your awayday. Admiral.'
Both sides the view was slowed and loosening
into familiar factories, the dull

surroundings of the station lengthening
away, it seemed, as long as the whole place,
HARTISLE in high letters, and a string

of green-red Christmas lights guided my eyes
along into the bustle of that station.
The slowing became complicated, noise

arrived as if the deepened throbs of motion
meant to survive, then suddenly the doors
into the carriage slished apart like magic

and somebody was there. 'This paper yours?'
he asked, he had a paper. Glen glanced back
and pointed, 'Take it, brother.' The lad's eyes

dwelt on him, who rose without a look
to get his things, but me they quite ignored.
Glen asked where I was going now. 'The Oak.'

He nodded: 'Think I'll check it, since I've heard
so much about the place. Then I'll be gone,
it's only twenty miles. I'll call my dad.

It sounds insane, but you're the only one
who knows me here, and while you're wholly nuts,
you seem a fairly holy ghost,' he punned

there heartily. We rustled into coats,
and faced each other. 'You're my other line,
Edmund,' he was serious, 'we're mates

in parallel, I'll stop now. Lead on!'
We went to the carriage end to await the doors
with the tall lad who folded out the *Sun*

to find the back again, and also there
there was a girl with him and she said 'Look,
it's him again, that danger man.' Her brother –

I knew they were the two, I felt the sick
surprise of feeling none – just read his paper.
Glen had some expression, half of shock,

half of being unrehearsed, a joker
part excluded, unsure where to aim
the smile he tried to loose, and he was whiter

even than before. 'So is that them?'
he managed brightly as we left the train,
infringing on my sweet returning dream

but somehow raising me. For I felt sane,
somebody sane, in Hell for nothing, he
whom Death deposited on a bare plain,

yet spared for these homecomings. Somebody
chosen, yes for horror, but at least
that. And on the brink of breaking free

now, this night. He was just someone lost;
I felt for him, that Glen. Also I knew
why he had come, to tell me how my curse

could end, it's what he had been sent to do
so far beyond his knowing. That was clear
from how his eyes fell when he didn't know

I watched him slyly. And he did seem dear
for knowing nothing, even twice as far
from home as I was if – if miles were years.

So I came home in 1984,
the year the Poet with his precious tale
appeared to me and told how very near

I was to freedom, to release, to full
recovery. And Love, as in my soul
I long imagined, was the rail from Hell.

A pledge of love, a promise, that was all!
Love was All, what else was true? And Clare
had seven years before on a dark stairwell

kissed me, said we could do, closed the air
between us, every space and molecule
she'd countermanded with that one desire:

Edmund. Fourteen years before at school,
she smoothed my poem on her desk in French,
and, pocketing it, walked along the wall

with others, and they told me at the bench
how she had mentioned me and said our time
was Christmas Eve. They shushed me over lunch,

and they were her best friends. A group of mine
were staring at me from the pudding line.

VII

Glen walked the slowest of our little crew
among the Christmas multitudes. The rain
made puddles all along this avenue

of shops and restaurants I'd never seen.
Umbrellas drew from under as they neared
the steps into the town, but we had none,

and bowed and damp I rose and reappeared
in Hartisle. 'You remember me,' I spoke:
'who am I?' 'Don't *you* know?' She was spike-haired,

shaved nearly to the skull: each single spike
was green. The little girl in the deep snow
she wasn't. She'd been someone I could like

like that. 'Am I Dark Vader?' 'Who? No,'
she sniffed, and never even shook her head.
'She ain't from here, so she ain't going to know,

is she, mate?' And that was all they said.
The rain came sheeting down and off they ran,
as if they knew a place. 'They're very good,'

the Poet said, who'd found in a stuffed bin
a snapped umbrella and was battling it.
'I mean are they on Equity rates, man,

and why exactly do they give a shit?
I mean, like who am I to have such care
lavished so? It's done with style, some wit,

and a cast of thousands but it isn't there,
Edmund. When you saw them in the snow,
that was a *fiction,* yes? So this new pair,

they aren't surprises, since they're in the know,
they're part of the whole project. I must say,
the girl's a throwback, isn't she? I'd say so,

and he's no actor. Still, it's a pay day,
and what did seem set fair to be the Christmas
Officially from Hell is now a play

I'm glad you asked me to. I felt quite hopeless
taking the wrong train like an idiot . . .
At least I helped you with your hopelessness,

because it *can* be hell, and it's been it
where I've been riding, seriously, Edmund,
it can be quite recurring, quite hot,

but it's not real, it pays to bear in mind,
and it does end, and it gets cool. I'm pleased
to meet you, we have traded what we've learned,

and that's been good experience, at least
it has for me. I'm hoping you can next
move *through* the metaphor, regard it just

as metaphor, you follow, it's complex,
this was in General Studies, stratagems
and signs you get, there's life and then there's text,

somehow, you know, I think Derrida claims
apparently somewhere . . .' I'd let his chatter
pave my way through the changed streets, the names

the same, the lettering bigger, all the posters
brash and new, new bands of course, a gloss
on hair, a gloss on clothes, the same Princess

beaming on some magazines. The cars
were different but they always are, one man
was begging, of all things, singles and carols

unending on Carew Street: one new one
kept coming back again, a mix of voices
asking do they know it's Christmas? Glen

sighed and with apologetic noises
dropped a coin for Ethiopia.
And as we came past Smiths and Boots I noticed

something had gone, had been a flowershop,
was selling big cassettes along with signs
for films, and Cravens News was further up

and not called that. Three windows of FINE WINES
were all there was of Record Time. 'That's right,'
Glen mock-encouraged, 'deck the hall with sighs

for the lost years, for now is the long night
of Number One! *Willkommen* to the Dream
of Riches, Meister Lea!' And the High Street

was brilliantly lit the colour lime,
the colour violet and the colour gold,
and thousands passed below where the street gleamed

all three colours back. 'Makes me feel old,'
the Poet murmured, 'Christmas. It's the lights.
It sort of makes you *want* to feed the world

in spite of everything.' There were spotlights
all around the Monument, which stood
rose-coloured at the base, and a hundred yards

along was the pink fountain, where a crowd
was gathered by the glow of a brass band:
music of plight, the melancholy loud

goodbye. The Poet offered me his hand
and said, 'You'll make it, man. I got that ache
I get when I just know. Go for it, Edmund.'

I wasn't clear precisely how to take
this kind advice from my Explaining Angel,
so I solemnly took his hand and let it shake

until he'd finished. Then he grinned: 'Hartisle,
thou art my oyster. Take me to your Oak,
obtain for me one gallon of fine ale,

regale me both with anecdote and joke,
provide for me one telephone whereby
I may contact my forebear, and one clock

by which I may tell Time most courteously
to fuck itself!' Then in this tone of light,
and arm in arm, we stole along the alley.

Then there was nothing where there'd been a bright
opening in my thought and that stopped dead,
like a song abandoned. 'But this can't be right,'

I said, and said it also when we stood
beside the silvered office block. 'It's here
it was.' 'It's very hidden, very shut,

your Oak, it's very reticent.' 'It was there,
the entrance to it. Carol singers stood
singing there, the kids were there . . .' 'Oh dear,'

said Glen, 'I sense a downturn in the mood.
The Oak has spoke. Look Edmund, that's enough.
Let's get a bloody drink. This isn't good.'

I turned a circle, then I turned a half.
There was a new place now, a blaze of blue,
velvet inside as if it dreamed itself

that instant opposite the site I knew.
Was it a pub? 'Edmund, this is, let's see,
a wine-bar, called – Websters Leisure? no,

I tell a lie, called Sleeks, it's a *brasserie*
is what it is. This town of yours is cool,
this place of yours is, Hartisle, Mr Lea,

if I were drunk I'd say you were a fool
for taking off for seven years, that Clare
and all. Now we need watering, the whole

world is sympathetic, plus we're where
they get you drunk for viable amounts
of sterling currency, so fair is fair.'

We crossed the empty street to the bright entrance,
and saw around the door a little group,
no one familiar, with an argument

it seemed as we approached, and walking up
two suddenly we recognised. A large
grey-suited gentleman in a grey cap

was talking with the boy, gave him a push
it seemed as we came close – and it was them,
the boy and girl again. 'She's under-age,'

the doorman said, 'I'm sorry.' I knew him,
his name was Michael Nelson, I had never
liked him, he had hated me, his name

for me had been Demundo. Pelly's brother
turned to me: 'It's Christmas Eve, you know,
but not wiv him. Wiv him it's like it's Easter,

why don't he nail us up like Jesus?' 'No,'
said Nelson, 'it *is* Christmas Eve, old chum,
and would you believe I'd rather be at home

with the wife and kids than listening to some
immigrant type give me a hard time.'
The lad stepped back, folded his arms. The doorman

turned his look on me and said: 'Blimey.
Edmund Lea. Or his *Spitting Image* puppet.'
He glanced across at Glen. 'Don't know you, chum.

You look eighteen.' 'I'm twenty-two, I'll prove it.'
'Will you now. It's simple,' Nelson said,
and now to all of us, with a sigh of effort:

'You're eighteen years of age and you're inside.
You ain't, you ain't. It don't mean I don't wish
you all a Merry Christmas, cos I did,

in case that passed you by. Tonight in church
we'll do the same, we'll light a candle But . . .
you want to come to Sleeks, you come of age.'

'I'm not the spit of Lea, I *am* him.' 'What?
You're what, his long-lost son?' I turned to Glen.
'How old do *you* think I am?' 'Don't matter, mate,'

the doorman said, 'don't matter, his opinion.
I don't think you're eighteen.' 'Of course I'm not,
I'm like you, you're Mike Nelson, thirty-one.'

He smoothed his hair and looked away. 'Now that's
debatable. Good evening, girls.' A line
of girls had come, made up and in dark coats,

so beautiful. Mike Nelson let them in
and smiled when they were gone. Now the black kid
came up the steps, 'Them girls are like fifteen,

my sister's older, look at her.' 'I did,
I looked at her, old chum, I came, I saw,
I looked at her, then I believe I said

no bleeding chance. You want to try the Bear
on Dunning Road. Fridays is Fright Night,
I see your sister being a hit in there.'

The kid turned round and stared across the street.
His sister looked at him, with her green hair
blue when the light was on a moment, green

again then blue. 'I never liked it there,'
she said in a small voice, 'they think it's it.'
Her brother said, 'I had a vodka there

when I was fourteen, so he's talking shit
in actual fact.' 'You can have a vodka now,'
Mike Nelson said, 'you can have eight brands of it,

but Scarecrow-Girl, she can't, and that's about
all there is to say.' 'Can I confirm,'
the Poet interposed, 'that anyhow

I'm in?' 'Do what you want, it's all the same.
Waste my time out here or waste some other
geezer's in the wine-bar, but your chum

is definitely not kosher.' 'Doesn't matter,
Glen,' I said, 'you go, you get a beer,
you need one.' 'Are you sure? We could meet up later,'

he worried with a frown, 'for example here?'
'Here it is,' I said. Glen gave a long
sigh and shook his head. 'It's so unfair,

this country. But the law . . .' 'And we meet when?'
I asked. He nodded: 'I'll be heading back
at some point, but, if plans change, well then,

say, eleven?' 'I'll be here.' 'Good luck,'
my Angel-Poet said. 'And don't forget:
a pledge of love, a promise, and you'll wake

tomorrow, right as rain in your own bed.
You'll need some other luckless plonker then
to tell your story to,' but this last bit

he shared with those nearby; then he was gone.
Now many lads came up along the street
and Nelson checked them all and let some in,

and chatted to the rest and was polite
but wouldn't budge and let them drift away,
while all the time I stood in the blue light

preparing to face home. The young black guy
quietly told his sister something. She
shifted her weight from foot to foot, said, 'Why,'

then shrugged. The boy went in. When I walked away
nobody moved. I went against the flow,
for soon it was a flow towards that grey

doorman I knew fourteen years ago,
and the new wine-bar beating its blue sign
and maybe some I knew, or once had known

when I was seventeen. I was seventeen
to look at now. The ride had left no trace,
no wisdom or experience. I'd been

nowhere and done nothing in that place.
Now nothing streamed like rain across my face.

VIII

I ran in it unflinching to a stage
I had to reach, though every step I made
removed me further from another. Each

was the extreme point of a narrow rod
that trembled on a pinnacle; the height
was giddying: to go too far, to wait

too long at either end, to hesitate –
there would be no salvation. I knew well
the cost was seven years. But I ran straight,

because it was my home. If it befell
that I was cursed again – no better place
to be the cause of that. It was my will,

and I had *had* none, held it like the ace
of a forgotten suit, and how I ran!
I ran on earth, I ran in earthly space.

I ran, the wrong man and the wronged man,
by left and right I splashed by in the world,
a man, a brother, and an only son,

towards the only house where I had held
and been held. And been held – I ran for Clare
away from where she lived, through the bright cold

I ran for time, I ran though the damp air
frisked me for the time I carried, let me
stumble on so free, so *debonair,*

then soon began to rain more thoroughly,
as if in mirth at all the time it took.
It made a troll of rain appear to me

beside the tended hedges in her mac,
hair flattened from its colour, and the green
as I slowed down was seeping on her neck.

Her skirt was short and raggy and her thin
harlequin legs were crossed, so that she seemed
scarcely to balance, seemed to need the rain

to steady her. It was as if she stemmed
from some long spell of filthy weather, rose
unseen, untackled at the garden's end.

Now I could see my house, and here she was.
'I know you're not from here. I saw you once,'
I called into the rain, 'about seven years?

You had a snowman. It was snowing then.
Hard to believe it does that! You were lost,
we made it to the station. I'm the one

your brother calls Dark Vader, and it's just –
it's just we seem to cross, I wondered why
we seem to do that.' 'Woz is getting pissed.

He let him in. He give that bloke the eye
and he let him in.' 'What did you call him?' 'Woz.'
'And what's your name?' She wiped her chinbone. 'Polly.'

'He used to call you Pell.' 'He calls me Poz.
But my name's Polly. You've got a trade name,
because your trade is Murderer.' 'It is?'

I looked up and the lights were on at home,
they all were, and a car was in the drive,
some twenty yards away. Now the rain came

sweeping up Laburnum Lane, as if
to clear it of us. 'I'm returning home,
Polly.' 'You're too young to have a wife.'

'I don't. I have two parents.' 'You have them?
Do they know what you are? They didn't see.'
'Why do you say I'm what you think I am?'

'Did you go to prison? Were you put away?
Did you do time?' 'You could say time did me.'
'He's always got his answers, Superspy,

Woz always says that.' 'What was there to see –
Polly, when my trade was what you said?'
'Woz always says he makes his getaway,

Superspy, it's worked out in his head,
he's got it sorted. I could be well scared,
but I'm not at all. I'm not at all.' 'I'm glad.

My murdering days are done, I can report.
I only dream sometimes.' 'You always dream.
I heard that on TV the other night.

It's true. 'Cos you can't stop it.' 'In my dream
I meet a figure but he's new to me.
But for some reason now I've followed him.

It does end in a death. Though usually
I get it though, he comes for me.' 'That's him.
You got to catch him in his cemetery

and pour some holy water.' 'In the dream
I do attempt to soothe him. I do say
nobody's hurt, I know we're in my dream,

I try to help.' 'But that would make him angry.'
'I die then, I wake up, I never know.
I'm going home.' 'All right.' She stood there, Polly,

a stalk untended as she watched me go.
That dream I had was with me on the path
towards the doorbell I began to slow

away from reaching. She had caught my breath.
Or none of it was with me as I stood
where the door opened brightly on my mother.

I was the rain forever. I was the Flood.
The look she wore was that, that there will come
what never ends. With the world's tilt, a nod

was how she held her ground. She gathered home
around her shoulders, gathered Christmas Eve
into her arms and curved herself in them,

then waited for the strength to disbelieve.
She was a mother and it wouldn't come,
however tight she held her red silk sleeve

with her white hand. Shrill was the voice that came
at first. She could see Polly on the street,
watching us and said, 'It's such a shame

her getting drenched out there,' then I was set
against a wall inside and for an age
held by her, held away, then by, held tight,

then held away for a fresh sob of rage.
I crumpled in her eyes, and am unclear
how long we lasted there in that bright passage

holding, held in fury and held dear,
for then the grief began and I looked out,
shrieked upon and calming at her shoulder,

looked out at Polly frozen in a crouch,
at how the Christmas baubles in the hallway
dangled blue and gold, magenta, each

globe there was displaying mum and I,
a trembling continent that split in half,
then joined or parted like all history.

And as the tears dried language formed above.
'We're having people, dear, what can we say?
The Andersons, where have you been? We gave

everyone your picture and we'd say
he's older than that now but now you're not,
Eddie, you're, you haven't aged a day

but I did that for you, dear, and, you're wet,
we have to get some warm things. Your clothes
we packed away but we can find them, Eddie,

they haven't gone! Your things won't take your father
hours to find, there's nothing thrown away,
not one thing, though it won't take seconds either,

but it won't take hours, oh God! You went away,
that's what you did, I said so to the Blakes
the other night it's what I always say

when people say you're gone. I say he takes
his time about it but he'll come, and then
you watch! They'll have to eat their words, the Blakes,

the stupid bitch, I hate that bitch!' Again
she fell to pieces at my feet, and wept.
The door had never shut. It was Caroline

who shut it. By that time my mum had stopped,
and we were perched and staring in the kitchen,
softly chuckling. Then my sister stepped

curiously in. She was a woman
now, in a black jacket and pink skirt,
and her hair swept and tinted, still nut-brown

as ever but with blonde in it like light
finding it. Her eyes were lined with blue.
She looked at me and lit a cigarette.

'Is this the Belgian cousin? Well are you?'
'Am I?' I said. 'Are you?' my mother chuckled,
'are we?' Caroline took a seat and blew

her smoke between us. 'Don't you think I look like
Eddie when he went away?' 'You do,
actually,' she said. 'You have that look

of cluelessness.' 'The Poet said I do,'
I told my sister: 'He's the one who found
the way it works. Me, I don't have a clue.'

My mother said: 'Cally, it *is* Edmund.
I only made the one.' She had a choke
and Caroline sat back: 'Have you lost your mind?

It's fourteen years. How do you think he'd look?
His skin's a kid's, good grief, he doesn't shave,
he's in his teens, Mum. Funny flaming joke.'

At that she softened. 'Edmund went away,
he's just at peace wherever.' Then to me,
bizarrely, 'Don't mind her, she gets that way

round Christmas. Every time she sees the tree
she sees him fussing round it. Who *are* you?'
'Cally, Casablanca, Cassy B,

your knight was called Sir Gengis, he was blue,
I broke him on your birthday and you said
I'd die and go to Hell. When I was two

you made me swallow ink. When Granny died
you ran away. I found you in the park
and you said she'd committed *superside*

was what you told me. You don't like the dark,
your middle name's Diane. You say it's Amy.
And fourteen years ago you went to work

at Allied Mills and hated it.' 'I'm sorry,
but most of that's all rubbish,' she declared,
though all of it was true. 'My name *is* Amy,

A-M-Y. And you must think I'm mad
if you think I'll believe you're my own brother.
Sorry to have to say, but my brother's dead

most probably, and, close your ears now, mother,
pretty disintegrated. If by some
miracle he isn't, then he'd either

never show his face round here for shame,
or anyway he wouldn't look like you do.
Coming here. He's a bloody schoolboy, Mum,

he's trying to con us. You can piss off, you.
My favourite knight was Denzil. Your research
was a great waste of time. You can get out now.'

'Caroline, I know he's not the age
he ought to be, he may be Edmund's ghost,
I've had my headaches lately, I felt strange

at Jeff and Jenny's morning thing, but at least
indulge me when I think I see my son
beside me.' 'No, I won't, Mum. Get lost,

you, you're preying on a sad old woman's
lost her only son. She's been bereaved
for long enough. I'm going to phone someone.'

She stood and so did I. 'Okay I'll leave.
I'll go.' 'Well good.' 'I'm Edmund, Caroline.
Why I can't seem to age you won't believe

if you don't think I'm him. But I'm her son,
and I'm your brother. When you see our dad,
tell him I like the crackliest bits of skin

so when he's carving he'll remember that,
because I'll come tomorrow. I'll be free,
and I'll be hungry! If I don't, am not,

if you don't see me, Mum, on Christmas Day,
you won't until the night of Christmas Eve
of 1991. If you go away,

show some sign of where.' 'Oh like *you* have?'
my sister snapped. 'Then you do think it's me,'
I said. 'No what I think is you should leave,

basically.' My mother looked away,
and murmured, 'Merry Christmas then, angel,
I'll remember. Come tomorrow, stay.

I don't care what you are.' 'Good grief, you're ill,
Mum, you're going to bed. And you, just leave.
My dad'll kill you. If he won't, I will.'

I touched my mother's red sleeve, and I left.
My sister stood and watched me like a hound.
Stars were visible, the rain had lifted:

Polly the girl was sitting on the ground.
I heard the door close, then the bolting sound.

IX

My wretched fellow-outcast had a watch,
a watch with Snoopy's paws to show the time
in all the ways Snoopy could show it. 'Watch,'

she said, and pressed the side that made it shine
fluorescent green. It showed eleven-ten.
She rolled the sleeve up further. 'This is mine,'

she said, she had a bracelet, a cheap thing
perhaps somebody made for her, with balls
of many colours jangling on the string,

she wanted me to see how they were 'All
colours you can think!' Then the thing broke,
the string, she stopped, I saw the colours fall

with others to the street and she said, 'Look,
all broken planets.' I was short of time,
I winced, I couldn't, I could not stop back

and help her and 'I'm sorry, I've no time!'
I yelled and started running. I made out
the light of the main street ahead, the name

of Sleeks, my destination, in the wet
surface of that street, and the fairy lights
were patterning in sequences, now red,

now green and red, now green, now green and white,
now red again: NOEL, it said, and SEAS
becoming SEASONS, and then SEASONS GREET

and there stood Nelson by the double doors,
processing out the revellers. The world
was drunk and dancing to its own applause

as everyone came through. A couple strolled
with purpose up to me and said, 'Do you?'
I wondered did I what and they said, 'Know.

Know it's Christmas time at all? We do!'
They said this to a bowler-hatted kid
who cried with laughter. In the spill of blue

the sign was making, Polly's brother stood,
an arm outstretched against the wall, his dark head
hanging forward. 'Overdose of vod,'

I heard a boy say, and his friend respond:
'Too much banana juice,' in a high voice
I froze and thought I knew, but when I turned

the face was unfamiliar. The noise
redoubled as the word was sent around:
'Strat's is where it's happening. You guys,

Strat's, tell everyone. It's going down
at Strat's.' 'Intriguing venue,' said a voice
beside me, which belonged to a tall man

in a duffelcoat with zips. 'Intriguing choice,
all things considered,' and I asked him, 'Why,'
and could not stop myself – 'Who's at his place

these days, him and his wife?' 'He's quite a guy,
in some ways,' said this duffelcoat, 'if not
particularly one's own *tasse du thé*,

but you, if you don't mind, are the dead spit
of my War-Zone Opponent, Long-Gone Lea,
I call him, as he is.' The man was . . . Pete,

Peter Binion . . . 'You mean Uncle Eddie,'
I heard myself blurt out. 'I heard he'd died,
I mean, I know he's died, he's family.'

'Just my luck,' said Binion, as he lit
a thin cigar that wouldn't light. 'Your uncle
owes me for that game. I took his White,

then he went down a Double-Horse with Eagle.
This isn't working, is it, my new look.'
'I'm Edwin,' I now told him; it was simple,

lying, no one knew or cared. With luck
I'd follow where they went: 'I'm Edwin Lea,
the nephew of your Edmund. And that's Nick?'

I sought to clarify, 'Nick Straton?' 'He
of many guises, few of them appealing,'
Binion chuckled. 'Am I right there, Lucy?'

he offered to a girl who stood there beaming.
'What is this, Binion, Trivial Pursuits?'
'That's right,' he said. 'Now look. Pretend you're dreaming,

Lucy, for a moment; by those lights,
who would you say *he* was, *this* man?' She . . .
I knew, a blonde girl with her hair in plaits,

she used to captain things. In 7B
she shared a desk with Clare. She was best mates
with Janet Bow. She'd passed a note to me

in History. I'd tried to ask her out
on the way home that week but Russ had said
she had a boyfriend. Now she'd gained some weight

and ringed her eyes with glitter for the night.
Those eyes widened: 'Edmund Lea?' 'You gain
your slab of cheese,' said Binion, 'but it's not.'

'Of course it's not! He's too – you're much too young,'
she reassured me. 'Edmund was his uncle,'
said Binion, 'and he died. He was long gone,

the case is closed.' 'He's dead? It was so awful,'
Lucy sighed. 'I'm glad it's yonks ago.'
I swallowed and began: 'If you . . . know people

that knew him, I'm—' 'We're on our way there now!'
she cried. 'The old reunion, the Team
on Crizzie Eve as usual! We're so –

predictable! But you'd be more than welcome.
Special Guest Star from beyond the grave,
you are! You come to Nick's and say you're him,

you're Edmund, we'll all freak!' 'And there's his wife,'
I said absurdly, 'she won't mind?' 'She minds
everything,' said Lucy. 'Her whole life

is minding.' 'You're related, you'll be fine,'
said Binion. 'Look, they're going,' and the crowd
was thinning out. A group was moving on,

and Lucy took my arm. 'This feels so weird,'
she giggled, and we set off on our way.
'It's odd to know he's – Edmund's – really died,

you know,' she sniffed, 'because it's odd to say,
because I sort of thought there was a chance
he hadn't done. It's only a white lie,

Edwin, if you keep it from these ones,
the Team, you know. It's just they like to think
he's out there somewhere.' 'Barmy as it sounds,'

said Binion, 'she's not wrong. You won't be thanked
for saying there's no hope.' I made a noise
assenting. Lucy looked at me and winked:

'Thank you, Eddie.' Passing by Old Cross
the gang were spread some hundred yards along.
We three had unlinked arms, the rain was less;

a car slowed down beside us, a white one
that curved on every side. The window seemed
to sink down of its own accord, and Glen –

my spirit rose to see that Poet – leaned
out: 'Mr Admiral Sir Edmund Lea,'
he called me, 'in dire straits?' My comrades turned.

'He calls me *Edmund*, Glen, but he's okay,
he is an English Poet. Catch you up,'
I told them. Lucy frowned. 'I know the way,'

I added, so they carried on. I stepped
towards the car. The driver must have been
Glen's father. Glen was grinning: 'Here's a chap

who ought to be on stage.' 'I found them, Glen,
my family, friends – and Clare! These up ahead
are leading me to where she lives!' 'Good man,'

said Glen. 'He's got this curse,' he told his dad.
'He only goes home once in seven years,
just for the night . . . Hey Lea, my dad just said

I ought to try that out.' 'I'm going to Clare's,
Glen, I'm going to hear that pledge!' 'That's cool,
you do that, Edmund, see to your affairs.'

'If I should fail,' I said – 'But you won't fail,
Edmund, don't you know Love Conquers All?'
'Remember me, won't you, if I should fail,

Glen, if we should meet, and you be old,
and I still look the same? Some Christmas Eve?
Remember Edmund Lea, in that new world.'

Glen slouched back in the car-seat. 'Fair enough.
Think I can safely say yours is a face
I won't forget.' 'But promise.' 'Fair enough.

I promise I'll remember. I can't promise
I won't forget. Did that make sense? Go on,
Edmund, get the girl, it's almost Christmas,

it *is* Christmas,' and he gave his grin,
the white car pulled away, the window rising,
until it showed the rain instead of him.

I set off after everyone, soon running,
then at some lights Binion and Lucy waited.
'Long gone again!' said Pete. 'Thought you weren't coming,'

Lucy added, 'now you've been invited.
I've sorted everything.' On the bright porch
of Straton's house – Clare's house – as we three reached it,

Moon was smoking, Moon, who was this strange,
slim, mystic type – guitar in the old band
we'd had in 1969. 'The image,'

he murmured to me in his smoke, 'young friend,
the living image of our memories.
We venerate your uncle, for he went,

he saw the light and vanished in the haze.
They say he died. I don't say that. I say
he woke one day with starlight in his eyes.

I see it sometimes, son, I think one day
I'll follow him.' He led me through the hall,
into the darkest room, where there were many

quarter-lit by crimson light. A girl
was clattering cassettes, and it was here
they sat me, Moon and Lucy, and to all

announced me. There was wine and homemade beer,
and all was cloudy, all I did was lie,
that Edmund lived in wilderness somewhere,

he had his road to travel, far away,
and more was drunk, while nobody who came
was Clare, though many came. 'He's Edwin Lea,'

they said again. At last I said her name,
like this I tried it: 'Edmund asked me once
about a girl called Clare? – Was friends with him?'

A low voice said, 'She didn't hold with friends.'
Dark in the door was Nick: 'She was my wife,
if that counts, mate, but I don't think that counts.

She never liked me much. She liked the life,
but not the sucker sharing it.' 'That's Nick,'
said Lucy, when he'd gone again, 'he's off,

he always says that, like his party trick.
The woman in the curtains, that's his wife,
Pamela, she hates it here. It's like,

it's this is where *she* lived, that Clare, their life
was in this house. All the men liked Clare.
But no one says a kind word now, poor love.

She's down in London with her kids somewhere.
There's pictures in the hall.' 'Her *girls* are here,'
said Binion, 'someone said, asleep upstairs.'

In the hall I found the pictures: *Rachel, Laura,*
a pair of daughters posing by a boat,
matching jumpers, yachts out in the harbour,

life elsewhere, the lemon morning light,
their holiday abroad. The younger sister
looked like Clare, her eyes had the same slight

mischief and her mouth was wide. The older:
tall like Nick was, with his long cheekbones,
shy to look at. *Clare*. I was so far

from anyone. I was so drowned, so gone.
My name had tumbled now, and my endeavour
always to be true. I was so young,

among reliving friends a lone teenager,
whose uncle burned out of the atmosphere
fourteen Christmases ago. Moreover,

I giggled, I was saying it, 'moreover,
I'm absolutely out of my own skull,
and if I go to sleep . . .' 'Don't do that, partner,'

said Moon as he was steadying through the hall
towards the back door, 'sink one for the lost boy.'
Then Lucy was beside me by the wall

that had the pictures. 'You are so like Lea.
You're so like Lea I almost want to do
the thing I never did with him! Stop me,

I'm *out* of it, young sir.' 'You wanted to . . .
you wanted to – ?' 'I really had it tough.
It's ancient history, but they stay with you,

the ones you wanted but you couldn't have.
The ones you wanted when you wanted love!'

X

A pledge, a promise, said that Poet, Glen,
to find the girl prepared to give me those
and wake tomorrow and be right as rain

in my own bed. That way I came to choose
Lucy Mizon, who remembered me
when I was in her world. *A pledge, a promise,*

and I had all the time that I could stay
conscious to receive it. The fresh air
revived me in the town. Her memory

of my last day among them (or, for her,
that of my Uncle Edmund) was a moan
of how she'd wanted Edmund and was sure

she had a chance of love – 'What happened then
was Clare told everyone she'd *chosen* Lea.
Chosen him, the nerve she had, that one!

when anyway she met this different guy,
and went with him and Edmund disappeared,
and she was back with Nick by Boxing Day,

you know, and said nobody understood.'
I filled with questions till I couldn't speak,
but Lucy was my hope, the Poet's word

insisted on it. In the cold and dark
we kissed and I was home and dry. She stared,
drawing away; so would I walk her back,

she wondered? 'Where, of course, but where?' I said.
'The station.' 'That's your house, is it?' I laughed,
because a chill had spread in me. 'I need

the train to Petchley Hill. I said I lived
in what you called the Hobbit House, remember?
It's just eleven minutes.' 'Right,' I shivered,

'I shall do that.' 'We're not being all that sober,
are we, Eddie, you and me, perhaps,
except it's in the stars, it said December

might bring changes, in some horoscopes.
This was the change I had in mind! You too?'
'Me too, Lucy.' 'I've been having hopes

just recently, of romance – not with you,
obviously, you're new to me, but then,
you look so like your uncle, you just do,

it all comes rushing back.' 'Will you be mine?'
I said aloud. 'That's proper,' she replied,
'like in a drama serial! What's your sign?'

'Libra.' 'Oh . . . What did it say?' 'It said,
mostly, quite a quiet year for Libra,
fair bit of travel, a certain solitude,

distant lands, et cetera, till December,
and then I'd – fall in love.' 'Did it indeed . . .'
She pondered. 'That means all of England's Libras

are happy now, tonight – or hopping mad,
they say they're the same thing! Do you think those two
are Libras?' They were waiting up ahead,

slumped on a bench. My heart sank. 'I don't know.
Looks like they're sleeping.' So we tiptoed by,
hand in hand. 'It's one o'clock *right now*,'

Lucy hissed: 'Edwin, we have to fly!'
We started running, pounding through the soft
light towards the station. 'Bye-bye,'

I grinned behind and neither one had moved.
'Remember me to Snoopy.' 'Who are they?'
'They're nobody.' The brother – Woz – did move,

he kicked out in his sleep. We turned away.
The train was in, two carriages, the slow
Cambridge train, we got on. 'We don't pay,'

said Lucy: 'no one's ever here. It's so
kind of them!' The seating, orange-blue,
was nothing like the velvet of my own

lit carriage; this design was cheap and new –
bleak, reassuring. It was 1.03.
We squeezed together. 'Can't believe it's you.'

She shook her head and yawned. 'Can't believe
it happens like it says. It says in Cosmo:
Eighteen Ways To Get Your Man!' 'Eighteen?

Which one is this?' 'I think it's twenty-two.'
She brushed her hair. The collar of her coat
attracted it. 'D'you like it? Honeydew,'

she said. I smiled as if I understood
what was. Now the train rumbled and it budged.
'Edwin . . . I've only got a single bed,

which only goes to show! For Christmas lunch
I have to go to Tricia's, but we'll phone.
They'd love it if – they always say I'm *such*

a single girl! I'll say I'm bringing home
an unexpected present!' The train lurched,
then pulled, then, almost quiet as a dream,

was going. 'We'd have slept on a wet bench,
you know.' She looked out happily. 'Mind you,
I *am* a Pisces, and we like a change!'

We glided past the backs of buildings. Few
lights were on in Hartisle. I imagined
Mum asleep, still saying it was true,

and Dad would have dismissed it out of hand,
like Caroline, but for a kindly reason.
I thought with a gut feeling of Clare Kendall,

lost, and her ex-husband with her children
fast asleep, the piles of Christmas things
along the landing for them. Glimpse of heaven,

waking up those days, the unsurprising
luckiness recurs . . . I was staring off
at mirror-Lucy, nestled and eyes closing,

then shuddered to my senses: whether love
was here between us there were words to say,
her words to say, words that would be enough

to free me from the nightmare – 'Wake up, Lucy,
I need to hear your voice, I need to hear
this matters to you, tell me!' 'But it's silly,'

she murmured as she rubbed her nose. 'I'm here,
I think that tells you something!' 'But the words,
I need to hear them from you, to be sure,

to know you'll never leave . . .' 'They're only words,
Edwin, at the end of the – you know –
day, to use the cliché. It's our deeds

that interest me!' She pointed on the window:
'Look there, I hardly know you. See that field?
It had chalk markings. It was called Chalk Meadow.

We had a game we played called Gain the Gold
and I still know the rules! You had to . . . there,
the river's there. That grey house was so old

we reckoned it was haunted! You'd see deer
off in those trees. I doubt if they're there now.
Those flats are new. I love you, said it, there,

Edwin, at first sight, I don't know how,
and if it makes you happy then of course
I say I'll never leave you! I – love you,

I do, I will, I – all I have is yours,
and all that jazz! I only think we ought
to take it as it comes, because—' The doors

slid open. They had caught our train. 'I thought
this was *our* train,' said Woz, 'as I'm that man
you heard about who had a famous heart,

the monkey heart.' He swayed and sat right down
opposite. I didn't care. His sister
took a seat across the aisle, alone,

curled up and peering out. 'I got pissed there,'
Woz informed us, 'in a private room.'
He looked at Lucy and I didn't care,

her Word was given. *Stick that in your poem!*
my mind was smiling at the shade of Glen.
'I was as a special guest allowed a room,'

the lad was slurring: 'I ain't goin' again,
cos they're all knobbers.' Lucy shut her eyes.
We slammed into a tunnel. 'I'm the man . . .

who had a famous heart. Do you know why's is?
A monkey heart.' He stared at me. 'But you,
you are the famous man who did the murders.'

I looked away, heard Polly say, 'Not two.
Only one.' 'He's got one in his sleeve,'
said Woz. 'We don't know what he's going to do.

I'm rat-arsed, me. But then, it's Christmas Eve.
Have you been good?' He aimed this one at Lucy,
who looked asleep and maybe was. 'I have,'

said Woz: 'I'm going to get my Apple Mouse
tomorrow, I was good all year, I was good.
I was *Woz. Wasgood, Wasgood. I was*

good, I *am* good. Changed my name to *Amgood.*
I'll get my Apple Mouse.' He rolled away
and lay there, lifted once: 'no time for bed,'

then went quite still. Now far in the dark sky
a plane was flashing. I began: 'I have found
the Love Forever. I am Edmund Lea.

I was afflicted and years without end
I rode the train. I now beseech the One
who caused this to acknowledge I have found

the Love Forever. By the time that plane
has come to land the dawn will be beginning,
and I will watch the world until the sun

is blinding me.' I felt the train was slowing,
I prodded Lucy and she vaguely rose
and slept again. 'How long have we been going?'

I called across at Polly. 'No one knows.'
'And what does *that* mean?' I did know the place
we now were inching through, it was Kenways,

a village before Petchley Hill. 'This place
is Kenways,' I said faintly: 'it's Kenways,
there's lights on in the manor house, those boys

still going strong! I cycled through this place
when I was twelve, with Christopher and Gav.
To think of that, and that was in the sixties,

you wouldn't think to look at me. I have
the smoothest of complexions. Why does *he*,'
I finally was asking, 'have this thing of

stating that I did this murder. Did I?'
Polly stared into the dark. Her image
stared into the light. 'I told a lie,

Polly, when I told you by the hedge
I'd had a dream of being killed. The dream
is a recurring one, that type, in which:

in which the same man always comes. He seems
a stranger, then he doesn't. On a bridge
he turns his head. In one most awful scene

he's falling in slow motion from that bridge.
He hits the railway line. I always wake
and ride the train again. The night on which

my old life ended I was in the Oak,
with many friends. I think the man arrives
and sits along from me, his clothes are dark,

or black. These dreams, they come at me in waves
but leave behind one tale. I should much like,
Polly, to ask you if you believe

that this I take for dream is – was – my life.'
We were still travelling. I could see a light
ahead that must be Petchley Hill. My love

was sitting there asleep, expecting it.
Christmas morning. Now I ached to feel
the sun below the ground begin to heat

the world, and the grass grow, and the light spill
across the close horizon. With a jolt
I woke and shook and saw that we were still

creeping forward by a flooded field
towards the village. Polly sat straight up,
then staring at the floor said, 'When I'm old

I'll live in California and grow crops
they got they ain't got here, there's too much rain.
Oranges, bananas, also grapes

they sell as grapes, or squash to make it wine.
Safest place to be, there ain't no wind
in case the Russians use their gas. Him,

Woz, he saw you. Body hit the ground,
splat! A mess. But I was just a baby.
My brother said I *wouldn't understand*

the workings of your mind.' 'Do you? Polly?
Why do I keep meeting you?' 'Dunno.
I don't like meeting you. I mean, somebody

died of meeting you.' It was time to go.
I pulled the plug myself. 'Why even try?
I am in Hell and nothing that I know

can spring me from it.' Then I breathed goodbye.
Soon you could see the ocean in my eye.

3 My First Poem

Edmund describes how, having failed to escape the Train in 1984, he rode across an ocean for forty days. He began to memorise his experience in rhymes, and only this preserved it, for all his written words vanished every night. Through this new poem, he began to recall the details of his last moments in the old world . . .

Autumn 1970. Edmund falls in love with Clare, a classmate, and believes his love is returned. He is the envy of all his friends, but on Christmas Eve a stranger, Cole, arrives at the Oak pub and seduces Clare. Walking the dark streets in misery, Edmund encounters Cole, who seems poised to jump off a railway bridge. Edmund tries to talk him down . . .

XI

Hereafter what you read
is stone. At this point we arrive
in separate elements. When this sound is heard

in me it's heard as crashing of a wave,
from nowhere forcing and receding home
to nothing. When it's heard in you you will have

stone to read it from, and, by that time,
by this time, there may be no sea at all
where I was passing. As you reach this line

know that I knew it well, for where I travelled
written words were sand-inscriptions, scored
briefly in the glistening shallows, dulled

by the first wave of daylight, by the second
slurred to mussel shapes, and by the third day
slobbered clean. Unliving in my mind

they had no life in land, sea, memory,
or history. I'd wake with eyes of sand
that showed me what my work had been, a dry

suggestion of it and, white bird in hand,
my book was empty and its emptiness
weighed everything. This state of things pertained

for one whole moonless month and for nine days.
The book would open like a baby beak
and feed on my sad scratchings. I would close

that book on nothing, on a mind as blank
not as the empty sky but a frozen sea.
One day I shut my eyes on the deep print

of half a beloved word, ground it in me
and woke to find it sleeping and alive
at the next clouded noon. For the whole day

I scorched against that sound its other half,
then for one week its echo and the line
arising from it. Soon there seemed enough

to go by, it was pegged to earth with rhyme
to keep it standing in the headlong rush
of chaos, and I used it to beat time

when I felt beaten. Stirring like a wish,
it rose and spoke, and told what I have told
through the long day. It would at twilight push

long fingers through the cloud to find and hold
tomorrow's infant reach, as if to pass
a thing of use in tissue to a child,

a lucky thing held out through prison bars
as evening turned its back. A poem formed,
or so I termed the outline of my years.

It lifted over days and nights, it seemed
to lead me, having followed me. The night
it asked recital, clamoured to be named,

I roamed the seven carriages, the bright
seven rooms and spoke it from the heart.
When I was done, I slept, and at first light

the shore began to spread into my sight.
Soon we were on land itself, we rode
no more across the ocean but beside.

The other view was of a plain, a broad
featureless grey lowland, though it too
transfixed me with the unrelenting blade

of its horizon. It was all I knew.
My words were hung from it as if to dry,
they fluttered from it when the day was blue,

it would swing near and shudder far away,
but I was strung upon it, and my poem
plucked upon it, softly, savagely.

Something began to be, as if a drum
were added to that string: it crept at times
alongside, it would fade, but it would come

afresh in yawning afternoon, the poem's
shadow on the spider-grass. It grew
stronger, and it strode. Far out of dreams

it leapt and realighted, and I knew
something was inescapable. There was something
pitiless, some fury to be true

unburdening itself below, unmasking
anyway. I ached to let my eyesight
in from the horizon. That was asking

thirsty bloodhounds to forego the twilit
water's edge. I drank and the dark hutch
inside me smarted at a birth of light.

So I recall that time. There had been no stretch
of ocean for so long, never so long
without a sense of land, a shard of beach

to reassure. Nor had there been so long
without a stop. I dreaded such a halt
out on that slate-grey ocean on my own.

It could be how the end came, how the world
allotted me would let me go, if what
decided so decided. But that world

was altered now, was altered at the heart.
I had remembered everything. The still
horizon had been waiting, and had brought

the burial to light. I was in Hell
with reason. Having ridden fourteen years
as innocent as you (who see a cold

lettering where once were moving waters)
I sat and faced and suffered with the soul
who'd done what had been done, the sorry cause

for which Hell housed us. Now I knew it all,
had had it told by the horizon's stricture,
by the wide ocean's urging to recall,

and by the pride and fuss of my mother English.
Like the sun, I warmed to it, and at a time
I calculate around the first of March

of 1985 the following poem
set itself in that blood-scribbled stone
I take to be my heart. Now written down,

it is all that heart is. It may feel warm
to touch, it may feel cold. It may depend
on what the ground is made of. Lift the poem

out from where it's bedded in the sand
and wipe its sand away. You'll be too late
to stop fresh water curling like a hand

into the hole it left. It can't forget
it had its time as ocean. Edmund Lea,
the author's name is, and the poem is set

in my home town. I only have to say
the names of roads and closes and the parks
to stand there in a wordless sunlight – I

now among them then. What is it makes
a memory endure? Few of these scenes
show anything or any face that speaks . . .

Lamps in the fog along a frosted lane;
a cloth set on the lawn; the dizzy hurt
of games on the great fields that in no time

were scrubs of land I glanced at – nothing learnt,
little told or treasured. Life could not
have passed so quickly to this puzzled end.

The innocence that wanders into sight,
the child I was a while – his innocence
is only that he could make nothing halt,

he couldn't hold, he couldn't know his chance
was now – he dashes out on Gully Field,
he slows down by The Pond, he sees his friends

who haven't seen him yet – was something held
a moment then? A feeling of *don't go*,
don't get there yet – a tilting on the world,

an act of balancing? One of the few
remembered – out there bobbing on a sea –
but he ran on, to what, or why, or whom?

No one is going to know now. Memory
has drawn its hand away like a child told
it's going to burn. My sister played with me:

she used to be the Queen of Marvel-World,
and didn't mock me when she ceased to play
one Saturday. She'd used a new word: *child*.

My father gently lowered his heights for me
in all his sports, my mum was there to say
my time would come. I went to Cooper-Gray

when I was young then Valley End. Today
would come and go, delights and wishes, pain,
embarrassments and furies, always I

was picturing a girl, rarely the same
from day to day, the name, the merest sight
made work unthinkable. My small bedroom,

my tiny mind: a hit, the constant clot
of lucky melodies, and her turning face
on all four walls for now. I was called bright

sometimes, a loafer, but begrudging A's
applied themselves to me. By the autumn term
of upper-sixth, 6E, I was advised

to try for university, my room
was tiled with glossy catalogues. I stared
astonished at how many lives now seemed

beginnable, so many sunlit gardens . . .
'You notice how it's never raining, though,'
a girl observed one afternoon that autumn,

sitting across and lifting up to show
the pictures in a pamphlet: 'They look weird,
students. Like they can't think what to grow.'

Her name was Clare. Her voice I'd overheard
in fact that morning, when a crowd of them,
the ring who stuck together, sat around

discussing death, how some guitarist, Jimi,
was the Last Breath of Liberty. Nick Straton
sat crosslegged: 'He wouldn't join their Army,

he had to go.' Stan Burke said, 'Out to get him,
they had to be, it fits, they had to be.'
Nick stroked a girl: 'He tried to fight the system.'

Across the room, Clare's voice said cheerfully:
'He tried to lay his own guitar, you guys.
And then he tried to eat it, and they say

he choked on his own sick.' Nick Straton rose,
as did the new boy, Moon, and others went.
The girl who'd bothered them was a surprise:

she tied her hair back, seemed nobody's friend,
was quiet in class, took Latin, had round eyes,
and parked her Beetle by the Science Pond.

They called her odd, but few of them could drive.
She got invited to their parties, first
as a joke of Nick's, then always. She'd arrive

on time, like nobody, then when the rest
turned up she'd leave. She never made us think
she wanted to be with us long. The furthest

anyone had got with her was drunk,
and that was Nick one night and though he swore
she said she fancied him, he'd drawn a blank,

he told me walking home. Now she was there,
a desk away, still reading: 'Look, it's you,
you're here already, Lea, you're in this picture!'

She showed me: 'In a lab with you-know-who.'
It didn't look like me. 'Who do you mean?'
'Far corner desk,' she said. A girl I knew

called Lucy Mizon sat there in a dream.
Seeing me she smiled. 'Forget it, blondie,'
Clare muttered in her breath. 'Don't know her name,'

I said. Those were our times in Private Study,
side by side. She drove past, I remember,
in town, late afternoon on a dark Friday,

smoking. Traffic lights at red-and-amber,
she wound the window down and jabbed her Benson
out into the wind. 'Lea, you're a member,

tell me the way to this,' – an invitation
somewhere. I could feel the entire town
screech to a halt around us, the commotion

blaring at us as I searched and found
a scrap of paper. Thus I did my best
to smooth her way to some forgotten friend's

that Friday night. I wasn't on his list.
She folded it and wound the window. Term
ended the next week. A poem I'd lost,

I later realised, was on that same
sheet I gave Clare Kendall. When I tried
remembering it, I couldn't. 'In your poem,'

her gloves were leather-black, she stood beside
her little car, 'you try too hard to see.'
I shivered, saw beyond her to the wide

field, the mist had thickened. 'Well that's me,'
I noted in the cold. She looked at me.

XII

In recollection what descended then,
that cold illuminated mist, remained
till Christmas, made a candle of each friend

emerging, disappearing in it, made
each smile a call to shelter, but in truth
it must have lifted on forgotten days

and let them by. What's kept of it is breath,
that's certain, fog-white utterance of gossip
overhead, a trade in rumour, myth,

complicity. The girls around the steps
at Record Time, Nick Straton sauntering by
in his hairy hooded coat, the talk of trips

gone bad in London, freakouts in the country,
nights of ill-lit deep emotional candour,
in blankets then, the sunrise ceremony,

drowsing. Christmas Eve in the town centre,
there they are – I see them clear as type –
Stan, Mendis, Russ, Nick Straton and some other

name that's gone. They're slouched along a step,
below the Great War Monument, their breath
is white with cold or brown with smoke. 'Slide up,'

Stan calls. 'I'm Christmas shopping.' 'Catch your death?'
says Nick, thudding a fag from his gold pack
to point at me. I join them. 'Hanging with?'

they're asking me. Stan says: 'We went electric,
Lea, we got a session round at Nick's.
You hanging with?' I smoke, the little frantic

sucks we used to take. 'Lay down some tracks,'
they're telling me. The Hunger was their band,
they started it one term, they played some gigs

at parties, we stirred drinks and stood around,
amazed at them for looking like stars,
just standing there. They made a muddy sound

and no one danced. We saw their bright guitars,
their skilful hands, their amplifiers and cords,
the nonchalance, the class . . . There are no chairs

in Nick's garage, it's dark, they crowd towards
the back for a band meeting. I'm alone;
I glide my hand along the chill bronze threads

of an idle bass guitar. The boy called Moon
rides up, he's excellent. Nick doesn't play,
he sings their songs, he sings in a low drone

I can't decipher. Now the band is ready,
counting four and starting, such a noise –
I sit on a sagging box and wonder only

when on earth I can buy presents now, in these
last hours of Christmas Eve. A light goes on
in mid-song, in mid-song, that memory

I swear by, and all six of them – Stan, Moon,
Nick, Russ, Dodge Mendis and the drummer – each
in some way falters. Nick says through the song,

down the loud blasting microphone: 'The switch,
the switch!' Out goes the light again, and I,
I think he's called the girl who's come *this witch,*

this witch to break their spell? And I'm wondering why
and who it is until it is Clare Kendall
who stands there listening, so improbably,

Clare, who halts there, tinted by the purple
bulb they use for light, in her long coat,
Clare who yawns and makes the cutting signal

past her throat. Nick Straton booms out, 'What?'
at which she rolls her eyes, and since the track
is not about to finish, turns her head

and stretches through between Stan Burke and Nick
to where I'm watching this. I feel my side,
my right side seem to warm or somehow quicken

at how she sits quite near and my left side,
I can recall it, seems so cold and dragged
I pity it. The Hunger play so loud

the noise is dreadful, but I recollect
these moments always as the purest silence . . .
Her scribble passed to me on a train ticket

suddenly in my hand: *Birth of a Legend.*
Mine passed to her: *Death Of A Christmas Eve!*
Hers on a shop receipt: *Let's save the patient . . .*

The song cranks to a stop. 'It's better live,'
says Mendis as the drummer peters out,
and Nick's complaining, 'That ain't long enough,

Staz, I got another verse.' 'Nah, mate,
my solo ends it,' and they're toe to toe,
while Russ asks, 'Dig it, Lea?' and I say, 'Great,'

as Russ and Dodge are standing near us now,
dumb about the girl. 'Jimi's returned,'
she tells them, 'but we're going to have to blow.'

Nick hears this and stops arguing. 'You can't,
you got to stay.' 'I *gotta wot?*' she wonders.
Dodge Mendis says: 'The next track's called *Burned*,

it's about some crazy chick.' 'Oh really, Mendis,'
Stan's now saying. 'Anyone we know?'
Nick storms out. Through the small garage window

I see him looking back, and I know now
he really liked her but it's me she takes
back into town at dusk, it's me somehow.

Her coat is long, dark green, and as she walks
beside me I am thinking of her coat.
Of how, on any field, in these last weeks,

those last weeks in that old world, I thought
always I might turn my head and there,
off at the edge and watching me, I might

see Clare in her green coat. Now Clare is here,
by Craven's shop, in town, we're on our way
alone together, never true before,

to buy last presents as the frozen sky
is lost above the Christmas lights. No sun
will rise out of the east for Edmund Lea

from now for many years. That chosen one
is shambling by in ecstasy of hope,
for sure the luckiest of the young men,

his one hour fixed forever on a tape –
its joke of lasting always. We were both
laden with our bags from the six shops

we went to (six I dimly name beneath
these words) and we were leaving the Town Centre,
our lists completed. I can see my breath

and hers go out and be a cloud together
past us as we walk, and all that air,
I watch myself considering, is over,

behind me, can be pitied, cannot reach her
now like I can reach her, and it's then
I seek to take her hand and match it there,

gloved, cold in my bare hand, and it's done,
it's swinging as we go. 'This isn't quite
according to my plan,' she says. 'This plan

is probably your plan. Mine starts tonight.'
'I've never had a plan,' I tell Clare Kendall.
'That's obvious,' she says, 'but it's all right,

we'll work on it, it's nothing we can't handle.
I mean, you're in my care, it's up to me
to sort you out.' The world is turning simple,

I wonder to myself, as from today
there's only this, and everything but this –
my family, friends, school, home, holiday –

is worth no more than what it's worth to this,
I see myself believing as we reach
Laburnum Lane, my road, this two of us,

this two of us. 'Oh here's where we diverge,'
I hear her sigh, both from two feet away
and through forever – *Here's where we diverge,*

and here's where I diverge: this Edmund Lea
who in a nightmare sputters to this page,
from *him*, eternal-envied shell of me

who holds her hands tight at the evening's edge.
She holds my hands and sees me as no face
has held me for that long – it turns to touch,

three seconds' worth of seeing turns from glance,
to sight, to heat, to something I'd depict
as touch, and four, five of the longest seconds

rust me to her future: at the sixth
we have a past together and her eyes
are the barred gates to it, which at the seventh

blinks into the distance. 'Where's your place,'
she wonders, and her hands are freed to find
a long soft pack of Bensons. 'That looks nice,'

she calls a home three doors away: 'We'll rent.'
I won't know what she means for half an hour
by that remark, we part around that moment,

till it ignites my bedroom like a star
and leaves me shaking. 'Eddie?' – I can see
my father lifting presents from the car:

he grins, unseeing what's become of me.
He's floundering in a time before Clare's choice
determined things. My mother's weary eye

that winks across the kitchen may express
some fluttering of such a time before,
but nothing in my elder sister's voice,

pin-narrowed as I hear it on the stair,
suggests she'd know me now. There is no help
I cannot give this evening when I'm there,

it strikes them all, my father's doubled up
with how I've altered and their jokey guess
is true: our Christmas tree's assorted bulbs

rustle up alibis up for my changed face.
Fragments left before the cold night air
assails me – few odd words my father says –

'Love, I read, has highs and lows like weather,
Eddie, isobars,' and Mum stands back,
yawning, from some cooling sauce or other,

and does just catch my eye. I get a shock,
I do remember, at how long that's for,
and it's no time at all, it's just a look,

not like my love, but seems to come from there,
I mean, a place one's looked at from – I'm mad,
you know, I am demented with despair –

but these were the same eyes. And soon I stand
out on the porch and leave and – now I think –
Russ is with me and he calls me 'Friend,

Ed the dark horse, eh?' and we buy drink,
beer from Craven's. 'Ed, you shadow-man,
you chosen one . . .' We head towards the Oak,

where everybody's going. 'It's the Plan,'
I tell him as we pass the Monument,
and wave to Dodge who sits up there alone,

drinking a tall can. 'You are my mate,'
says Dodge when he comes down. 'You, Mr Ed,
and You-Know-Who, you dating her this night?'

Nothing needed saying. That new world
spun on regardless: 'When she says it's time,'
Dodge carries on: 'you'll probably be signalled,

right, will you like sort of say my name,
Mr Ed? Coz then it's like I'm there,
if not in spirit, then, at least, I mean,

I do mean spirit.' Russ breathes out blue air:
'Coulda been me, weird thing is, coulda been.'
Hartisle centre's lamplit like a fair

and the old Fountain's turning red to green,
leaping and foaming. 'This, it's just my time,'
I say to Russ, 'that's all . . .' (As in a dream

Here comes – again and always at that line –
my Intercessor now, here comes my Judge)
we reach the Fountain's wall and we sit down,

the trio there, I give a light to Dodge,
smoke dies between us. Through the rushing water
I see a man is standing at the edge,

staring in the pool. I'll wonder later
why he carries nothing. All his clothes
are dark, except red writing on his sweater

unreadable from here. But then he rises,
and makes his way around the Fountain's rim
towards us. NAVY as he comes up close

it says, although he wears no uniform.
He looks in his late twenties, maybe more,
and vaguely lost, or drunk. We'll call him *rum*

in the Oak pub, together, in an hour.
He asks us are we 'bound for anywhere?'
at which we chuckle. No one says we are,

but as the water changes colour, 'Where?'
he calls, then cries it through the streaming air.

XIII

'The Dog and Duck.' 'The Lions.' 'The Green Man.'
'The Bull, The Bear, The Cricketers.' 'The Forge.'
'The Ace of Spades. The Man in Black.' 'The Man

From U.N.C.L.E.' 'The Green Man.' 'The Extremely Large
Cock and the Horny Hen.' 'The Happy Hen.'
'The Pregnant Hen, The Banged-up Hen.' 'Which

is no mean boozer, man.' We were crammed in,
five of us, into a space. The Oak
was heaving when we got inside, and Stan

had got the only chair but we saw Nick
and pressed around him, five of us, 'The Duck,'
said Dodge above the noise, 'The Pregnant Duck!'

and we all smiled. Nick said, 'The Tired Joke,'
and we all laughed. He said, 'You lose the guy?'
and Russ said, 'Sure we did, we dumped him back

I don't know where. It's mainly down to Lea,
Lea told him hit the Bird-in-Hand, this place
his parents go to! Sucker.' Passing by

there was this girl called Janet Bow, her voice
could cut through all the crowded rooms. 'Rock stars,
I hate to put a dampener on your Christmas,

but Michael Nelson hates you.' 'Why?' 'Because.
Because his girlfriend digs your music.' 'Hey,'
said Dodge, 'you heard her what she called us, Russ?'

'*I* think it's just a noise, though, personally.
I can't make out the words.' Nick stared at her
until she left. 'That's cool, you walk away,'

he added, 'you eternal amateur.'
'He doesn't hate us, does he, Mike the Man?'
Dodge was asking Nick, who didn't care

but looked at me and said, 'So what's the plan,
Eddie mate, we're talking wedding bells?'
He scowled, as if I might mistake his tone

for friendliness. Then Russ and someone else
spoke up for me, said 'Leave it, man, that chick
she's stringing him, she's like them London girls,'

and Nick was nodding: 'Do I give a fuck?
Answer: No,' and, 'Eddie, score some beer,'
said Russ. I was relieved to turn my back

and push into the crowd, be anywhere
but where Nick Straton was. It didn't seem
important what he felt. His sense of Clare

was lost on me, as if he knew the name
but little more. I pushed. The place was heaving,
hot and loud, I couldn't raise my arm

to wipe my brow, the crush was such. 'You having
fun here, Lea?' was shouted by one girl,
her make-up smeared across, 'you ain't seen nothing!'

She shoved past to the bar, and in the hole
she left I glimpsed the blonde hair of a girl
who went to things with Clare, round a small table

six or so of them, and when they all
tipped backward with a squeal a single one
was visibly untroubled by a smile.

I shivered on two legs. (That girl was mine . . .)
Clare prodded round her glass with a red straw
and started saying something. (All the time

I'd waited . . .) 'Wizard, what can I do you for?'
cried Peter Binion with a tray he set
before me like a miracle. 'This beer!'

I yelled at him and hoisted a glass out
in peril overhead. Now I could turn
and edge towards the girls, I was without

anyone, unwatched, I felt unknown,
and strayed towards her seat among her friends
as if wound in like yarn. She'd had my poem,

had scanned it in her bedroom, with her things,
my work, had had it in her schoolbag, smoothed
it out and read it thoughtfully again,

so I imagined. Suddenly stools moved
for me to sit, between a girl and Clare,
and, as I bent to sip, my back was shoved

by someone passing and I spilt some beer,
not much. 'You going to lick that up?' she said,
then grinned when I was shocked. I looked at her

and sat among them. Someone at my side
was asking, 'Are you bassist in that band?'
'I hang with them, but no.' 'Come on, it's Ed,'

said Clare, 'we checked them out together. And,
we found them pretty miserable.' 'We did,'
I nodded. She said: 'Find this man a girlfriend,

that was my first thought,' then all her crowd
were staring at me. 'There's a thing to think,'
said one of them. I couldn't say a word,

in case this went away. I took a drink,
then conversations started. For a while
I made no contribution, drank my drink

and set it down, with an all-purpose smile
I got by. Once I glanced across at Clare
and she was frowning at me. 'Like the style,'

she said, and she was pointing down at where
she'd noticed my new shoes, brown shiny shoes
I got for my job interview at Homecare.

She let her shoe come off, and, with her toes,
made golden in the tights she wore, she touched
my ankle for a while: 'Some day we'll go

and splash your Christmas money.' Then she reached
her hand around behind her where her skirt
had pockets and she showed me a white edge

of paper, my old poem. 'Then we'll start
on all that stuff you're trying to say,' she added,
hiding the sheet again. 'See you've been caught,

Mister Lea, the game's up.' I just nodded,
staring past her legs into the dark:
'no need to struggle.' Everything was vivid:

the words on someone's matches *Longleat Park,*
the one shoe on, the one shoe off, the song
'The Tambourine Man' always on the juke-box,

and Janet saying, 'I'm smashed enough to sing,
but not to be the only one.' I remember
someone tapping me to show her tongue

jump back inside, a pill on it, her brother
thinking I was with her. 'Are you nuts?'
she screamed at him, 'Are you like my own mother?

He's with *that* one,' while Clare just piled the beermats
and wondered was it Christmas yet. I see
the band off in a corner, fairy-lights

on faces and his name was Gary Cholsey,
the drummer, he was dancing. 'Paint It Black'
was on again. A red-haired girl – Sue? Sally? –

was shrieking something like 'They're playing *his* track!'
and pointing at the door to the public bar,
 – where had appeared our NAVY man, our dark

and misdirected friend of long before.
Lost in the crowd, a concentrate of loss,
he looked around him, slender and unsure,

until he caught my eye: I read no message
there, he went on peering round the room,
and then retreated out to the short passage

leading from the smaller bar. 'Do we know him?'
the girls were asking: 'Do we? That's a poser!'
Clare got a light: 'Jesus, do come in,

wipe your feet, why not.' 'He's a rock biker,'
said Janet Bow, 'I knew they'd come.' 'He's not,'
responded Clare: 'He's just the man from *Psycho*,

he's shopping for his mother. Reckon that's
way over all their little heads,' she noted
sweetly. It was over mine, in fact,

so all I did was grimace. I'd decided
I ought to hold her hand and I moved mine
near to hers, and in a movement took it,

held it like that a moment. 'Well that's fine,'
she said out loud, 'there's nothing in the handbook
either way.' A girl asked, 'What's his sign?'

so Clare said, 'At the Sign of The Blasted Oak.
Let's get a drink,' and up we stood, conjoined,
and somehow not towards the bar but back

through the connecting passage hand in hand
we went, and by the cigarette machine
had space to stop, alone. 'This was half-planned,'

she said, and with her other hand took mine,
and was on tiptoe to be kissing me,
with her peach lips a moment, and, again,

more forcibly, a third time tenderly,
then stood back, and I said, 'I love you, Clare,'
imagination and reality

meeting in an eclipse of both, a roar
that was a silence, shadow that was bright –
she lit her cigarette and asked, 'What for?'

then we were out again in the shone light,
her turning once to look at me, the bodies
swaying between us, then a sudden jolt

and she was out of reach. I heard Dodge Mendis
yelling to me drunkenly, 'He's there,
man of the hour!' 'Lea, mine's a pint of Harvest,'

said Nick up close: 'Look, cat, don't fall for her,
she'll screw you up no end.' 'Yeah but she'll screw him,'
Russ said boldly: 'That's what this is for,

he'll get to where you never.' 'So you reckon,'
Nick retorted, 'so you reckon, Russ,
you fucking virgin.' 'Oracle has spoken,'

Peter Binion piped up, and was pushed
and almost lost his footing. Lucy Mizon
swung across me, she was pretty plastered,

we'd never seen her drink. 'I've got a question,'
she bellowed at me: 'What do you call a woman,
I'll start again, What do you call a *person*

who never, What do you get when you cross a person
with Miss C Kendall? Do you know the answer?
I know, it is my joke, but I've forgotten.

You would have laughed.' I grinned and I got past her,
fell against the bar but nowhere near
where Clare had got to and by now they'd served her,

so I called and signalled but she didn't hear,
or look in fact, she had hold of three glasses
and backed into the crowd. 'You got them, Clare?'

I heard myself cry out in a boy's voice,
as if her name were slipping. I would wait
God only knows how long for any service

now it was near eleven. In my seat
was Clare when I got back, and on her stool
the NAVY man who had arrived that night,

who wore all dark and wasn't from our school,
who lit his cigarette and was engaged
in deep talk with another listening girl,

I noticed, on his other side. I reached
our table and knelt down alongside Clare,
the other side from him. Gently I touched

her hand and she looked down. She said, 'He's here,
he's coming through the rye,' and carried on,
quarreling with Nick about some war

he said was not 'true war'. The NAVY man
was scrutinising him. The atmosphere
was purest smoke through which I led my hand

towards her thigh, gold-coloured and so near,
and let it rest and have her move away
as if earth had itself marooned me here

by quickening. The stranger had his say
about all kinds of things I couldn't follow,
and 'Time!' was called to a great choral cry

of disappointment. 'Christmas Day tomorrow,'
a girl proclaimed unsteadily. The whole
gang was round our table. 'To the Mallow!'

Stan was shouting, 'To the Protest Wall!'
Now everyone was out in the yellow mist,
and clapping in the chill. 'His name is Cole,'

Clare quietly was telling me. 'It is?'
I wondered, 'who is Cole?' 'My heart's delight,
obviously.' I looked her in the eyes,

but clashed with shields and stood back in the night.
'Now don't forget,' said Clare, 'it's still our plan.
Don't think you aren't still in my care, all right?'

Her lips were open, she had silky skin,
her breaths were cherry-flavouring the air,
and each was marvellous and none was mine:

and every step I took away from there
put off a light, until the night was bare.

XIV

I'm in the greenest spot. From where I sit
I see the hills begin to rise, the clouds
muscle along them quickly, and I wait.

We've been decelerating for some hours,
I know our noise like birdsong, can divine
our speed from it, I know how when it roars

it won't go on. Then for the longest time
the land prepares, it grows a path away
across the nearest field. There is no sign,

no settled route, it's an instinctive way;
it's trodden, though, which keeps me from despair,
it's trodden somehow. On some empty day

a soul discovered it and walked it. Where,
who knows. The sun is hidden, and a rolled
cloud is half the sky and staying there.

Choice is present now, the relentless child
that points its sticky fingers both the ways
the day could go, the rail or the empty world,

and pauses. There's a sulk on its pale face
the longer I do nothing. By the time
we stop it's fast asleep. All the world is.

And all of Hell but Edmund Lea and them,
or him or her or what it is that strokes
the carriages to standstill in the gloom

of growing cloud. We stop by a dull lake,
a track around its edge. If I get out
I have within me thirty hours awake,

my all-time record gloriously set
in April 1982, in warm
weather walking on the alpine plateau

lovely to observe. That long a time
ought to produce some people. Empty houses
I often reach in five hours, but a town

I thought I saw that night from the high places:
a twinkling in the valley. I was chained
to where I was by weariness. Old voices

bubbled from my life. When I sat down
to rest I felt my eyelids fall towards
the deep, I let them close on that dear town

so far away, released beloved words
and sank to earth. I woke – but you know where.
However far, however long my strides,

however full my lungs with loving air,
however clear my thought, I never reach
a settlement of humankind before

I yearn to sleep. From miles away I watch
my train become a toy on the horizon,
I walk some more, it is a pen, a match,

it is a pin. I walk and it is nothing.
But by the time the night has come, a night
that bestially has never thought of ending,

I'll pass a hedge and meet the silhouette
of carriages, with all the nightlights burning.
I'll know then it's soon time. My skeleton

will jig for joy. The rest of me is howling.
I drag it all to jail. If now I choose
to walk by this grey lake in early evening,

I have no expectation of release,
arrival, conversation, English chatter –
nothing but the land's varieties,

and the sky's lonely scroll across forever.
This time I wait an hour to make the choice.
I help myself to food from the strange counter

that stocks itself. I listen for the voice
of he who serves returning to the carriage,
but hear this time only the fractured noise

of my own talking. I can make a sandwich
last twelve minutes. Nobody this time.
I am unspoken. I am a dead language.

I'm going nowhere and at last the train
is satisfied I'm not. It moves me on
past the dull lake I'll never see again

and further into night. I am the one
who lives in Hell, who rides alone in Hell,
remembering. My eyes are on the line

of land in the faint light, it is a gentle
drawing out of pain, till pain becomes
normality. It is the winding spindle,

winds everything, it neither spares nor blames,
it just recalls to mind until that mind
divests itself of day, and then of dreams.

It's fourteen years ago I left behind
the crowd outside the Oak. When I looked back
she still was in their midst, and Russ my friend

was talking with her. Cole, aloof in black,
had hold of her gloved hand on the top step,
and then I turned the corner. And I walked

wherever, I could not foresee a stop
for any purpose. It was Christmas Day,
I bleakly iterated at the top

of Wheaton Hill. I stood and had my say,
a plummeting self-pity and the need
to weep, it too was hopeless. The word *why*

crawled into and emerged from this absurd
oration, then it fluttered on its own
on the deserted junction, like my standard.

I had dreamed of this girl Clare, and had not known
there would be nothing. I had sat all night
in ecstasy of likelihood, and now

I had fresh air, I had the deathly white
beyond the poem. I thought of that, it still
folded in her skirt, there came sick heat

of jealousy towards it. 'Terrible,'
I judged the thing in fury. 'Take it out
and burn it in your room.' Then with a dull

professional expertise was built a set
in my imagination, of her room,
a place of softness and her on her bed,

the other actor quickly there on cue,
the action starting. 'Cut,' I giggled, 'cut!'
but couldn't stop and had to see the two

together now, the shimmer of her tights
under his hand, the journey of their lips
across the air, cool subtlety of lights

dimmed down to pink, his hands in nerveless steps
on newly naked legs. 'It's Christmas Day,'
I said to my illusion in a bookshop.

I wandered through the streets, I made my way
to Mallow Park, heard nothing but the trees.
Cold and fit, I felt, and strangely ready,

but that mood couldn't last. There were the days
to get through now, without what I believed
would happen to me, 'Love,' the uttered noise

I only once had made. 'My love.' I shivered,
went quickly from the gates of Mallow Park
towards the Monument, went by, 'Go forward,

press on, away, go bravely in the dark,'
I murmured, a medieval fool. Now birds
mistaking dawn rose over me, a flock

of words she'd said: *No need to struggle*, words
so sweet they dried and stuck and now I ran,
a target, through the town and out towards

St Catherine's. I stopped on Quillers Lane,
and panted at the wall. There, far below,
the oily darkness of the railway line

rusted and ticked. I peered and thought for how
long one would be falling, and I guessed
four seconds, then I shuddered. There came no

inclination. I got my breath and crossed
to the other wall. The station was in view,
the last train lit and waiting there. Surprised,

I checked my watch but it had stopped at two.
'Milk train,' I said aloud, so it was named.
'I used to be in love, now what I do

is name the trains. If *you* want your train named,
ask Edmund Lea.' 'That train already is,'
a low voice said. I know I all but screamed.

He sat some twenty feet along the bridge,
scarily, on the parapet, one hand
slightly behind him. With the merest nudge

he would be in mid-air, would hit the line
or hit the train. He wouldn't live, I thought.
But I felt glad to see him for a time

before I recognised him. Something stirred
and brimmed in me, rejoiced in him: in Cole,
I realised. I said, 'You know we've met,

me and you.' He looked at me. His pale
face had sunken eyes, a narrow nose;
his lips were thin. He looked fatigued, and ill,

somehow deteriorated in the hours
since I had seen that face. Where had he been?
I thought he'd be with Clare, go back to Clare's,

be with her there, I'd trusted what I'd seen,
embraced the worst – now here he scarcely hung,
over the frightful drop. 'What have you done?'

I started, 'I can't – think of any . . . thing
bad enough to make you think you want
to jump from there. I think there is no thing

so bad you'd want to do it.' 'But I don't,'
he snapped at me: 'It wouldn't do me good.'
'It wouldn't,' I agreed with him and went

a little closer: 'It would make you dead,
and what would be the good in that?' 'Wrong twice.
It wouldn't make me dead, though, if it could,

it would be welcome to. It would be nice
to get away.' He said this with a snigger,
and almost went. I jerked and saw his face

crease with pleasure at my fright. 'You'd never
make it if you fell,' I cried, 'the drop
would kill you, or the rail, or both.' 'Or neither,'

he said. 'What makes you think I want to jump?'
I stared at Cole and answered, 'Where you are,
is what. I thought you'd be—' 'You thought I'd stop

at Thingummy's? You thought I'd be with her?
I do not stop, I never stop, I reach
this place and I take anyone. It's where

I come to when I'm thirsty. It's the ditch
I drink in.' 'That's my town, that is,' I tried
to lighten things. He said, 'Pick any bitch,

I may. I've had the pick since a bad night
before this town was here. I come from nowhere.
Dream-destination, that, it makes them wet,

the look of the dark stranger. I'm aware
of everything they feel: you would be too.'
My thought was now to get away from there,

this madman on his watch. At least I knew
he would be gone, and it was hard to care
which road he took away from me. 'Are you

interested?' he asked. I said: 'It's Clare.
Is she all right?' 'She's average. Had better.
First time, you see, first blood, first visit there,

it's always *yikes*.' 'I mean, you didn't hurt her?'
He raised his hands a moment, and my heart
reared, I thought he'd go. 'No, I'm a master,

really, she's all curled up like a cat,
thinks I'm with her. I've become pure cad.'
He settled on the wall. He said some word

I didn't catch. I couldn't leave. 'You said
it would be nice to get away.' 'Not bad
for euphemism, Edmund,' he averred:

'Just tell it like it is. I should be glad
to die.' 'You said you didn't want to fall.'
'I don't, it won't solve anything. The crowd

I run with doesn't recognise a fall.
It wipes it out and wakes me up, it's happened.
A miss is good as half a million miles,

runs my proverb. I prefer "a friend
in need." I wonder, could you try that role?
You could effect a happy ending, Edmund.'

'How do you know my – I know yours is Cole,
I know, she told me. But I'm not your friend.'
'Not yet you're not, you've still to sprout a soul,

so what. It could be thundering round the bend
and carry you to Heaven.' 'What's the word
you keep on saying to yourself?' That sound

he made again, too muffled to be heard.
'Destroyed, old lad. I want to be destroyed.'

XV

The word departed from him with a sigh,
as if it had held on too long, as though
the wind dislodged it from him finally,

decisively, as if required to do so.
It blew away and left us quiet, both
staring at the railway down below,

at the shadow of two carriages. Our breath
went out and in again at the same time,
children asleep. I didn't want to breathe

when he did, had to hesitate with mine
to lose his. It was difficult. At last
to speak was the unwelcome one solution.

'That is – what you will be, Cole. At least,
if you let go. Destroyed is what you'll be.'
'I don't want to *be* anything. The dust

is greater than I want to be, the sky
more intimately human. What I need
is to be shot from life. I need its eye

to close on me, its brain to bear no thought
I thought again. I cannot kill myself.
That will not hold. I have to be destroyed,

unmade, become forgotten, grow unheard-of.
To reach the garden that was never there,
nor will be, to be unknown and unthought-of.

I have been riding for a hundred years
and five. The earth is paced into a yard
that I could flood with shedding of three tears

if I could shed them. I have wrung the world
so tight it's in my throat, a sugar bolus
I would expel before I go. The girls

you drape across the sky – as if they'll waltz
you beaming through your life – they are the spots
that slide about my cornea. It rolls

to reach them and they quicken out of sight.
Born by accident, I've been preserved
by pitiless design. I would complete

the trinity tonight. I have deserved
no more now for so long. Your presence here
I take to be a pledge, to be a gift,

your disbelieving face the very door
that leads me from all light.' I turned that face
away towards the trees, became aware

of its convulsing, how incredulous
I looked. I'd never met a man insane.
My cheeks relaxed, my forehead and my eyes,

into a holy gaze of pity. 'Train
can't seem to make its mind up. The poor driver.
What a way to – typical, this line,

always a nightmare! Hope his shift is over,
by and by.' I stole a look along
at my confused companion. He was either

drunk, I reasoned now, or really wrong
in the old signal box, my mum would say.
Her fleeting presence was a strengthening:

that I would have to save this man, would stay
and talk him from the brink. I'd be well-known
for doing that, or would be if the day

would only come, with someone, anyone.
I took a breath, began, but all the words
that came emitted from that lightless man.

'You are about to hear a thousand words
you won't believe, my friend. It makes no odds
how wild you think they are. That they are heard

alone is of significance. These words
were proffered to me on this very lane
when all around were fields and hedgerows, woods,

and the brightest lights Orion. The slow train
waited down below, and, as I walked,
bemoaning my financial troubles, sprang

from out the hawthorn bushes Dr Creek,
a man I'd only met that night. We'd played
brag and sank a hatful at High Oak,

parted the best of friends. When he explained
himself to me he seemed a man demented.
For in all calm and seriousness he claimed

to be of the last century, a spirit,
he did insist, who *paid a heavy cost*
for but one ancient sin, was how he termed it.

He said for that one trespass he was cursed
to roam the earth, returning only once
in every seven years to his own house

and family. These desperate occasions
he sought escape, he sought release – by dawn
would find himself removed from all connections,

bewildered and elsewhere. I was a man
of decency, I think, but soundly failed
to keep my bearing even. I began

to strain. Through my hilarity he called
to me – *Two rivers lead from out the fire.*
The first is to be known and to be killed

by he who knows. To find a soul out there
who knows and loves you, yet desires your death,
still wants you gone. This is the first: Despair.

The second – a roar ignited on my breath
and I was racked with laughter. Dr Creek
kept talking through it. I controlled myself,

apologised and asked him to repeat it,
which he refused and said: *It is delivered.*
I begged his pardon. Thoroughly entreated,

he added only this: *The second method,*
Hope, I do not have the strength to try.
Nor to repeat to you. Now I have suffered

long enough. Next moment, he and I
were locked in combat in a mulch of leaves.
He started it, but he's no match for me,

I knocked him out. Abruptly he revives
and flails at me, he also starts to talk
the most unspeakable filth about my wife,

my son, my mother, everything! – this Creek
I thought an excellent friend an hour or so
before, he's Judas in a velvet cloak,

but he wasn't taking *me* with him. I know
eventually he'll come at me too quick,
when I'm against the wall there, just like you:

I swing him over, and dear Dr Creek
is history. Was *I* the soul out there
who knew and loved him but would have his neck?

He must have thought so. First way out: despair.
I didn't love him. Did I? One must love
one's neighbour . . . Do you, Edmund? Do you care,

now *you* know?' The one answer I could give
was yes, of course I did: 'Of course I care,
of course. Though I can't tell you I believe

a word of your whole thousand. But I'm sure
your life is filled with pain, and anything
there is to help that I can do – I'd rather

that than see you fall. It's – you belong
among more helpful people, there are now
places with them, they have special wings—'

'You want to love me but you don't know how.
I said as much to Clare.' He'd changed his tone
to a dry sneer. 'Don't really want to know,'

I changed mine too, to casual, 'what's done,
you know, is done, you weren't a friend of mine,
you didn't know, it's cool, there's no harm, man,

and you don't care, so why should I? It's fine,
you're into that "free love"' – 'You call it free?
It took an hour of the most precious time

on earth to get her to do right by me!'
'Do *right* by you?' 'I call it what I please.
I make the most of will on the one day

I am permitted will.' 'And I don't believe,'
I rode my indignation, 'that in fact
she "wants to love you." Why should I believe

you even took her home?' 'Oh, I expect
you do,' he softly said, 'because I saw
how you would always follow where she looked,

so would have known that for perhaps an hour
she stared at my right cheek. We made the most
tri-cornered entity. It wasn't fair.

I take no pleasure in how much you lost.
You are a child, and I have lived some six
times your tiny span. I was surprised

she mentioned you at all. I'm sure it makes
your heart a measure lighter to be told
your name came up between those berry lips

when you were gone, as if she had half-felt
some aftershock of you. She did express
a sadness at your conduct. She'd been *thrilled,*

was actually the word, on having first
discovered you in this most unengaging
banlieu. She showed me on her desk

some piece of yours she said she found quite touching.'
I tried to let it go, I couldn't. 'Why,
my conduct? What was wrong with it?' 'Who's judging,

Edmund, I'm not judging, who am I
to tell a teenage boy the do's and don'ts
of how to melt the maid? I'm just the guy

who's doomed to get it right, and get it once,
and shuffle home to Hell.' 'You're just the guy
who's lost his – bloody marbles, mind my French.'

He was five feet away. '*Alors, mais oui,
mon frère, je suis d'accord. Cet homme, c'est moi.*
But I'm the man with raspberry-coloured knees,

not you. Unless you whipped it out somewhere
and stuck some sorry local in the mist.'
'Because you've told me this, right, I'll make sure

you're put inside, because you are a rapist,
on top of being nuts. And I'll tell Clare
you didn't know her name, she was your "conquest."

Which means tonight was all you'll see of her
forever.' 'I know that, I have no hopes.
I knew that when she led me through the door,

and put her pretty fingers to my lips,
then squatted to undo my boots and led me
tiptoe in her stockings up some steps

into the dark. I knew it when she said
under her breath *you now are in my power,*
and lit a candle by a queen-size bed.'

'I didn't ask for details.' 'But you wonder,
you wonder what it's like to reach the place
you dream of, to undress at last a lover,

who looks and wants you to, whose arms are raised
for you to lift her shirt and show her satin
top she bought in town today, whose face

is hot and serious with having chosen,
as if I cared, whose lips are licked and needy,
whose little skirt, deftly unclipped, has fallen

dark around her ankles. Who is greedy,
acrobat in bra and stockings, winds
her leg around my back and pulls my body

down upon her there. I think you wonder
what you might have undergone, had I not
visited your town. You might have heard her

tell you you were *in her care*—' I coughed
to cork his noise. I knew there was no lie.
'It's Christmas Day,' said Cole, 'and there's a gift

we each can give.' 'I don't care if you die.
I'm going to walk away from you. I have
nothing you might want. You have already

taken it. Now it's not yours to give.'
His hand was still behind him, as before,
the other now he pocketed. 'Your love

was thinking of you, Edmund.' Now I saw
an edge of white appear between his fingers,
emerging crumpled and uncrumpled. 'There,'

he said, 'delightful, *billets-doux* of lovers.
She's dashed you off a little poem, sweet.
Smells of her things so far as I remember:

lavender rose . . .' – I ripped the thing apart
to get at it – what would she write to me
now everything was ruined? The torn sheet

was what I'd written, my own poetry
for her, unwritten on and I was blind
at that, I gripped him. He was asking, 'Why,

it's only love . . .' I felt the rush of wind
that took his place, it took my empty hands.

4 *The Once*

Horrified, Edmund flees on the last train. He meets two little children, Woz and Pelly, who saw everything. When he wakes next day on the Train, the children are gone. Slowly he begins to understand the nature of his plight . . .

The Ghost Train has seven carriages. It is staffed by three figures speaking gibberish. Whenever Edmund wakes it is afternoon, so he sees neither sunrise nor morning. Over the years he comes to believe that perhaps he is in Hell, at other times that he is insane or comatose. He passes through land-scapes both beautiful and desolate. Sometimes the Train stops and he walks for miles, but the Train is always waiting for him. On his walks he begins to encounter lost men speaking lost tongues. Briefly he recalls his homecomings of 1977 and 1984, then prepares to return again, aware of his crime and penitent, on CHRISTMAS EVE, 1991.

XVI

His shape receded, spinning to the end,
and struck. I'd thrown a shadow on the lines.
He had been sitting, and he turned enthroned,

rose out and turned, and once with Mr Hinds
in Chemistry we'd watched as a pale stone
had hit a box of water from a height

and spread it into crust: that turned our form
to open mouths – it hit and made a drink
dead matter, unpotential. It became

oblong, with a chilly web of cracks.
The stone had done it and we grinned in awe.
The cracks, he said, are travelling so quick

they've ringed the world three times already, four,
five. What if they meet, does the sliced earth
begin to break? Bob Filer asked. For sure,

the teacher told him, just to hear his breath
wasted on that. The ice when Cole dislodged
and turned and struck between the rails had spread

to the dark blue horizon. It had switched
the land to still – not *still*, the word for *still*
had always had some breath of motion, touch

of light to it, regardless of how still.
This didn't have. The world was white, opaque.
Touch of him I'd been the last to feel,

touch of him. I found myself set back
and loudly bleating I had not touched Cole.
I'd gone to him, and that dire lunatic

had swung out into space, let the world hurl
out between his ears. The freezing stone
was dropped again, in me, the chemical,

and I was stiff with lying. Death was done,
and I had touched him. When I swallowed now
the bubble broke the skin of a white pond,

made a hole, a dreadful tiny thaw
in total winter. I had killed that man.
But I was mitigated: *You were there,*

I hissed into the molecules at no one,
he begged me to. I might as well have told
a fire it wasn't hot enough to burn.

His every act and utterance had ravelled
into him like backward smoke, and vanished
utterly to where his body curled

face down on the line. *It's what he wished,*
I told him. Had he pushed away? Or had he
lunged to save himself, or had he stretched

to take me with him? Had I caught his eye?
I thought so then, I didn't think so now.
Only a trap my mind had set for me,

as if in league, in on it, in the know,
which left Lea flesh-and-blood alone to bear this.
The breath I took was short, but felt somehow

the first in an eternity; its brothers
jostled after hopefully, and one
trod on a sound, a shard of voice, a nervous

squeak above the chasm, like a sound
a child gives up in sleep. Was what it was,
I realised. Borne lightly on the wind,

a baby's cry, no relic of my voice.
It had to be the train that all this time
had stood there, lit but silent. Six red eyes

ahead along the track had stayed the same
throughout. I hadn't thought a soul was here.
I could remember giving out my name,

that it was Edmund Lea, and I was there
to name the trains. Thereafter was a blast
of noise now in my mind. I was aware

of what I'd done but not how, or at least
not why. A little child was on the train.
I said it, to accept it. In the east

no shred of light. I backed along the lane
towards where, leading down to Hartisle station,
there was a street I walked along. Unknown

I moved, the train was steady in my vision,
it trembled, made a guard-rail. And below,
behind, beyond, the thought of every person

known to me. They bristled, row on row
of leaden standing infantrymen, stark,
unbreakable and nowhere else to go

but shepherded downhill in the blue dark
towards the one warm place. It came again,
the baby's cry. I saw the station clock,

3.21. The windows of the train
showed nothing, no one, no light in the cabin.
I climbed the fence and jumped down to the stone

platform. I saw no one. I was even
dabbing at the edges of a smile,
and doubting what I'd done could truly happen,

when straight ahead and clustered to the rail
I saw him. All the limbs were gathered under.
I said, *We must report this, we must dial*

Emergency! I was picturing my father.
This thing could make him like a son to me;
he'd smile as if included. *Tell another.*

It wasn't in Mum's universe. A lie
would walk with me forever now, a shade
would form behind me every time the light

of question shone. It would be gone in cloud,
at night, or only sensible to me.
The sun would never see it, nor the God

I didn't think there was. The baby's cry
now started into wailing, and it came
from somewhere in the second carriage. Why,

I wondered, like a citizen, the same
as anyone would wonder, any man
would care, was there a baby on the train?

It was mid-winter, Christmas Eve, the dawn
was hours away! I stood. *It's in my mind,*
I said, *it isn't tenable.* The train

came suddenly to life, with a low grind
of engine, and I heard a different voice.
'Are you a Venger? Are you Mr Bond?'

I rattled through my hearing every noise
the world had ever made so near to me
in hope of finding something else it was –

but in the doors a dark-skinned little boy
was looking at me. He was very young.
Four or five, I thought. 'You made her cry,

you fathead. Now I got to sing a song.
You woke her, cos you gone and done that man.
You frightened her. You ruined everything.'

Now I could see the baby, laid along
the seats in a pink coat, out jerked a hand.
I couldn't see their parents. There was no one

anywhere but them. 'That's right, I'm Bond,'
I heard myself begin. 'But him back there,
he was a Soviet spy.' 'Is it The End then

now?' the boy enquired. 'Yes, this is where
it ends.' He nodded. 'Is he dead and all?'
'He's dead and all. Are you on your own here?

Where are your parents?' 'What, you gonna tell?
You tell, and I'll tell them.' 'You'll tell them what?'
He frowned: 'You made him fall.' 'I made who fall?'

The baby cried again. He went and sat
beside her and said something. Sure again
how very much alone we were, I stepped

up into the carriage. 'Does this train
ever leave?' The little boy stood up
as if to shield the baby. I sat down

across from them, to calm him. 'It's our stop,'
he said, 'we got off here. My dad's a butcher,
he don't know how I done this. In our shop

I got this basket hidden.' 'And your mother?'
The boy sat down. 'My mum plays the tom bone.'
'What's your name?' The doors slid out together

suddenly and shut. 'This is the train
with magic doors,' he said. 'I never touched 'em.
Stop crying, will yer?' 'What's your sister's name?'

The boy sat back and frowned at the presumption.
'I'm taking care of her. Our dad he said
to go away. I'll take her to our mum's then,

in Cressle.' 'Creslet?' 'Yeah.' 'Your mum and dad
don't live in the same town?' His face was bleak.
He stroked the baby's arm. 'My name is Wasgood.'

The train was moving slowly in the dark
and he kept stroking, 'Chelsea is our name,'
he said. I breathed in and our carriage stank.

'Pele, she done a shit. I'm not to blame.
You are. She got frightened. She's Pele.
Nothing frightens her. She got that name

cos she's the best. Better than Italy.
Better than England, better than you. She scored
a goaw, she scored ten goaws!' 'I saw them play,'

I could assure him, 'best in the whole world.
In Mexico, the yellows. He's the best.
It's good to call her that.' 'She's still a girl,

but now she got good luck,' said Wasgood. 'Most
days I call her Pell, it's just Pele
when she's all crying, like when we got lost.

She scores a goaw, then we get home.' 'Today
is Christmas, Wasgood. Will your mum be there
in Creslet when you get there? She might be

terribly worried now.' 'She got short hair
our mum.' 'Does she expect you're at your dad's?'
The baby cried again. 'Do you change her,

or what?' I wondered and he shrugged: 'My dad's
got stuff he uses on her. So's my mum.
I'm getting a new bike. I'm getting loads

of Germans, and a fort when I get home.
What are you getting, James Bond?' 'I'm getting
nothing, Wasgood.' 'Chelsea is our name,'

he sang, 'blue is our colour . . .' 'I've got something,'
I said, 'I meant to give a friend.' I felt
the string of beads, my only Christmas shopping –

well too late now, I realised with a jolt,
itself collapsing in the vertigo
of *who in heaven cares?* – 'The thing I've got

might cheer her up,' I brought them out to show.
He moved across to opposite me, took
the beads in his small hand. 'It's a ringbow,'

he said, 'it's really good. That's what it makes,
when you get purple at one end and red
at one end, and all colours. Pell, it's like

a ringbow.' Now he loosened the pink coat
around her, sat her up, and hung the beads
in front of her. She saw them and went quiet,

her eyes went side to side with them. Wasgood
put them in her hand. She made a fist
to hold them in. 'She likes 'em, cos I made

a ringbow in my school.' In the blue mist
around us I saw lights of what I took
for Speltham. If it was, then Hatch was next,

Kenways, Petchley Hill, New Lady Park
and Creslet. 'She can have the beads – Pele,'
I said. I saw my mind had been at work

the whole while, was ready to explain
everything to anyone . . . I had left
the Oak when time was called, I walked alone

into the mist. I saw the train arrive
and climbed aboard because I was so cold,
and far from home, without my key and loath

to wake my family up. I would be told
a man had died and I would raise my brows
in horror. They would say his name was *Cole*

and I had met him. I would say I know,
the once, on Christmas Eve, and to my mind
he was disturbed. *Did you address him?* No,

Nick Straton did, Stan Burke, a girl there. And,
now I think, I think she drove him home,
in her car to Lower Fisher. She's a friend,

she won't mind if I call her that. *Her name?*
Clare Kendall, you could ask her. You could test her.
She may have information. It's a shame,

but he's at peace. 'She's saying thank you, mister,'
Wasgood prodded me. The little child
again said, 'Sackoo, mist,' and I said 'Pleasure.'

They had forgotten everything. She held
her brother's hand. My present meant the world.

XVII

Cole struck again, he talked to me again,
he fell again. The cards of it returned
in randomly dealt order to my hand,

I read them all again and saw they meant
I couldn't win. I set them down face down.
He fell again, he spoke, he raised his hand,

he fell far, he was killed, he reached my town.
I'd stood with Russ beside the fountain spray
and seen him coming, Cole, seen him come round

slowly like a second hand. Yesterday,
yesterday. Russ Parrish, Clare Kendall,
Hartisle, Valley End, my family —

like saying, deal again, I'll have them all,
three deals ago I had an ace of hearts,
four deals ago a flush! If you only deal

again to me I'll beat you. Gold-backed cards
flitter through the night again: he falls,
he twists and thumps the rail, he says kind words

about my loss, he tells demented tales
of olden times, he's grinning and he lifts
his trophy to my sight; on the oiled rails

his body lies, he talks of trading gifts.
I fill with sickness that I took his word,
I did his deed. One of the human lives

was halted by me. One who had made proud
at least a mother somewhere – all the germs
that dot the air, the dangers of the road,

the terrors out there, accidental harms
inherited or met, they all had failed
to end him but I ended him. The arms

that held him at his birth had failed to hold
him back from mine, and these had let him go.
They rested like a gang, the fingers curled

into twin arks of sleep. *He begged them to.*
Back came the grave committee: what I did
was try to reach his shoulders, for I knew

Cole was about to jump; my action failed,
regrettably, and the unfortunate man
did fall, did jump. I listened for the world

to note my findings. Nothing but the train
absurdly slow through Petchley Hill, the mist
about a boating lake, no trace of dawn,

the baby sleeping, in her tiny fist
my only trinket bought in the bright day,
and little Wasgood with her, his eyes closed.

They were alone. He must have run away
and got his towns mixed up. His mother must be . . .
somewhere. What had happened here would stay,

my mind smouldered on, it was down to me
how much of all my life would suffer. Yes,
I thought, sat forward, stroked my hair, now *I*

had power to be broken, to confess,
see all come down in ruin. From my cell
see visitors, explain. I could be blessed

by catholics, church people, I could tell
my story fully. I could meet one day
his family, inform them how he fell,

beaming at me, how his tone was gay,
accepting, light. Or I had power to sink
the memory like a galleon, to pray

from time to time but otherwise *unthink*
that hollow vessel twirling down to rest.
I raised my dozing hands and made them link,

compact the thought: I choose, *it's as I list*
came somehow to my mind. They made a ball
of brothers in embrace, they were hard-pressed

but would forget, they vowed before they curled
back home into their fists. Where were we now?
I saw a barn, some horses in a field,

and on a night like this? I wondered how
I'd make it home tomorrow, play the lost
apologetic son, keep my head low,

THE ONCE

feign an affliction when my sister asked
exactly where your presents are? I'd say
I need some help, my mind is overpressed,

I need the doctor now – or Boxing Day
will do! My body rested, then it shook,
rested again. Who'll soothe it? Who'll soothe me?

Why, Clare, of course, my skull cracked as a joke,
Clare Kendall will! My hands were in my hair,
examining each prickle, donkey-work,

police-work. *Tell me, are we sweating, sir?*
If I might ask some questions . . . At long last
my eyelids couldn't hold, as if the air

increased in weight. I stretched, and stretched across
the seats, much comforted by the deep breath
of Wasgood and the baby. We might miss

the stop; someone would wake us. They were both
infants, I'd be questioned, I would say
I couldn't find who they were travelling with,

I stayed here to protect them. Men would ask me:
Are you aware a man is dead? I'd answer:
That's such a shame, on the Nativity,

I wish he was alive. I wish he *were* . . .
Sleep came. I calculate it must have struck
beyond New Lady Park, by where that fair

goes on in August; through that misty park
the train rolled on, and three, oblivious
to shivering discomfort in the dark,

were dreaming. Now a curtain falls on us.
Let it fall, you are protected. Now . . .
something tall is striding through the years,

makes steps of them, steps up and spirals down
into the rooms, across the rooms, the rooms
are decades, and a century the town

that something tall is striding through, long arms
lean and holding boxes, and its eyes
are fixed ahead. It has a host of names,

it trails them. It is fireproofed to lies,
coated against reason. It is drawn
by smell, a child could draw it, often does

if you look hard enough. Where it was born
there's nothing now. It isn't in the scope
of such as are affixed to oxygen

to know where it will die. It's speeding up
through years *you* know, it is a fantasy:
that never stopped it walking. Now the rope

is tightening. Sleep seconds, Edmund Lea,
let every second stay you hours, each hour
stay you a year in dream, in memory,

because the sand of time for you is shore,
and the next moment foam about your shoes.
I sing this to the soul I was before,

though I know it doesn't save him. When you lose
every soul there is, you have to burrow
doggedly for more, make all you do

a mine of them. This spokesman of tomorrow,
as all that's written is, he leans across
the lap of time to guide him in his sorrow,

Edmund Lea, who for his lone trespass
is picked from his own time. I'll play the dream
he had, I had, before this came to pass,

and leave in the distress of the to-come
a token voice for him, a sign of hope
to hear, though he had none. And I had none.

When the train stopped I started and woke up.
An English Field, my mind amused itself
to specify, is the next local stop,

English Field. Many an English Leaf
on many an English Hedge. Some English Trees.
I shook my head at it: it ought to have

an English Man to see. Our stopping place
was quite deserted, couldn't justify
its status as one. 'Total waste of space,'

I didn't finish saying before I
divined I was alone. And furthermore
could not remember for the life of me

whom I'd assumed was there. No one was there.
I shook my head, it hurt with lack of sleep
and shoulder-ache and overload of beer.

I'd gone and got a train at the wrong stop.
And then it broke on me: the great defeat
of hopes, harlequinade at the Oak pub,

the fool again, and Clare gone where, the street
outside, a blur of shouts and faces – now
hang yours, and I hung mine. 'It's over, mate,'

I offered to the empty carriage: 'How
appropriate, don't tell me, Coventry,'
I said with my stage scowl. 'The perfect town

to send me to, deserted, dark, and wintry,
a place to call my own. Now we were where . . .
We were nowhere. *I* was up a gum-tree,

I heard Mum say. With an authentic roar
the tide came further in: 'It's Christmas Day.'
A wince, a further slump. 'God.' Any more

recall and I'd be slithering away
through ventilation ducts. I'd done it now.
I'd be, I grinned, a subject. You know Lea?

He's cool, he went and hopped a train somehow,
Christmas Eve, went miles he did. To where?
Where. Where. Between the English Towns

he went in style, to breathe the English Air,
observe the English Leaf and Further Leaves.
Five, Gold, English, Rings . . . Dear Clare,

nowhere, nowhere. 'Now separate those lives,
was said on high,' I murmured to the floor.
'Choose any night, but do choose Christmas Eve.'

I rose and sat back. That's what I was for,
I thundered on inside, to make a map
to get the girl from A to B, for Clare

to roam the English Fields, though at each step
an English Man appears. And who's the latest
lay-by? I could bear it, I could cope;

I sat and waited to recall a face.
Bound to be a friend, it was, a friend,
a trusted one – nobody filled the space.

She'd telephone. Perhaps she'd telephoned
already to console me, as she lay
unwrapping presents with the world on hand.

Christmas Day had dawned a cloudy day,
I saw, and more than dawned, the light was strong.
Surprised, I scanned the white expanse of sky

for its still whiter heart, the stain of sun,
and it seemed high. Delightful! I had spent
all Christmas to mid-bloody-afternoon

comatose, bravo, ace, excellent.
We hadn't moved. I felt for the first time
suddenly far, remote. I had a sense

the tears had mustered in an anteroom
already. They were swallowed back. Since when
was there a Christmas service? And it seemed

pointless, unrequired, the kind of thing
nobody needed: it was bound for where?
I reckoned I'd been shuttling between

two points, Kings Cross and somewhere north of there,
all night, all morning, and there'd been no staff
to find me, throw me off. The place we were

said nothing to me. It was flat enough
for Fenland, or the Midlands, not the south;
the fields were wide, no cottages, no huts,

not much at all in fact. With a slow breath
I counted all I missed. There was no wire,
nor gate, no steeple far away, no path.

There was no road. I'd travelled awfully far.
Where the rail stopped at an unfenced divide
the grass began. 'A child could be hurt here,'

I said. I nodded. Gingerly I stood
and started through the train. I counted four
swept deserted carriages ahead,

plus mine, a closed food bar and then one more,
a first-class area in the old design,
enclosed and private and nobody here,

first-class or otherwise. 'This is my train,'
I grinned in it. 'It carries Edmund Lea.'
I thought I'd tell the driver I alone

was with him! He would laugh. It was Christmas Day,
why not? I deeply breathed and made my way.

XVIII

You couldn't reach him, as you never can,
there is a door that's locked, you have to wait,
you wait there swaying, you're a travelling man,

you've come this far and would now like to put
questions to the staff. It's no surprise
it's understaffed, they can't be blamed for that:

you knock again. There was an unlocking noise
and nothing more, like it was down to me
to act on it, as if I had the keys

to anything, like I had EDMUND LEA
in orange stitching on my jacket. Lines
I'd never crossed I'd have to cross today,

this was for sure. I knocked two, three more times,
then tried the door, my thoughts already cool
and holding out no prospect, but my arms,

uninformed, were furious, and pulled
uselessly a while at the locked door,
then stiffened with new principle, and hailed

blows upon it. Now I shouted 'Sir!'
bizarrely, 'Merry Christmas! Have a heart!'
in vain. I grinned the grin of the done dare,

and gained admission to a welcome thought,
that all was a planned trick, a prank, a game,
and I was had, fair landed, I was caught,

I'd be the butt of jokes, that day would come.
I sighed. I would be sporting. I went back
still grinning to the carriage I came from,

still nodding to the empty seat I woke in,
and sat, the prank concluded. Now outside
the fields were grey and the day darkening

already, and my mouth on either side
lifted itself to hold the appalling weight
of everything. Then couldn't, and I cried.

And when I cried all Hollywood broke out,
no star went uninvited, every face
of every joy was driven to the site

to build the fire: my family, my house,
my friends rotating past, and always there,
uprising through the story with her eyes

the dark in every frame, her honey hair
its texture and her voice its theme of strings,
she was, and she was there when it was over,

coughed away like nothing. 'We have things
to cope with you,' I said in the ashen growl
that follows tears. 'God gave us the good things.'

And *God* I hadn't said since as a child
I'd had to go to services, my scalp
still ringing from the comb. I'd used the word

before our football matches, for His help,
and when an uncle died, before he did,
to save him, and then after, looking up

one evening to the sky. That had been God,
I there conceded, but I'd lost Him now,
and, if asked, I said so, calmly told

my friends I had believed, but did now know
He had departed. Nick was satisfied,
chewed and nodded. Russ said, 'Told you so,'

and queueing at the pictures I once heard
some kid say, 'I believe like Edward Lea,
He *was* here, like He did create this world,

but *now* He's gone, so no one's actually
watching us, like what they say in church,
that's all old hat. The new hat is we're free.'

My friends were proud. I meant to tell this titch
my name was *Edmund*, but Nick pointed out
it wasn't cool. 'Can't have the local sage

baring himself to nobodies.' 'You're right.
Edmund's gone. I'm gone. Like Him!' 'You made
your world,' said Nick, 'and now you're out of sight.

I call that cool.' And that was it with God
for quite a while. Forever, now I thought,
forever up till now when I'd said it.

I staved Him off and stood again. 'It's wet,'
I now observed, 'it's raining where we are.
This could be the express that runs all night

to Scotland, doesn't stop at anywhere.
That's what it is,' I firmed it up. At last
the thing made sense. And soon at last appeared

a soul to share it with, my reflected face,
my straight man so the joke could work. We met,
both bowed confessionally against the glass;

improperly we kissed. He was a Scot,
I dubbed him for good luck, he was my guide
who joined me at the border. Like a shot

his face lit up, a tunnel flew outside.
I turned away and all the train was lit.
I rose, I had sensed movement, now I stared

one carriage back. The buffet car was bright,
rattling for some custom. And I knew
no way could it be open, but the sight

located hunger in me like a new
discovered growth: it swelled to my own size
and in I went. The seats there were pale blue;

some places had been set, were set for teas.
I swayed and sat. *Had* they been? I stared
at knives and forks and napkins, plates. 'Oh please,

let this, let this,' I shivered, and I heard
then saw the blinds of the shut counter lift,
roll upward and be gone. There a man stood

polishing a spoon. He was stout and clothed
in black with scarlet piping, and his cap
was red with a black brim. He saw me, moved

briefly out of sight, then back, looked up,
then said – I didn't understand a word.
I reached the bar, cried, 'Christmas Day, old chap,

three beers and all your sandwiches – my God!
Where are we going, sir? You see, my friends,
they got me sloshed on Christmas Eve, they're mad,

they must have put me on this train, which means
I spent all Christmas Day, can you believe,
heading to bloody Scotland and – this train's

bloody empty as I live and breathe,
where were you? You weren't here. Your driver, he's,
he's deaf or else he's crazy, or he loathes

sixth-formers, eh? I know for sure he does,
your driver.' So I bought and ate and paid
with my last fiver, now it was just pennies,

had I not bought a bracelet? That was odd,
that wasn't there. I drank the barman's health,
watching him. 'Are you, are you a Scot,

heading home, are you?' He took a breath
as if to answer but he let that go.
Words came in with the next, like the whole truth

washed up in another world. There was no
syllable I understood. It came
with a wry smile, I fancied, and a glow

of goodwill in his eyes, but I was dumb
and cold with fear. I drank the beers, and more,
feasted on carrot cake. With my money gone

he crouched and rummaged underneath the bar,
then reemerged with whisky of his own.
He talked about it. It was Glenamore,

I pointed to the word, and with a grin
he said his own without a consonant,
then poured us both great glasses of it. 'When ...'

I lifted up my slabs of sound, 'at Scotland?'
He shook his head and drank and I drank too,
till the lights danced and my disabled friend

was helping me by stages to my pale blue
seat and brought me sandwiches I ate,
triangle lardy cake which I ate too,

with beer beside 'to wash it down,' I said,
as he sat up behind the bar and sang
this strange and folkish tune I'd never heard

till I was sleeping, for that halting song
was my last memory of my first day.
I woke in the next carriage, one along,

where I had slept before. The sky was grey,
it looked like afternoon, in every field
you could see stones. My right hand came away

from my coat pocket clenched. Open, it held
the money I had started with. My mind
was clean and clear. I was seventeen years old.

 – That's all of twenty years ago. I have learned
I am still seventeen: add on perhaps
those seven hours in '77, that grand

time with the Poet in '84, my hopes
that lasted for whole hours. It's '90 now,
as I write this. I've taken giant steps

towards you, you who read this. You know how?
There's not a word that isn't known by rote,
it's how I brought it here to this new town

of black and white, the page. Now every night
I sit in the same food buffet with the same
macabre servant present and I write,

I make the thousand copies of this poem
I'm going to need in – I can calculate –
four hundred and five days, for when I come

to Hartisle once again at Christmas, late
on Christmas Eve of 1991.
All these copies can survive the night

because I've backed them up. I took a carbon!
Look at my smudged fingers, indigo
with memories I call my claws in Heaven.

 – But I can't desert myself, before I know
a thing about the world I'm in . . . I looked,
and found the day half gone. The breakfast toast

was buttered in the food car, but he'd locked
the counter and was nowhere to be seen.
I walked the empty train again and knocked,

and this time not a sound. This had a claim
to be the worst of all the days. So dark,
so fearful. But it's hard to reconvene

my feelings. I was well beyond the joke,
and clung for a short while to an idea
that some great crime was underway, some crack

red terrorists were taking this train where?
Gave that one up. It was as if I'd stood
with everyone I loved on a top floor

which suddenly gave way. Through wire and wood
I tumbled, through a room of people shocked
and so too slow to help as with a thud

I holed another carpet, dropped and smacked
the kitchen tiles that gave like chocolate, down
into a dusty cellar, then a crypt,

and now a shaft, and still I flapped and clung
at twig and bone and flint of what in real
life could have befallen me – what thing?

By the next afternoon when still I fell –
what now? I dabbled in a dream of dreams,
I reasoned it the realest dream of all,

the one so real to touch you make it home,
you make it where you are. It was my last
hold on light, the last idea to seem

escapable. It rained that day. By dusk
I felt what I would feel for seven years:
that I was *in* my mind, and that was lost.

Then hours of nothing, hours of stillborn tears
cold on the cheek as I stared out. Times spent
talking through the driver's door, or the beers

like skittles on the counter, and my friend
relating something in his garbled tongue.
I'd ask the word for 'beer' or 'nose' or 'hand'

but learned that it would change, that I'd be wrong
with the right word tomorrow. Happy Hour
I christened him: he was the only thing

I waited for. My money was good there,
I'd be expected and I'd drink my way
to dreamless sleep again. When the Driver's door

opened at last he didn't look at me
but shared a word with Happy Hour, who sat
commenting on the mountains. 'Edmund Lea,'

I said. They spoke in whispers. 'Today's date
is January 1st,' I said, 'New Year.'
The Driver's hands were large, I saw, his head

a fright of yellow curls. 'Be of good cheer,'
I told them, 'Yellow River. Happy Hour.'

XIX

He must have had the thinnest skull I've seen,
a shaven man who woke me. He was a yard
away in uniform and in a scream

berated me with a recurring word
made of all *f*'s and *s*'s. There was sweat
emerging from him though the world outside

was wintry grey, a land of freezing wet.
He held his hands behind his back, and leant
bizarrely forward like a figurehead

foaming in anger. 'I don't know what you want!'
I cried, 'you're meaning nothing!' So of course
he heightened the tirade, as if I'd spent

my breath in reinforcing his. 'It's yes,'
I cried again, 'it's no!' and rising up
to face him felt the air between compress

and bounce him back to stumble in a heap.
I giggled, I'd repelled him! Mrs Lake
in Physics would be proud. I and this creep

were poles apart, the red end and the black
of butting magnets. 'Clip that, bony fucker,'
I told the ticket man – Inspector Stick,

I came to call him – 'I don't have a ticket.
You have to pay *me* to be on your train.
Do *you* have one?' He stood, hands in his pockets,

aggrieved. He hoisted his blue-black machine
up to his chest, then ratcheted it twice.
He went on down the carriage. 'Busy time,

we're having, are we?' I could hear his voice
replying in some tongue. This was a scene
we'd play and play, though he never brought his face

so close again. The others were the same:
they couldn't touch me. Those two never tried;
they were polite, good listeners. My chum,

Happy Hour, he'd amble through at five
to open up, suggesting with his brows
a different tipple? *'Edmund, what'll you have?*

I'd say for him. *You know it's on the house.*
I'll have some wine, HH, Hungarian red
I fancy. *Coming up. Slight hint of rose,*

aged in oak, a liberal wine, well-fed,
a little spoilt, good at cards. Oh yes,
a dab-hand, I can tell, it's very goodly.'

I'd take my drink away, sit down across
the aisle from him. He'd scan the book he owned,
his tall thick book of graphs. It was embossed

with something he was pleased with. He would find
three-coloured graphs to show me. For a while
I'd look, then gravely nod; he'd move his hand

to turn the watery pages past until
another point of interest. *'Same again,
Edmund?* Thanks, HH. I think I will,

it's nice. *We an authority on wine?*
No, not at all, HH. Don't know a thing.
I'm dead, you see, except there's still this brain

that's dimly going. I was seventeen,
I made it to. I was about to spend
my eighteenth Christmas Day, it had begun,

at least I think it had. *How's that, my friend?*
I'm error-prone, HH. I fell in, well,
love, I fell in, if you want a sound

to stand for it. But this was with a girl
I couldn't have. I wound up on a bridge,
I think, and I'd been drinking, and I fell,

it seems to me, down to the track. Or each
time I wake I sense that fall – I see
a figure, her perhaps, but by a hedge

at sunset, so before . . . It may be me,
HH, then I feel falling and I wake
in my beloved carriage. *Who was she?*

Her name was Clare. She got me, like a joke.
She did this to me. *Devilkind, they were,*
the ladies. Lips as red and hearts as black.

You're safe aboard the train. I am? You are.'
I tried to give him character, to find
a world behind him, he was always there,

but all I needed from him was the sound
of asking me and answering me. HH
was like my writing book until I found

my memory in the years ahead – a stage,
a sounding-board, a mirror. Since to me
in those dark years he was a mere vestige

of form in an illusion, I felt free
to cast him as I chose. To that poor shade
I moaned the piteous tale of Edmund Lea,

his love, his loss, his lucklessness. He poured
Courvoisiers into the flutes so thin
a drop was inches high, then he said his word

for *your good health* and so we drank. 'We're gone,'
Happy Hour, we're gone. *Why so we are,*
Edmund, we're the goingest of men.'

The night outside was black as death, as fear,
as evil? Tarot cards. The night outside
was black as being unaccounted for.

The hands that stalk the face cannot avoid
the times they cross, and I would chime with pain
each time it happened, when the tears were set.

I thought of us, Mum, Dad and Caroline,
I thought of us in boats escaping out
on those hot breakers, better to be gone,

while the great hulk was burning black and bright,
its cabins crumbling and its sailors doomed,
and we could sail on a small boat all night.

I saw our fleet of boats, the sea becalmed,
moonlit, my friends hallooing from afar,
familiar. Chosen spokesman, now I named

all of them, no losses! There'd be Clare,
wrapped in a woollen blanket, all her mirth
gone out, expended, she'd be helped ashore.

The thought would peter out. Dry land was death
to all my fantasies. I sat alone
in the abysmal train, my deepest breath

my dearest friend. Now Happy Hour was gone.
He'd made his goodnight sound, and left the rum
for my convenience, and a small light on,

as on we hammered into kingdom come.
 – I lost the days that first year, had a sense
of never-ending winter, but it came,

the spring, as in all lands and neverlands
I know it seems to when it all seems lost.
I was painting. Happy Hour had found me paints

and paper; I was sitting up in first,
trying to get the hills – I was no good,
but everything was grey or went too fast –

then passing trees had second trunks, or had
shadows, shadows, from a light up high,
much higher than I'd thought. The whey-white cloud

that never lifted and was all our sky
had for a moment (which was gone again)
been caught by light and pulled reluctantly

the shadows from its pockets. Now the line
of leafless souls between the chilly fields
appeared expectant and recalled the crime,

forgave, and waited. Over many miles
each was rewarded with a russet sash
and shade restored, new pattern to the hills.

The light was so much higher than my wish,
I saw again: in miserable hours
depending on it I had kept my watch

two thumbs off the horizon, sobbing there
until the shrug at twilight, unconsoled
in the buffet car. Now it had reappeared

so high, so lofty, like an old friend's child
to whom you cry, 'You've grown!' and get a look
so blank you merely smile. I merely smiled,

and painted shadows for about a week.
Then Happy Hour found me a pastel set.
To my relief the white of my sketchbook

would do for this spring sky. I'd be about
to reach for my mixed yellow when I saw
the white assailed, but I'd not touched it yet;

I basked in waiting. It was hard to care
how good I got, since every page I filled
was empty the next day, or wasn't there.

This seemed the custom here in this dark fold
of my diseased interior: that all
expression was extinguished, as if reeled

backwards to me. Every syllable
or sentence written, every stroke or dab
of paint or pastel spiralled to a hole

like water and was gone when I woke up.
As sure as I could never lose my money.
As sure as Happy Hour would touch his cap

and talk his freshly alien mumbo-jumbo.
It took another lifetime to discover
how to keep. In the meantime I was somehow

chalk on an old blackboard, many-coloured,
daily free, nightly erasable,
the dark outside the closing of my cupboard.

Imagine what it meant to see April –
or so I estimated – and the sunshine
often in a week, and the new pale

lime and petal tints, with my attention
hourlong, even daylong, to the sight
of that soft, undulating, grassy region

we passed the month in. Think of having thought
time dead to you, then feeling the new pulse
of any season, let alone the great

bestirring Spring . . . for I had little else
those early days of my despair; these joys
immeasurable to you as molecules

were measureless to me, infinities.
After emotion, and the glasses raised
so many times to many sunset skies:

the reasoning, the wonder rationalised.
'HH, you know, my brain is such a god.
Though it can't let me go, it's realised

I once existed somewhere where we had
these season things. Poor god, it's trying hard
to make me think I'm living. *Just so, Ed,*

perhaps a top-up there, that's very shrewd,
very astute, that is, if I may say so.
And what came after this in your old world?

For it couldn't get much brighter. You don't think so,
Happy Hour? You wait until it's June,
it's brighter still! *You think so? I know so!*

You wait until July, then. When that's gone,
maybe I'll be. I'll tell you when we're there.
Be sad to leave you, really. *Oh come on,*

be honest. Are you sad to breathe the air?
Yes, these days. *Drink this, it's sad as you.*
Nudged forward suddenly, I held the bar

and swayed. I stared at Happy Hour. 'It's true,
we're slowing down. We never have. We are.'
I couldn't give him words. I didn't know

what they might be – he did give a thick murmur
in the vaguely Slavic sound he made that day,
and settled to his book of charts. 'We're somewhere,'

I whispered, 'there's a place along the way,
we stop there, there are people there – this spring
is consciousness, it's my recovery!'

He looked up for a second and said nothing.
The train had slowed between two grassy banks,
misted with white flowers, too high and sloping

to give a clue to why we slowed. 'Give thanks,'
I told the ghostly barman, 'to my brain:
we're not abandoned!' He was pouring drinks

in any case. There was a jolt again
and we were really slow now. And the sides
lowered away and levelled to a plain,

unfenced of course, unfeatured but for woods
at its far distant rim. It fell away
to nothing then, until the rooted clouds

of misted berry hills, then the real sky.
There was no sign of life, or of my kind.
Ahead the rails were curving: I could see

the front five carriages, and, like a friend
thought lost forever, I could hear the wind.

XX

If you are with me, you do not know Hell.
If you are with me now, you don't. I know
you were not with me then. There was not a soul

but the recurring three who at the window
watched as I stepped down to the still land.
I knew a hundredth part of what I now

believe: I thanked God on unmoving ground
for this dim shred of light to my dumb brain.
'HH, look, I'm Armstrong!' I turned round

to tell him, but they all had gone. 'The moon,
I'm on,' I said alone. 'I'm stepping forth,
mankind is watching,' and I wandered on

into a first great sandy field. Your breath,
your breath can no more smear the ink of this
than I could leave that desolating path.

I'd lost whatever lets us try, the thrust
into the dark, I followed where the trail
was clearer, had my eyes on a sharp crest

of hillside. I would stop there for a spell,
munch my provisions and observe the land,
strike out again for the next highest hill,

then on until I dropped, or else could find
a human sign. By the fourth hill the train
was barely visible. Richly I dined

on cheeses from my bag. 'If it's my brain,'
I said aloud, 'it's empty, so let's eat.'
I shouted for the echo, as I'd done

once in a gorge with Dad. He said I'd started
landslides, and we ran, but then he laughed.
I started nothing now. The stone ignored it,

the wind engulfed it. I was one, bereft
of even echo. At the next high point
the train was gone from sight. Now I would brave

the emptiness. This ruined continent
was mine to cross and I was its to suffer.
Birdless, insectless it was, it wasn't

bearing anything but me, its maker,
unechoed, unacknowledged, and alone.
I walked another valley with no river

lining it. On a denuded stone
I fought my eyelids open. On a height
that oversaw a further dusty plain

I curled away and spoke into the heart
of nowhere. As I do now, twenty springs
removed from him I picture at the spot,

no nearer freedom, with the selfsame lungs
that plump and shrivel as the view goes by.
Sleep crept to him, to me, on the worn rungs

of every breath, and packed the day away
like a good parent. Soon my body woke
exactly where it always wakes: one eye

lifted to bright afternoon, one cheek
cold flesh against the glass; the crew unfazed,
my pockets full, my head clear, and my artwork

crazily undone. Who is amazed
at what he daily lives? You, who have seen
in the last twenty years the yellow sunrise,

do you prize it now? To Edmund it would mean
his life returned to him. Your spine would freeze
at these phenomena in which I'm spun,

but I was soon inured to my disease,
deep-settled in these cells. We slowed again;
about a week went by when in a place

of long grass meadows and the warmest sun
so far I walked a day or so. I found
neat hedges, tended and I cried, 'Someone,

some work, some time!' I saw a flowered mound
that seemed created! It was what I chose
for bed that night, befriended in my mind

by supposition of some local souls.
I told all things to Happy Hour each day,
over the sandwiches or the chicken rolls

he set before me as I jawed away.
And so I lived in limbo, ever holding
my dear demented brain itself to be

the theatre of this emptiness, rebuilding
slowly to a species of new life.
It was a hundred days (I was now counting

carefully) since my first striding off
into the land. I reckoned it July.
It had been raining, but was warm enough

and sunny now, and the light bright and high,
for wandering some way. So I stepped out,
shouldered my good bag and a flask of wine,

and ambled off into the wooded heat,
thought lucky by the rainbow at my back,
the air the blessed damp of a washed sheet

billowing on the line. This was a trek
of new delights and sadnesses: the first
white roses set in rows, and the first brook

chuckling by a grass shelf where I rested,
gazing at the cirrus. The first fly,
the second, the first running water tasted,

the birdsong finally when that grand day
was in its blue decline, and I could hear
repeating notes. For then I heard a sigh

that froze the skin and bristled every hair.
A time had come. Some yards away, between
two silver birches, on a wicker chair

there sat a man, a plump man with a green-
grey hunting jacket, and he rose and stared.
'You are the first,' I blurted, 'that I've seen,

in the great space. I am – a son – that's dead,
you see, but for life-images that play
forever in my mind. The place I died

was at a station, so every night and day
I travel on one train, awaiting either
freedom – or an end, a seal on me.

In life I was in love – but my only lover
fooled me. Were you told of me?' The man
resumed his seat and with a pudgy finger

pointed off. The seven-carriage train
had rolled into the field adjacent. Tracks
I hadn't noticed led through the green corn

into the distance. Soon the stranger spoke
his patternless half-penny's worth of noise,
and had me burbling praises in the dark

for what had brought alive this figure. Others
followed: after days of walking, shades
ever alone, uncomprehending boys

in bluebell vales, or stranded on hillsides
and seeming lost, or older men by streams,
bootlessly fishing, resting in the glades

of yellow woodland, elderly sometimes,
or young in fiery bracken in bad moods,
or darting from me too late, like dreams.

They formed my thinly scattered brotherhood,
these apparitions, each of whom cost miles
of wandering. Some spoke, though never words

a tongue could spell. Some halted me with tales
in which recurred one little stab of sound
that seemed defining. Some were happy souls

who only smiled and some were round the bend.
But all were male and all were on their own
out walking; none I've ever seen again.

Reel in, wind on, whatever will was done
for seven years. My life in its vast cell
prospered in silence as the spectral train

ran on through worlds transfixing to recall:
gold hills, ash hollows, beaches with the sea
too far away to hear, a streaming gale

that blew for weeks, the lilac ice that seemed
in constant motion and a land of snow
behind wire fences – we'd begun to see

more signs of artifice: an amber glow
on one horizon, a stark crucifix
picked out on a high ridge. They'd come and go,

the men, I'd come and go. For what seemed weeks
I'd scarcely leave my carriage; there'd be days
I'd keep my seat, with all my sketching books.

And when you find these words, it's in that place
you find me. Now I've led you through the time.
It's as I told the Poet. Seven years

had passed, in the dimension of a dream,
when suddenly around us were real towns,
then towns I knew, then loved. It was my home

in 1977. I staggered down
into my world wound onward, where my friends
had aged and I (unrealising then)

was as I was. Briefly I held the hands
of her I'd pictured, yet was unaware
that other hands were holding me, the hands

that hold me still, and I was brought from there
home into Hell, for, in the desperate age
of my return to nowhere, Hell was where

I knew I was. Despondency and rage,
a pass or two at self-destruction, these
were features of that spring. Flights from the edge

of cliffs were favoured – I discovered those
could really put the days behind me quick.
That couldn't last; it came as no surprise

when each attempt would earn me seven weeks
without a stop. Just one infernal rule
I had to learn. What else did I expect

but pain and sanction? I was lodged in Hell,
my Hell. Yours may be stuffed until it shrieks;
mine, love-avoiding, gapes like any skull.

And why I'm there, and why for the angels' sakes
I leave it every seven years, I leave
to angels to explain. What action breaks

me from this place forever I believe
I'll learn in time. In 1984,
my guess was right. Aghast, on Christmas Eve

I found myself arriving home, when there
appeared a Poet with an empty book,
who listened to me closely, held me dear,

told of a curse he knew, that was unlocked
by declaration of undying love.
I tricked a pledge from Lucy, and awoke,

alone again, deservedly unsaved.
After the loss in '84, there came
my forty days of ocean, the white waves

lapping at the rail, and the clear time
of recollection – Cole, Cole on the bridge
inducing me to take his life. The crime

of doing so – the unreceding image
of his throned body through the air, his voice
before he speaks. The deed of it, the damage

dwelt on, then the strength to memorise,
to seal the hurt in – now began the years
of having it by heart, whatever was,

committing it, the cold and facing hours.
This is the thousandth of a thousand books
I made of this these years. The carriages

are piled with them, undiffering. My works.
A thousand times I own up to the murder.
I pray that this time, for these thousand acts

of truth, when my tormenting is considered,
I shall be free to dwell where I began.
The afternoon is long, and when it's over –

one night to wait. It's 1991.
The train will slow. When the first streetlight gleams
tomorrow, on the twenty-fourth, and towns

of England form again, my thousand poems
I'll throw from here, paving beloved ground
with these exact confessions of my crime.

You who have read so far, this is your town
I inch towards: you do not know my face.
It cannot age, and aches to. No sun

it's seen for more than twenty years can rise:
they only sink. Its eyes do little more.
Its mouth is starving for a word it knows,

its throat is rust, its ear is caked with air.
It might be that of anyone you see
at Christmas on his busy way somewhere,

weighed down with thoughts of home, or one whose eye
is on you ages after you pass by.

5 *Mallarea*

CHRISTMAS EVE, *1991*. Edmund hears Wasgood and Polly (now twenty-six and twenty-three) talking on the train, and knows he has come home again. He has made a thousand copies of his verse confession, hoping that this will redeem him. But only Polly seems to remember what happened. They drift together through a vast shopping mall, where Edmund is dimly recognised by an old friend. They visit Edmund's home, only to find his family moved, and a drunken party in full swing. They find the house of Clare, now thirty-eight and much changed. At a new pub on the site of the brasserie, Edmund finds old friends not so changed. Desperate to avoid the railway station, he tries to get arrested . . .

XXI

'I said I'd get him cards, a pack of cards
I'd get him. And he's all like *ma'moiselle,*
the French for women, he's got all French words,

Arthur does, he says how them other girls
he thinks I'm one of, how we swiped his things
when he and the boys came off his boat. He smiles

and says he's here to do a job for his king,
him and his boys. I want to say well, ta,
Arthur, that job's done, is what I'm thinking.

Shame he thinks it's still like it's his future.'
'What king is it, he reckons?' 'I don't know,
but *he* don't know they done that job – Arthur,

him and his boys. He thinks he has to go,
go there, do his stuff.' 'That's some sad shit,
Pell, him thinking that, 'cos he's our hero

is what he is.' 'We all, like, tell him that.
Mrs Bailey does, and the Paki nurse,
and the new bloke who does our garden. *Great,*

they call it, that bloke says, to end all wars
was what they reckoned.' 'Yeah, only it never.'
'The garden bloke, he says, they called it *First,*

it being first like worldwide one, but after
they had to call it *Great,* 'cos of the second,
but he's forgot he fought in that, old Arthur.'

'He hasn't. Fuck.' 'He's not forgot it happened,
only him being there. Instead it's all,
this morning, like, I'm getting his bed straightened,

doing the rounds – ' 'Up in the morning, Pell,
that's really you.' 'It's not but now it is,
I got to, bleedin' five o'clock this girl's

setting the branflakes out!' 'That's mental news.'
'He's by the window, and I'm going, "Arthur,
what the fuck are you up to?" 'Cos the view,

it's not, I mean it's back of Marks and Spencers,
know what I mean?' 'You told him what the fuck?'
'I told him anything, he don't remember.

He says we nabbed his kettle, at the dock.
He says he docked this morning with his *chums,*
came in on the *Southampton,* says we took 'em,

me and my *ma'moiselles,* his pots and pans,
nabbed 'em for souvenirs. And I say, Arthur—'
'Tell him he kicks arse, tell him he wins,

Pell, you tell him he gets home, poor tosser.'
'I go, *M'sieur, we're glad you're here.* He's come
to save us, 'cos it's what we said whenever,

nineteen, *I* dunno.' 'Fourteen, you tell him.'
'Then I say eat your meal. How's Allied *thing?*'
'Shit. I got this boss, I'm going to kill him.

I had to work till two today, typing,
yeah you can laugh, typing, like I do that.
Christmas Eve, I'm typing.' 'I do typing,

but orange words on black.' 'Well ain't we *it,*
you and me, Pell, tell our dad we're really
almost famous now, he'll be dead proud

to see his children typing on the telly.'
There was a silence then, as the Estates
went past and the sun sank behind, a chilly

crimson eye below the budding streetlights,
and a star picked itself to be the star
for any child out in the cold that night.

We hit the tunnel and the rush of air
ruffled my few remaining manuscripts.
I thought of Happy Hour, how he wasn't there

suddenly, when I stood among the heaps
of work and asked him for his help, and how
I ran to the driver's cabin, caught a glimpse

of someone new who waved at me to go,
then swore in English and the time had come.
I lifted up my work and wandered through

in sweet delaying ecstasy, numb
with knowledge, golden-legged in the grim awe
at being granted freedom – one night's freedom –

panic and pride at the stern height of law
that walled my life within. As we shot out
into Tows Hill I was already there,

bolt upright in an unaccustomed seat
in what had been the buffet car. Those two
were there, I heard them, heard the sister's bright

impenetrable chat, her brother's low
and doubtful mutter. So, these were the shells
on the wet sand of a new world: by now

they were my witnesses, my sentinels,
my keepers of the gate. Soon they would glimpse me,
but now, as a lost soul when the church bells

he knows and loves are heard at last distinctly,
far away, I listened, just to know
my world returned alive and turning in me.

'I got him this. About four weeks ago
he said he needed one for the new motor,
but I bet he thinks I'm psychic, that I'm just so

tuned in to him.' 'I got him these cool letters,
you know, to write,' said Pell, 'but it's all posh,
for special letters.' 'Like he can be bothered,

know what I'm saying?' 'It's what I got him, Woz.'
'Too bad, I got him software.' 'What's that?'
'It's WriteWord, number 3, some shit, it's this

packet you can get. It's what I got.'
'He'll never work it out, Woz.' 'Like instead
he'll write on *classy* paper.' 'He won't write,'

said Polly, 'cos he's got no worries, Dad,
but it's the thought that counts.' They were then quiet
as if to try the theory out. Outside

we went by twilit playing fields, the lights
of Hartisle just beyond, the twinkling cars
illimitably lovely on those streets

I tried and failed to name. The seven years
I did with fingers, curling two in one
confining fist, for there were no more prayers

to say today. In late blue afternoon
the sun went down again, beloved eye
of snake, beloved end of tunnel, gone,

put out. 'When I next see you may you rise,'
I said, by accident aloud. The kids,
who were still talking, ceased to. So I rose

and went to them. Woz lay across three seats;
Polly read a book and they weren't kids.
He was broad-shouldered in a black tracksuit,

he wore enormous running shoes. His legs
were longer than the seats and in my way.
His sister sat between two canvas bags,

one red, one silver. Something in one eye
was odd, she wore a yellow-black peaked cap
with LAKERS on it, some boat holiday

she'd been on, and her hair was gathered up
into the hat. Her mouth, diminishing
from what she'd smiled at, shut now, her top lip

jutted out slightly over. Everything
she wore was black: jeans, sweater, her scuffed boots.
Only a narrow silver neck-chain hung

a little fish in plastic at her throat.
I stood there with my manuscripts – a man
they knew for a cold-blooded killer. 'What?'

Wasgood moved his feet. 'What's going on?
You want our tickets, kid?' I had to laugh,
to be called kid by those two, whom I'd known

as infants! 'Want my fucking autograph
or what? Is it my typing, like you heard
I'm on this train?' 'He wants to get a life,'

his sister said, 'for Christmas.' 'Listen, kid,
do I look like fucking Santa? Someone singing
Shady Christmas, are they, kid? Well get

the hell out of my grotto.' I said nothing,
waited for them to see. They didn't see:
he carried on. I sat and he was swearing,

calling me all kinds of things. 'It's me,'
I said when he ran dry. 'It's me, James Bond,
Dark Vader, you remember? Superspy?'

He stared, he read my face until it meant
nothing, then he sniffed. 'Is he for real,
or is he some bleedin charity event?'

Polly zipped her coat: ''s just Hartisle.'
'You know me,' I began again, 'last time,
seven years, we met. He calls you Pell,

but really your name's Polly, your nickname
was *Pele* when you were a child, and his –
is Wasgood, that was his idea.' 'My fame

spread far and wide,' said Wasgood: 'Pell, this guy he's
out there, he's like Spock. I'm going to lose it.'
'What's the point, we're nearly there, it's Christmas,

he's just some nut.' 'I know. It don't excuse it.
He's saying stuff he don't know.' 'You came here
to see the coloured fountain, for a visit,

to show it to your sister, in the year
1977 – she was ten,
or nine, you'd made a snowman. I was there,

you talked to me. You'd done your hair bright green
next time I saw you, 1984,
a bar called Sleeks, they wouldn't let her in,

or me, and we just wandered – you were there,
threw up outside the place. You caught the train
I caught, and you remembered it, the murder,

I swear, you knew me then!' 'No swearing, son,
God covers up His ears,' and he sat back,
glancing at his sister, who looked down,

grinning. Woz said: 'I ain't ever sick.
Sleeks was a hole. What are you, mister stalker?'
Polly snorted: 'Yeah, at the age of, like,

two he's seen us, sure. Ignore my brother
because he's shit at maths.' 'I'm thirty-eight,'
I told them, and I was, 'The curse I suffer

requires I look the same as on the night
I killed – a man called Cole. I was seventeen.
You saw me do it, Wasgood. You cried out,

I'd woken her. You'd got on the last train.
You were trying to get to Creslet.' 'Were we, *chaps,*
were we,' he repeated. 'What are they?'

inquired his sister, nodding to my scripts.
'They're all the same, they're poems, you can each
take one away, they tell you—' 'Spock. You're nuts,'

said Wasgood. I'd relaxed him: now he lodged
his hands in deep side pockets, 'You're a headcase,
you, you're like my sister, you're well-matched,

she wrote a poem.' Polly's foot knocked his,
and she curled up. I said: 'In this long poem
I tell how I was cursed, and why I was.

I tell how I am lost to my own home.
And how I threw a man from this exact
bridge we're going under now. It rhymes,

because that's how I learned it.' 'Actual fact
there's someone on my mind,' he said, 'someone,
couldn't be you, some kid, but way on back

that was, couldn't be you. I saw the sandman,
I told 'em, Pell, I saw him fall like, quick,
he was, and fucking bang and, like, with bone,

X-rated, know what I'm saying? It was sick,
man, it was, I must have been well young.
I do know no one ever gave a fuck

I told it to. *You having us all on,
Cassius Clay?* I's like well fuck you all,
I saw it. *You been on the ganja, son?*

they go. I'm just this youngster. That for sale?'
He took a script from me. '*Edmund* – Lay?'
'Lea.' 'That you?' 'It is.' 'Yeah. You don't spell

Lee like that, I hate to have to say.'
'*I* do.' 'I see you do, don't make it right.'
The train had stopped, as usual some forty

feet from platform five. We were inside,
I saw now, we were sheltered, there were screens
along the platform. We were in this wide

expanse of shops that stretched away. 'This town's
the fucking business,' Wasgood said, and tossed
my poem into his sister's holdall. 'Thanks,

there, Lay, you going home?' 'He said he's lost,'
said Polly as she stood and zipped her coat,
'how can he do? He's got to find it first.'

Her brother stood and said, 'We getting out?
You gonna hang with Spock? What's that about?'

XXII

At times there's little mystery to how
I felt, it takes you little to get there.
And, should you want to, you can set out now,

take map and money and go anywhere
you never went in England, where a mall
spreads from the railway line. Should you want to share

further, only stand in that high hall,
look upward, be the only one to, stare
out the grey skylights, be the only still

contemplative creation to be there,
then say, with force and clarity, bright tones
to bring detectives running: *I am where*

I used to live. These people are my friends.
This was my only home . . . This simple game
may help you picture me. Picture my hands

grasping the other shoulder to be warm,
my feet unsteady in a world at last
of many and on ground that stays the same;

picture me peering at it, see me pushed
past by accident, me chuckled at
for my old coat, observe me spun to rest

on a sun-yellow bench where Polly sat.
They'd lost me or I'd lost them in a crowd
around a band of drummers. There the beat

had got me swaying and I sang aloud
whatever words came by. Then when I looked
they'd gone. At least I'd found her. 'I'm afraid,'

she said while doing lipstick, 'that, in fact,
you're really lost up here.' What *up here* meant
I couldn't tell. 'If you was all an act,

if you was all an act or if you weren't,
eachways it's just as lost. I hate this place,
I done my shopping, Saturday I done it,

only time I could. It's just for Woz
I thought I'd come here so he gets his done.
Get the last train to Dad's.' She lined her eyes

with a violet crayon: 'Know what this is? *Poison,*
that's the shade for *Poison,* someone thinks
in Paris . . . I could do that, be like spectrum

colourer, some shit. I'd make a mix
of gold and black and name it *Wasp.* Instead though,
instead I'm down the Centre with the stiffs,

and that's all different skills. But I got those.
I'm in a structure, Lee. If you ever make
old age, I'll sneak you in. You can write poems

in the canteen, I'll clear up round your work,
you'll be still celebrated, like, the man
who don't get old. Who broke some punter's neck.

I'll look like this!' She nudged me, it was done,
her face, it was white-powdered, with both eyes
and lips in purple, crudely in outline.

'My brother dared me go to work like this,
scare the old hoppers half to death! He's mad, him.
That's why I got a job with people. Woz,

he's better more behind the scenes. They made him
supervisor last year. Like to know
who's such a pillock at his work they'd put him

second to Dr Dense.' 'I have to go.
I don't know how to, but my family
lives somewhere here.' 'Are they the same as you,

all seventeen? That's fun on holiday,
but naff all other times, I reckon.' 'No,
they're older, getting older.' 'That's the way

it normally pans out.' 'I have to go.
The street is called Laburnum Lane.' 'You reckon?'
'I know it is.' 'Well, Lee, it's up to you,

I got no say. I'm stuck in here till seven,
when then he wants to meet with his old mates
who work here. Gonna meet him down the Virgin.

That's fun for me. They're more or less the pits.
See by that red sign YOU ARE HERE?' 'What, there?'
'Mm-hm, it's got a town-plan. You could start

by reading it.' 'My God, I'm really here.'
'Yeah, them red signs do come in quite handy.'
I scanned the map, and traced my finger where

I would have walked, before the 'mall', and found
the way to the town centre. From the star
that meant this place to the blue pointing wand

that meant the Fountain ran a sheltered path,
a tiled and covered lane of only shops;
once, perhaps, Carew Street. Now no cars

were here, only the clacking of footsteps
above a haze of undivided noise,
the teeming windows and the darting shapes

in coloured light, a flashing world indoors.
It was impossible to place a foot
on something I could name. 'This town of yours,'

Polly explained beside me, 'now it's got
the chains and all, so in from round November
the place is heaving, I don't go for that,

then the godawful sales they have, whatever,
finish, then you know what this is, Lee?
It's, *hello*, anybody here? It's over

and out, it's shot, it's dead. On Saturday
you'd come here for some kip. We ain't from here,
we only come by Christmas, we're the same

as anyone. See the nice lady there,
she's ogling you, Lee. You can't be lost
forever.' Someone was, a loopy stare

from a stout woman I assumed at first
was someone Mum knew. She had silver hair
tied back, and she wore glasses. As we passed,

she raised her hand towards her mouth. I saw
this bloke, her husband, reaching her, and how
she spoke and pointed over to us. 'There,'

said Polly. 'You been sighted, you're home now,
however shite it's got.' 'I have to go,'
I hissed at her. 'She's calling out, poor cow!'

'It doesn't matter.' 'Does to Mrs Moo,
it looks like, and there's kids as well, hey Lee,
your generation's coming after you!'

I glanced and saw two boys breaking away
from the plump woman and her man, whose frown
had deepened as we hurried on. 'Well hey,

you *are* the Superspy,' said my companion,
running, rapidly out of breath. We lost them,
cutting through a shop called Candle Canyon,

and into a wide Smiths. 'You really missed 'em,
didn't you, your mates. Give 'em a poem,
you could've, Lee, only you hadn't lost 'em.

Too late now.' I had, I saw, mislaid them,
the last of my one thousand. 'Never mind,'
said Polly brightly, 'No one's going to read 'em,

not in what's the culture. I've a friend
who would, he's ninety-two. He's still alive,
still in some war.' We trod towards the end,

the exit, where the day was, the sky mauve
and chilly, the outdoors! – when from around
an artwork came a family of five.

The father stopped and mouthed a word: *Edmund*?
His wife was blonde. I groped for either name.
The wife was flustered, tired: a step behind her

the children she was tired by wore the same
green jagged pixie costumes. 'Edmund's son,'
the man said, 'or his double.' 'Can't be him,'

the woman snapped, 'for Christ's sake use your brain.'
The man approached us. 'Look, is your name Lea?'
I answered yes. 'I knew it. You're his son.'

I needed to reach daylight, to be free
of this distressful alley, yet I'd sworn
over the years to answer truthfully,

and did so. 'No, I'm Edmund. I was born
in 1953. On Christmas Eve
of 1970 I was seventeen,

and, for the murder – ' 'What luck,' said the wife:
'care in the community.' 'No, wait,'
said Nick – Straton – 'Come and have a coffee,

son. It's nothing. Pam, he was my mate,
his dad. I want to talk.' 'You're taking them.
Damned if *I* am.' 'Fine,' said Nick. 'All right,

you frights are with me. Go, just go on home,
whatever.' 'Class. And you'll buy the tree lights,
I'm right in saying? And the Nintendo game

he won't shut up about? You'll do all that.'
'I will, I said I would, are you quite deaf?'
Polly stepped up: 'Lee ain't got time for this.

He has to reach Laburning Lane.' The wife,
almost amused, thought better and was gone,
then Nick was herding us to a café.

'Your dad was first, son, but we all moved on,
all changed. He must have had you in his teens
or nearly had you then.' 'I'm not his son,

again, I'm him.' 'You want a glass of wine?
I told the bitch it's coffee but, you know . . .
We're split these days, it's only for the gang

we do odd spots together. Like, you know,
reunion gigs. They're great kids, they're twins,
the two there scrapping: Gemma and – you two,

please – the Liebfraumilch – I loved her once,
Pame-*lah*. Your dad would know her . . .' '*Man*,'
Polly had zipped her bag and reached across:

'you've ninety seconds.' 'That your girlfriend, son?
Same as my wife. Get the general Rorke's?
The general drift? Rorke's Drift, it's just a pun.'

'Seventy seconds.' 'Must be the great sex,'
Nick Straton winked at me, 'That might be it.
Warm, am I? She's *goth*, I think, she looks

ooh, twenty? Just a kid like you.' 'I'm not.'
'I know, you're Edmund Lea.' 'You know I am.'
'Of course I do. Oi, mate. I said the *white*,

the *vino blanc* – forget it. Waste of time,
let's swig the fucker. Look, I liked your dad.
My first wife left. She said I wasn't him.

Too right I wasn't him. I'm me, I said,
I'm me! That's why, she said. Bloody whore.
And anyhow, I go, the fucker's dead,

but look, he isn't, is he, he's right here,
he's probing his espresso like it's some
mystery to him.' 'Your wife was here,'

I said, 'you said she left.' 'No, not their mum.
The mother of – I got a snap – their mother,
Rachel and Laura's, look. I got one. Them . . .

Oi you, Nirvana, why don't you come over,
clock my children, there.' 'They look like you,'
said Polly, 'mouth and nose.' 'Oh yeah, they're clever,

don't miss a trick. Difficult stuff, though,
son, your dad missed out on it. My wives,
bless their cotton hearts, they make it so

difficile, you know. See my little elves?'
'No, point them out,' said Polly. 'Very sharp,
razor-keen, you are,' said Nick. 'Poor loves,

there's no love lost. Pam and Clare, good job,
very humanely done. I rate this wine,
for café fare, I rate it. Ain't no pubs

in all this mall, mall-area, that's mine,
mall-area, malaria, as in:
bad air, mosquitoes, i.e. any teen,

bloodsucking high street chains, that's what I mean
by that, *mallarea* . . .' He drank some wine,
and looked at what he left. 'We all moved on,

is how it – if you do see your old man,
tell him it's okay, his thing, it's cool,
tell him. How he went. The being gone

was what impressed.' 'Is your – first wife still –
is she—?' 'Why, do you want her? Go ahead,
who gives a monkey's? Pam and I, we're real,

we fight, but we're *au fait*, so we both made
alternative arrangements. But – Clare's –
I mean, the first one, probably getting laid,

odds on as we speak, in the very house
we shared . . . That house was mine, would you believe?
Look at us. Got to hand it to the girls,

son, they got us where – they ride the wave
and we get soaked. My God, you look like him.
Between us, where'd he go? He still alive?'

'He's told you who he is. You're out of time,'
said Polly. I said nothing, then the same.

XXIII

So unfamiliar and unreal had seemed
that bright arcade, that semblance of a street,
I half believed the rest would be unchanged,

left as it was, balancing: it was not.
The former High Street lived on as a lane,
truncated, paved, laced up with fairy-lights,

remembering itself in its own dream.
Brasserie Turquoise. The Monument
remained, but with its old stone scrubbed to cream

it did look stripped. Across, where was our fountain?
'It's never there,' said Polly, 'or it's there,
this pool of water people lob their junk in,

only it's never on when I come here,
except one time it was.' 'Does it change colour?'
I wondered as we passed it by. 'Colour?

No, it's water, Lee.' As we walked further
some streets were right, the ones that led along
towards our haunts. A place called 'Happy Eater'

was where the Oak had been when I was young.
'That's a new pub,' I said, with my brave face
meeting its. 'Is it? Well we got one,

we got one where I work. That's where that place
we went to was,' she said, 'It's an ice dance
centre place. The bloke was in my class,

he was a wanker, Lee, his name was Vince
and now he's like he's *loaded*. It's not fair,
you know, he asked me out to bowling once,

I told him sit on this. A millionaire
I could have been, now I like mop up piss.'
'Sleeks,' I said, 'Your brother stood right there,

they wouldn't let you in.' 'Lee, you're like this
bleedin' quiz-show.' 'And you had green spikes
for hair.' 'For the big bonus: was I pissed,

true or false . . . Do we care now, do we fuck.'
Behind the Ice-o-theque there was a pub-
bar-restaurant complex called The Virgin Oak.

'I'm meeting Woz here later. Want to stop?
You got to get home, though. Can I come as well?
Being as how you're lost.' 'I'm here, I'm not – '

I faltered, 'lost from here. It's up this hill
and the first left, but I'm not even certain
who lives there.' 'This gets better, like, I feel

bad for you, or weird, but it's exciting,
being how we're your special subject, Lee,
and how you know stuff everyone's forgotten,

being as how you'd win a holiday
for two on what we did in such and such,
a year, you know, like 1968,

what happened next, you know, on the first of March
what happened, Lee, for thirty points, a hundred,
your holiday in Malibu! Not much,

not much was happening, only I decided
today's the day. Cos that date I was born
is the right answer, Lee. I was awarded,

you know, the cuddly toy, well thanks. Come on,
let's get you back to where you started from.'
And over Wheaton Hill we went, and turned

into my street together. And my home
was as it was, a glass door where had been
a panelled one, but everything the same,

the hedges taller now by the front lawn,
and a paved path, and the old cherry tree
was filled with Christmas lights. 'There's someone in,'

said Polly, 'plus his mates,' and we could see
the place was full of people. Up the path
I didn't look, but 'Look at them,' said Polly.

'We're being watched like anything, we're both,
it's the red carpet, Lee, hanging with you
's like having fucking Di to hang out with,

like people give some serious shit, they do,
they're opening the door.' And two or three,
others, more, grown men and women, no

one face familiar, grouped there, greeting me.
'Edmund?' said one woman: 'Edmund Lea?'
I nodded. 'Yes!' The crowd in the hallway

applauded now. I saw two hands raised high
and their palms slapping, different people's hands,
saw a pink fish on a tray. 'It falls to me,'

the woman said, and quietened her friends,
'to do the official honours at this time
of, how shall we say, much – ' 'Sampling of fine wines!'

a man roared in the background. 'No, welcome!'
announced the unknown woman, and she drew me
gently in through everyone. My home

was not my home, I knew immediately.
It had its form, as my hand has the form
of your hand, but I knew they'd moved away

by everything I saw. In the small room
my dad had worked in they had spread out food
and here it was they sat me down. 'You came,'

the woman smiled. 'I didn't think he would,'
said someone else. '*I* didn't. I owe Margaret
half a case of plonk!' 'Good on you, lad,'

another man was laughing: 'Knew you'd make it!'
They offered me a glass of beer. 'Where's she,'
I wondered, 'who came in?' 'Take off his jacket,'

a woman screeched: 'hard evidence!' 'Oh, Fee,
you *would* say that!' 'I did!' 'Margaret Lovell,'
the woman said, the one who welcomed me,

'you must excuse these horrors!' 'Aren't we awful?'
a lady hooted as some plates appeared,
one plate of cheese and salad, and then several

saucers of white pudding. 'Chow down, Ed,'
the plonk-man said, 'It's in your honour!' 'Gordon,'
said Mrs Lovell sharply, 'give the lad

his personal space.' They clustered in the doorway,
observing us as if we were these two
shy lovers on our date. 'Monsters, aren't we,'

said Mrs Lovell, 'when we've had a few,
given the yuletide – bit of a double-whammy,
probably, for you this. Good for you, though,

coming round the mountain, through the rye,
so to speak.' 'You know me – for some reason.
I don't know how you do. My family—'

'Moved out of here in 1987.
Moved to Sackwood Drive, and then again,
to Cutters Row. I've met your mum. No, Edmund,

don't go, because they're not there, they're in Spain
this winter, on the CDS, I know,
because she told me. It's their winter plan,

that's all. A week before they meant to go,
she came here with a letter that was sealed,
addressed to you. She told me all about you,

Edmund, that you travelled in the world,
had always done so – but you look so young,
you're Marvin's age! – but somehow she'd been told

you might arrive tonight? I may be wrong,
and it may not be my place but could it be
your father doesn't – well, they're always going

round the world themselves, Spain, Capri,
the hot spots as it were. It's always Spain
in winter, though, and cocktails by the sea,

the lucky ones!' 'It's 1991,'
I said, 'it's Christmas Eve,' I don't know why,
I knew it was, I asked where was it gone,

and she looked soothing, waved a glass away
somebody was approaching with, and said:
'Where has it gone indeed,' and she stroked me,

actually touched my shoulder. 'Where indeed.
I don't know where last week went, let alone
last year!' 'I meant the letter that was sealed

and had my name. I mean where has that gone?'
She shrieked with laughter: 'Oh, I thought you'd turned
all existential on us!' 'No.' 'It's in,

well, a special cabinet, Edmund.
She said it was a secret, that your father,
you're probably aware, was – never mind,

Edmund, and don't mind this big palaver.
We always have a bash on Crimbo Eve,
we thought we'd watch for you, the tall dark stranger,

tallish, darkish – well, the girl you're with
takes care of that – but as of now no call
to *be* a stranger, you've been the great myth

of recent weeks – will he, won't he – well,
you showed the doubters, Edmund, you did come!
You do exist!' 'It's Father Christmas nil,

Edmund one!' announced the one whose name
was Gordon. Plonk-man said: 'The wandering Jew,
more like . . .' 'A little un-PC, old chum,'

another man said, and one not in view
added, 'The age-old mariner,' so deeply
the room went quiet. 'We all believed in you,'

beamed Mrs Lovell, 'and you came exactly
when we needed you.' 'Can I have the letter
now, excuse me, can I,' I said bleakly,

emptily. 'It will be my great honour,
Edmund,' said this lady, 'Follow me.'
She took my hand and led me through the others,

who clapped me on the back and chuckled. Polly
was standing on the welcome mat, ignored
by everyone. 'This crew are pretty deadly,'

she reckoned as I passed, then the parade
was marching up the stairs, my stairs, to where
in what had been my bedroom a book-cupboard

was ceremonially opened wide. 'There,'
said Mrs Lovell, 'I declare the message
officially delivered!' A brown, square

envelope was handed to me. 'Postage
paid!' somebody giggled, and they made me
leader marching down again. One image –

a small girl staring from a dark bedroom,
once my parents' – was the last I saw
of it, of that, and, crammed into the food room,

they wanted me to read my letter there.
One brought me a brass slitter. 'Jesus Christ,'
I heard a voice say, Polly's, 'like I'm sure

he wants to share this with you. You're the first
I'd come to. Lee, I'm out of here.' 'Of course,'
said Gordon, 'right you are, it's as you please.'

One said as we went by, 'Hey what a swizz,
she didn't rhyme! I thought we'd hear some rap,
some funky rhythm music!' 'What it says,'

said Fee, who was quite drunk, and propping up
the bannister, 'is Dear son, three pints,
three pints of milk, milkman.' 'Fee, do stop,'

said Margaret Lovell. 'You two vagabonds
are welcome any time!' The cold night air
came in and found us. 'And don't mind my friends,'

she added, 'they're all jealous, they don't care,
that's their way! But you, Edmund, you've brought
a certain something to the yuletide fare,

yuletide, we call it now.' Cold, on a seat,
on Brilson Road a stolen cigarette
made Polly's breath a brown smoke to my own white,

and I read my mother's letter, my mum's note
she'd written on lined paper with a robin
in a bare tree at the top of it:

*Dear Eddie, you'll have no idea how often
I tried to write this letter. A hundred times?
I don't know if I'm mad, but I know someone*

*visited us once who was the same
I felt as my dear Eddie. My dear Cally,
your sister, and your dear dad, my Tom,*

*they do not think it's possible that could be
you who came. They hope I understand
it is not possible. But who can blame me*

*for hoping? So this letter I will send
to the new people who are living now
at our old house. So then, if you returned*

*from where you are, dear Eddie, you will know
you weren't forgotten by us all! Our home
is a new cottage at 8 Cutters Row.*

Cally has two children, Kyle and Kim,
they live in Berkshire now. Kyle has your eyes,
which splits me down the middle! I have time

to say more but I can't. Love, Mum. PS:
sometimes I think you're better off! God bless.

XXIV

Another well-lit house, another gate:
the sight of it a child's sincere attempt
to build with bricks the castle in my thought,

now I had dangled from a final glimpse
for fourteen years – Clare stumbling in the snow
to reach that door; I stowed two picture frames

in the mind's attic where it's mad to go.
We came, my odd companion and myself,
my witness, one of two, who years ago

haplessly crossed my path and could not help
recrossing it; I with my mother's note,
a bird in wintertime that should have left

with all its flock for somewhere far, sunlit.
Into the huge imagined haze I cast
a small true message. Polly folded it.

She'd held it to streetlight and read it first,
unbidden. 'Look, you didn't say their house
is full of scum. Call me the Christmas post,

call me the chimney, Lee, I'll handle this.'
She pocketed the letter with a sniff,
and frowned into the distance. Though her eyes

met mine they didn't mean to, and glanced off.
(The words I wrote are a mere further loss.
They died as they were done, they had short life,

though in their time they gave one stranger pause.)
We stood outside the house that was Clare Kendall's,
as the wind whipped up ironical applause

at those outdated names. I heard a cackle
of TV through the door. From the garden gate
Polly reported faces at a window,

but no one came. I rang again. The wait
was falling, in a well. Then two girls' voices
rose inside the door and yellow light

was opened on me. Girls in two black dresses
stood there, teenage girls, one long, dark hair,
one curly, fair, the younger. Their blank faces

had had expression once – there by the stair
I saw the photograph I'd seen: a boat
one morning in the sun. 'I stood just there

seven years ago,' I must have said
instead of thinking. 'Did you,' said the fair.
'I stood there half an hour ago. It's good,

it's really a cool place to stand.' 'I'm there
now,' the darker said, who was. 'It's great.
Other locations you've appeared in here,

just let us know. Yes? As in, yes what?
As in—' 'Go on,' the fairer said, 'I'll sing
the note and off you go: *Sigh . . . Silent Night,*

Holy Night . . .' 'You can't have anything,'
the darker reached the door again. 'We gave
a load to the Samaritans, who sang

really well, considering.' 'You can have
a biscuit,' said the younger one. 'No they can't,
don't listen to her, they're for Liz and Dave,'

the dark one said. 'You said they were for Santa.'
'I didn't, Laura.' 'Yes you did.' 'Don't lie,
you little sleaze.' 'Stones and sticks.' 'Whatever.'

'*She's* the sleaze,' the fairer said to me,
'but if you're Greenpeace or that type of group
and you can prove it, I *will* give you money,

so long as you don't sing that holy crap.'
'So rude,' the older said, 'it might be he's
Jehovah's, he can't help it.' 'I can help,'

said Laura: 'He can hold a debate with me
on spiritual stuff. I may not be religious
but I am still spiritual.' 'I'm Edmund Lea,'

I spoke into their chat, 'and I wonder is
Clare, is Clare, your mother, Clare Kendall
your mother—' 'Yes. She is.' 'Is she in this house?'

'The person you refer to as Clare Kendall,'
said Laura, 'is Clare Straton, legally,
so her full name is Clare Straton *née* Kendall,

although she goes by Kendall day to day.'
'In fact she goes by Mum,' the darker said,
'and who should I say—' 'Who's that down there, Rae,'

her voice exactly as I knew I heard
upstairs. 'It's a religious caller, Mum!'
said Laura, 'We're discussing Christian thought.'

'She's being a fascist, Mum, he says his name
is Edmund Lea.' 'He got your surname wrong,'
Laura said. 'No he didn't, little madam,

he got it right. Mum, are you listening?'
Laura noticed Polly by their gate
and asked was she with me. 'No I don't sing,'

she said from where she was, 'not on this street.'
There was a shadow on the staircase then,
boots and jeans, brown jumper – into the light

Clare came, her hair with static, wild and long,
her eyes dark, she was hugged with her own arms
and reached the lowest stair. 'Is he going to sing?'

she asked her daughters. 'No, there's two of them,'
said Laura, 'but one's hiding.' 'Which one's hiding,'
said Clare, 'is this one hiding?' 'This is him,'

the elder sister said: 'We were deciding
what to open when, when he showed up.'
'With his assistant,' Laura said, still meaning

Polly, who was now by me on the step.
Clare sat on the stairs. 'Well, let them in,
it's cold, get that door shut, maybe they'll help.'

In a warm chaotic kitchen we sat down,
around about a hundred presents, each
wrapped in red or silver or pine-green,

some with a tag. 'See, Rachel, we *are* rich,'
said Laura as we took our places, 'here,
these are all ours. I said it was too much

considering it globally.' 'Well, dear,'
her mother said, 'why not consider it
some other way, like greedily.' 'I'm there,'

said Rachel, 'are you, Edmund Lea?' 'He's not
Edmund Lea,' Clare said, now lifting out
a silver gift to look at it. 'He's quite,

he's welcome, he's quite welcome, but he's not,
are you, can you be him, I don't think so.'
The girls were staring. 'What school are you at –

whoever you are!' the daughters asked. 'I go
wherever I – ' was all I managed. Clare
leant forward to the table. 'What I know

is, we've no lights. Take this young lady there
and maybe they'll get fixed, while this young man
can tell me what he's on about.' The pair

leapt up together and with all three gone,
Clare stood and got two glasses and a jug
of sweet warm drink. 'It used to be mulled wine . . .

It's now just close your eyes and break a leg.
Think of England.' She drank and I drank.
She gazed around their kitchen. 'Want a cig?

I do, I don't have any. But, I blink,
you know, and you are Edmund, you could be,
so young though now, the only thing I think

is you're . . . his son, you are. He never told me
he had one when I saw him, it was years,
you must have been alive—' 'You can't believe me,

I understand, Clare, no, but on the stairs
at mine, my old – house fourteen Christmas Eves
ago, we were, together, almost lovers

all those years ago. You wore black gloves
and you had children.' 'Did I? I had one.
Laura's June of '78. That leaves

seven, no, six months, I was pregnant then,
dear, when I'm being groped on your old stairs.
I'm not convinced. Pity, it sounded fun.

What do you mean by *almost* lovers? There's
an all-embracing concept. *Almost* love
accounts for my whole life. *Almost* careers,

almost success, *almost* slim, *almost* Dave,
how many's that?' 'Your beautiful – two daughters
are – beautiful.' 'Because they *almost* have

a beautiful old mum.' 'They do have that!'
She looked at me across the pile of presents,
and then out through the door. 'That's almost sweet,

Edmund. I shall almost pass your comments
on to them, because I'm almost pleased
you like them, fancy them. You're a mate of Straton's,

aren't you? Saw he could pass you off as Ghost
of Edmund and he's doing it for a trick.
Warm, am I?' 'No, but yes, I'm like a ghost.

I can't grow any older but I'm stuck
outside of – you could call it a disease.
I do, I have. I know it didn't work,

with Nick, I mean. You know I'm Edmund Lea.
In love, I was, with you . . . It took me years
to think I'd ever say but now it's easy,

saying it . . . I know that's what it was;
it's easy now I've met you. On this date,
twenty-one years ago in a warm place

that isn't there, with a good crowd of mates
all gone now, I was kissed by you, held hands –
then this man came we had no plans to meet.

Cole, his name was, and he had no friends.
You left the place with Cole.' 'You mean the Oak,
that godforsaken hole. It's where we went

when we were kids, they served us. Some weird hoax
you're part of here. You've got to be the son.'
'You left with that man Cole. And when I next

encountered him I killed him, Clare. That man,
Cole, he asked me to and I obliged.
I pushed him from the bridge on Quillers Lane.

He fell still looking at me and was crushed
between the lines. I got on the next train
to get away. I woke somewhere I wish

on no man ever. Something has been given,
bestowed on me—' 'Rave on. I don't recall
this man, this Cole.' 'You don't?' 'Like it's *so* often

I meet some man – what kind of a showgirl
d'you take me for?' 'You must remember him.
You would have loved me if—' 'Oh is that all?'

She sighed and traced a line across her palm.
'No sign of it on this. You two are gone,
whatever you got up to in a dream.

You may be Edmund. You may be the man
who found the beauty product to end all
beauty and all products, but you're gone.

I don't remember loving you. I feel
sad you do, there have been some I loved.
I functioned like that once. I did have spells

of lust, you may have been one, but you left,
Edmund, if it's you, and if it's not,
you still left. You became a disbelieved

thing, they don't come back, they come at night,
they want to be restored to what we knew,
but we can't let that be. We had to wait

while they were rotting in us, had to stew,
waiting . . . We can't sweeten, Edmund. Look,
look at me, I'm old, and if you're you

I'll have that virus or whatever plastic
surgeon you've been using. If you're not,
you've been put up to something I find sick,

to trail those times in here. I'm thirty-eight,
Edmund. I'm divorced. I've teenage kids.
You say you're outside time, but you're too late

to ring a bell with me. Somebody's dead?
No one I know. I never heard the name.
You say you killed him and I hope you did,

I hope he died in pain, taking me home
as if he had some right to. Those days
they snap their fingers and we're in their dream

delighting them – they've gone. It was a phase
we probably enjoyed and were designed to,
Edmund, biologically, but please,

whoever you may be, it was a window,
one we liked to sit in but it's shut,
gentlemen, forever. It is with sorrow

we announce its passing but with no regret.
Have a mince pie, squire. Not a bad dream
you make tonight, some fantasy, some fit,

but no, there's not one cell of me the same
as her. Only the name. Or one of them.'

XXV

We sat in the upstairs. I'd never seen
an upstairs to a pub, but this new place,
the Virgin Oak, had galleries that ran

the whole way round above, where we found space,
with ones above them too, like a third tier
of people eating, drinking, shrieking. 'Mice,'

was all I said, and to nobody there
at our small table. Polly had gone off
to find her brother and if not some beers,

and I was thinking of my other life,
fondly suddenly, for its tendedness
of all things. I was shaken out of breath

by thinking that, I jolted with the loss
of oxygen. Like the neglected flower
in some dry nook I was, then felt the wash

of bright and close attention. By the chair
opposite, which Polly's jet-black top
was fitted to, an overweight long-haired

man in only denim stood. 'This pub,'
he said, 'serves eighty beers. This one I got
is Danish. Do you mind if I draw up

the old proverbial?' He took Polly's seat,
and leant towards me. 'Eddie, Eddie Lea,
you're always someone that it's good to meet

and natter through old times. The other day
some bird was doing you down. I said you watch
exactly what you're saying! Because he,

Edmund, is a friend of mine. That bitch
she shut up then! She backed off, she chilled out.'
He was so big. 'That's good of you, that, Dodge,

sticking up for me.' 'You got to, Ed,
stick with your mates. You may have been outside
the group in terms of musical output,

but when it all began, when it all started,
back there in way back when – I was on rhythm
then, though I'm more known behind a drum kit

these days, or, more accurately, tom-toms.
And the old backing vox.' 'You mean the band,
the band is still—' 'It's under brand-new brand names.

Bit of a mouthful, true. We're now The Wand.
Can't be The Hunger now.' 'Why can't you be?'
Stan Burke had brought a bar-stool. He explained

through a smoke haze the sad and winding story
of how they'd had their hit, how Michael Nelson
managed them back then and how one day

he sacked them all except 'the nameless person'
(Moon, he meant, the Indian kid), how Moon
had been a star until for no reason

he vanished without trace – how his one son,
Meadow, owned the rights to all the songs;
how Nelson had adopted him by then,

how all of them were rich and lived like kings,
'Excepting us three losers, Ed. Because
that cunt he took us big time. And he brings

our Christmas song out every year, then buys
a penthouse with the proceeds.' 'We don't mean
the magazine,' said Dodge, 'but a whole place.'

'He's totally sold out, of course,' said Stan,
'can't hold his head up. Comes in here, he does,
trying to gloat. As for the nameless person,

he *better* have expired.' 'Are you two guys,'
asked Polly, who was back, 'at all concerned
about what Lee's been going through? Or is

your useless combo all that's on your mind?'
'He's Eddie,' said Dodge Mendis, 'comes and goes
like the cool dude we know and—' 'Who's your friend,

Edmund?' Stan inquired, 'from overseas,
I take it.' 'I'm from Stortwood.' 'Like I say.
What's the difference.' Next to come was Russ,

but not for long, he said it wasn't me,
it couldn't be. The pregnant woman with him
was introduced as Russ's fiancée,

and stared at me two seconds. 'Lucy Mizon,
you'd know her as,' said Dodge. 'Not possible,'
the woman said: 'I don't know any children.'

'Not yet you don't,' said Russ with a half-smile,
as the woman drew him off, away. 'They're here,'
said Stan, now glancing into the lower well

of the Virgin Oak, 'the Nelsons. Nightmare.'
Polly had jerked her jacket from behind
Dodge Mendis, who tipped forward. 'Do we care

this much?' and she measured with two hands,
'or this much?' and she measured with two fingers,
and took my arm and led me from my friends,

Dodge giving two thumbs up, and Stan, his shoulders
hunched over the balustrade, threw a bleak
and vaguely hateful look our way. 'Real charmers,'

said Polly: 'Heard them play. My mate Monique
had them at her eighteenth and they were shit.
They said they could play garage. Could they fuck.'

We went down spiral planks into the hot
and heaving crowd below. 'Woz isn't here.
They said he had six pints and picked a fight.

That's really made my evening.' By a door,
through which about a hundred families
were eating, rose two figures from before,

the couple in the mall: with them two boys,
a tall pale one, a little dark one. 'You,'
the woman said, 'I know you by your eyes.

You're Edmund Lea, who went away.' 'She knew,'
the husband said: 'She got that gift, you see,
it's no great shakes to Linda. I'd a clue,

I have to say, but tended to *no way*,
it's been too long. Mike Nelson, we were pals
of the old school days.' In fact he'd hated me,

harassed me, hit me once. He was all smiles
as he filled in a card: 'That's phone and fax,
but home and work's no difference. No hols

for Mikey now.' 'You never do take breaks,'
sighed Linda. 'Dad,' the taller of the boys
declared, 'you're never schoolchums. This bloke's

not old, he's bleedin' under-age he is.'
Mike Nelson muttered: 'Second warning, Al.'
'I'm only saying, Dad. Check out his face.'

'The Lord has His scenarios, that's all,
and looks is nothing, is a thing you'll learn.'
'He's cursed,' said Polly, 'and he lives in Hell,

and can't grow old. He lives on a ghost train.'
'You're him!' The darker boy was shocked, 'the soul
my dad wrote songs about.' 'You sing 'em then,'

now Polly snapped, 'We're going to the mall.'
She got my arm, and so did Nelson. Al,
the pale boy, winked and had a card as well

he let me have: NELSONIX KLASSICAL,
and now I saw the wife was shocked. 'It's true,'
she said, 'it's you, but it's a miracle –

isn't it?' 'That's not for us to know,'
her husband said. 'You ever need a chat,'
said Al, 'you call this number.' 'He's bound to,'

said Polly, 'he was hoping you'd say that.'
The small dark lad now touched me. 'You've inspired
an album, you have.' Out of his coat pocket

he brought a little square of plastic board
and opened it in two. I saw the face
of Moon inside in midnight blue, remembered

Moon was gone, this was his son, this case
must be his souvenir. 'I'll sign my name
and Dad's.' The case was called *Mystyryus Ways*.

Inside there was a flimsy leaflet. 'I'm –
honoured,' I responded. 'It's a bound
booklet of poems,' I noted. With it came

a little silver disc, an ornament
I pocketed. 'They were all friends of mine,'
I told the boy, 'but I wasn't in the band.'

We left them staring after me. The time
was half past ten. We hurried through the cold.
Above, the stars were out. I said my name

in steam and said I wouldn't let this world
cast me off among them, I would keep,
I would attach to it, I would be held

by the remotest stranger in his sleep
on some Siberian wayside, by a stream
in India they'd grip me like a hope –

not one so distant he could not redeem
me from my curse, I cried, there is not one,
I called into the sky, without a name,

not one: 'I will be free! What I have done
I've paid for! I confess it on this night,
this very night, with twenty-one years gone,

I killed a man, he died, I stopped his heart,
I took his life! I know if he were here
he'd beg you to restore me!' 'Well he might,'

said Polly, 'I'd be on your case forever
if I was dead, I'd haunt you. Now shut up,
or Woz'll beat your head in.' We were there

at the Mall's Virgin entrance. Though the shops
were shut or shutting, still so many people
thronged the place, laughing and shrieking, groups

making their way towards the station, several
perched on litter bins; one wobbly girl
was singing carols terribly. 'Hartisle,'

said Polly, 'it's the business.' And then all
I clearly recollect is two policemen
in caps befriending me, Constable Dale

and Constable Devine, who was a woman,
who tried to calm me down, how they explained
their reasons for deciding to, how someone

passing by said, 'Officer, need a hand?' –
how Polly rolled a cigarette they pinched
and said she couldn't. 'Men, I killed a man,'

I told them. 'Yes, we heard you, son. You managed
to make that fairly clear.' 'His name was Cole.
He died by falling from the railway bridge

on Christmas Eve of 1970.' 'Well,'
said Constable Devine, 'Mr Poirot's
been sweating over that one.' 'Ain't no call

for that tone,' Polly said. 'Oh is that true,
Miss Addams Family?' said the man. 'We out
larging it, are we? The mistletoe

been kicking in? What's Christmas Eve without
some chocolate coins?' 'I been all the time
with Lee, he's lost his family, he's got

scum in his old house. He did this crime,
he's trying to say but you won't listen.' 'Love,'
said Dale, 'In 1970 I'm home

getting my first Subbuteo, I have
a team in red, a team in blue. I wear
shorts to school. I collect the Famous Five.

Your boyfriend, on the other hand, is out there
on a sub's bench in the clouds, a good ten years
from getting picked at least, a good few more

from his first murder rap. Do us two favours,
three favours: One, shut up. Two, go home.
Three, have yourself a merry little Christmas.'

I'm said to have then said I had a bomb,
I was a Soviet spy. He said, 'So what?
you read the news, we won in extra time.'

I threatened the Royal Family: 'This plot
goes everywhere!' They shared a weary grin.
'I'm after Margaret Thatcher!' 'You're too late,

alas,' said Constable Devine. By then
they'd started walking off. 'His real name
is Finnegan,' said Polly, 'off the plane

from Belfast.' They were careful when they came,
sorry even, 'being as how the season
is on us,' but they took us all the same,

for routine questions, searching of my person;
I do remember Woz was also there,
for hitting someone when he saw this happen,

his sister in handcuffs. We had to share
a cell, Wasgood and I, and he was pissed.
He shouted at them for about an hour,

but they sang 'Silent Night' until at last
Wasgood sang it too, and so did I,
my counter-spell against what it expressed,

like thinking walls, a ceiling and a key
could keep the light from rising to release me.

6 A Child's Recorder

During Edmund's next seven years, he begins to see distant figures of women and meets his first fellow-passenger. He fancies that Happy Hour is advising him to find a man who will murder him, as he murdered Cole, and end his suffering that way...

CHRISTMAS EVE, *1998*. Wasgood and Polly are glad to see Edmund. Wasgood has started writing about the 'phenomenon' and regards himself as Edmund's protector. They accompany Edmund to his parents' new house in a gated community. His mother and father, now in their eighties, have different ideas as to who he is, and send him on his way. Edmund, in despair, tries to induce Wasgood to kill him by way of an enormous lie, but the plan fails, and an old friend is waiting in the shadows...

XXVI

And it was policemen who when I was nine
one awful night arrested my own dad,
then drove him off for questioning alone.

Mum cried, we had digestives. He was cleared,
I know now, of a crime of robbery
relating to the school he taught at – kids

he taught had done it – but that couldn't free
my mind of how he'd had to go that night.
How nothing he could say to them or me

could make it better. Nothing but the sight
of him being driven off against his will
engrossed my every hour. The world was not

a place he could protect me from, and all
beyond the door could take him if it chose.
Because against the window he was small,

and could be only smaller as the days
flew by and my arms grew around him. Lost
again from him, my mother, all I was,

lost from my place, and dismally recast
into my sentence on the nameless train,
I knew that pang – that that place I exist,

a named and numbered human citizen,
the English earth where I am Edmund Lea,
the laws of time, of physics: all this meant

nothing at all to *that* by whose decree
I suffered. It was insignificant
what steps were taken by humanity

to love me, hate me, give me what I want
or take it, help me, hide me, let me in:
distinctive colours worn against a wind

that strips them without sensing anything.
If it was making life in its own form,
that wind, making it empty with such long

rewardless pain, it was by that cold time
in the ghost-nineties getting there with me.
I was the bluecoat sailor of the same,

a creature of five habits. Past a sea
of stone that yet had waves like sea we passed
for the first winter. Once I made my way

across and only once. Once in a mist
I found a grass-piled barrow, heard a song,
saw one – a girl? – halt on a distant crest.

Was that a parasol, now it was spring?
I worked on the old poem, and on a new;
I painted every scene I could. The long

summer evenings I would watch the view –
first taste, delight in, gorge on, then be damned
by scarlet colour till it begged to go,

be healed in the blue-grey. HH, my friend,
leafed through his book; Inspector Stick would march
out of the air and scare me for one second;

the Driver drove and spoke his double-dutch.
I thought about the three of them. I tried
sums with threes and sevens: filled a page

with threes and sevens minused, multiplied,
divided, written Roman, upside down,
made into points and notches. As a kid

the threes had been important – how three sons
were sent to find a treasure. If the threes
applied somehow to what was going on,

the next time what I did might count. 'You see?'
I sought a nod from Happy Hour, 'First time
I tried with love, to get a girl who'd say

she loved me, see? But that's no good to them,
they don't know love, don't deal in it. Okay,
second time, I owned up to the crime,

you see? I said I did it and would pay.
But they don't care, they're not concerned who dies,
their sun can only set, the only day

they know is one that's dying. The sunrise –
you don't know what I mean – it's what they fear.'
I drained my whisky glass. 'That's a surprise

I'll spring on them one day. And that I swear,
as God's not listening. That's what Wasgood says,
him and his sister. Can't get rid of her.'

Whatever words were next were Happy Hour's
in his own language, but I voiced them thus:
'Edmund, you're quite right. I think the powers

are asking something of you. What it is
you can't imagine and you won't be told,
so you've forever to discover this.'

With him beside me did the words of old
return: *'"Two rivers lead from out the fire.*
The first is to be known and to be killed

by he who knows. To find a soul out there
who knows and loves you, yet desires your death,
still wants you gone. This is the first: Despair."'

Remember? Word for word I do. *And the other?*
'"Hope, I do not have the strength to try.
Nor to repeat to you. Now I have suffered

long enough."' Said when that Creek was only
seconds from his death, as if . . . *As if
the riddle was itself the cure, the way?*

And I – I murdered Cole a moment after
he told me the same story – so, I need . . .
to tell it to another, find another

who'll hear the words! It's cracked! *Well yes indeed,
Edmund, that might do it, if your will
is death. I thought your will was to be freed.*

My will. What if my will's impossible?
What is my will in that case?' And this question
circled every day and made a spiral

I had to look down daily, nightly, wishing.
Yet this age was a kinder one: some mercy
I felt, rain can possess it; the confession,

I reasoned, had been good for me. The country
was green and warm, the autumn marvellous,
the winter short and glisteningly snowy,

single lights far off that I could guess
a family behind. And yes, at last,
a woman in the distance, on the grass,

and gladdeningly through a smoky mist
one afternoon a passenger – a man
climbed up aboard and took his seat, the first

in an infrequent but a constant line
of fellow-travellers. He was neat, well-dressed;
I asked him what was in his case. The sound

he made was otherworldly, or mine was.
I understood now, his was of the place,
and these days I could hear in it a gist,

a sense, a song: the treble and the bass,
the rise and fall, the force and reticence,
began to play upon me. My discourse

with Happy Hour was little but a chance
to seek for what I felt in a new voice,
but theirs was language out of the Expanse:

these were inhabitants, the men and boys
who came and went within half-hours, their talk
mournful, hopeful, wittering or wise,

I felt I knew. I read my poem back
and saw them nodding as they stared away,
absorbed. When they were gone, and in a blink

they often were, I seldom failed to try
to fix them there as sketches or as lines.
Beneath, I wrote what I had tried to say,

and, overleaf, what if they came again
I'd tell them I'd beheld along the track.
None ever came again. I had seen men

who looked like others, boys from a year back
who might have been the sons of these; one lad
did seem a twin of one seen by a haystack

early in my travels, but he'd had
brown eyes not green. I tried to make him see
I'd seen the other, but I went for food

he looked so hungry, and he'd gone away
when I got back. The world could be a size
so terrifying that a man was lucky

once to see another. Though the ways
might cross in this, the chance of any soul
discovering a soul it recognised

were infinitely low. 'And this is Hell,'
I was explaining over the rosé
as the sun set in the sky, 'and this is all.'

And Hell had made a number out of me.
I suffered on that page I couldn't turn,
fell headlong into calculus, x, y,

and z my sole companions. One equation,
cold, recurring, would confide with glee
Love couldn't win. It could be likewise proven

Repentance couldn't help. I could now die
the way the riddle told, or I could hope
against all hope to learn that other way.

But this world, this enormous empty shape
I floated in (I hesitated now
to name it Hell, so differing and deep

it seemed) knew nothing, or the life it knew
it couldn't tell. Nothing was there to seek.
Which left me with the one knot to undo –

that deed I did for Cole, and Cole for Creek,
and Creek for whomsoever long ago
condemned him to his journey. On a rock

above a wildwood that I'd made it through,
I took time to accept – but I did so –
my death, that it was freedom, that I knew

no way of hope, no second path. I knew
who'd be my Edmund Lea: the only one
to see my crime and be infected too,

albeit mildly, now and then: my man,
my mate, my cellmate, Wasgood. Christmas Eve
of 1998 would bring the curtain

down on me. I would make Woz believe
my story, I would find the words to bare
the killer in the citizen. I would leave,

fall smiling from the bridge through the dark air
on Quillers Lane and lastingly be still;
be found, be an abiding mystery there;

be to the world thereafter what the world
has been to me, a catch in every breath;
be something gone that never could grow old.

I spent a cold night on a forest path
about a month from home. There I prepared
the details of my passing from the earth,

my visits to endure or be endured,
on Cutters Row, my family one last
sight of – any friends I once had made

whose voices I might beckon from the mist.
But Wasgood was the key. 'You see the girl,'
I told a soldier who was sinking fast

into his beer one night. 'I can never tell
exactly what she knows. She thinks I'm mad,
you know, she's very strange, she's like a ghoul,

she's always there. She's from this place Stortwood,
it's always been – you wouldn't want to go.'
I'd never gone far in the life I'd had,

but in those years, the last years I would know,
I missed no stop, no moment to leap out
and see the world such as it was. I grew

those days an instinct for the whereabouts
of human breath. I fought with conscious light
against the never-conquered heavyweight,

sleep; once I went days before defeat.
And I had come by little chalets, rooms,
broken places, and a radio set

the rain had ruined bore the faded names
of Asian cities. All I wrote in books,
stabbing myself awake with the cheap pens

the driver gave me, books I meant to take
into the town when the last day arrived.
'This world I loved as well,' in the last week

I knelt and said aloud. That day I breathed
the last of its outdoors, a rainy day
in a great park. 'These sights I have believed,'

I added, and I made my stately way
towards where Happy Hour forever stood,
turning through his charts. 'I'm going away,'

I told him as I poured my beer. I poured
until it foamed. 'Because it's time I did.'

XXVII

'She's got this tape recorder by her bed,
it's ancient. *That* belongs in a nursing home,
not her, I tell her. When you press *record*,

she's like too weak to, *I'm* too weak to! I'm
like asking Bob to help, and Bob, he's like:
"In *my* day . . ." I say, "*You're* not one of them,

Bob" – he does our garden – "Make it work!"
And you can hear them turning, the two reels,
and her old tapes are always getting stuck,

and all you hear is clattering at meals,
which she records. I go: "Clarissa, what
exactly are we taping here?" "X-files!"

she goes. I say, "We don't let you watch that,
sweetheart," and it's true, Woz, the whole place
can you imagine? Like, *Coronation Street*'s

enough excitement.' "Shit . . ." 'Clarissa says,
"He's coming back." We're all, "Who's coming back?"
"The boy who has some questions," she goes,

always the boy. Bob says it was this bloke
came by while I was off on holiday,
he was some kind of poet, and he's like

asking stuff, like old town history,
as she's from there, his town.' 'What town, Hartisle?'
'Can't remember, some old dump.' 'Who's he,

famous?' 'He's a poet, Woz, get real.
Anyhow, he said he's coming back,
Clarissa says, she says he's got this file,

this project that she's helping with. I'm like,
you *sure* he's coming back? And then she's off,
she's telling me all stuff she told this bloke,

about her dancing on a lawn and stuff,
like dancing in formation and I mean,
it's yonks ago.' '*This is Your* bleedin' *Life,*

know what I'm saying?' '"Who was your gentleman?"
I'm like, and she sits back and has this smile,
and says "Are we recording, are we on?"

I go, "It's off the record, not on file,
you go ahead, Miss DH." That's her name,
Dudley-Henchard. Classie to her pals,

we call her Deadly Nightshade. One time
she rings the bell, I go up there, she's all
dressed for dinner, it's like five a.m.,

the birds are singing and the poor old girl
is looking for some – *line* to say. I say,
"How will the evening be?" "I'll dance my fill,"

Clarissa says, "I'll dance the night away."
I help her back to bed. We had this guy
thought he was in the war, in history,

Arthur Hulle, his one fresh memory
was that. You get that, though. Bob says it's like
you climb so high the only thing you see

worth seeing is that far away. The landscape,
lie of the land, you know.' 'I don't remember
yesterday,' said Woz, 'way out of shape.

What's my name?' 'Search me. You someone's brother?'
'I'm someone's father, man, this is his third
Christmas, Pell. First one without his father.'

'You'll see him.' 'One half day. That'll be good.
Season of goodwill.' 'You got him them?'
'Yeah, I got him these. He wanted red,

but they're sold out, the little fuckers. Next time
I'll do this stuff in bleedin August, Pell.'
'Sure you will. We've stopped. Leaves on the line.'

To hear again, hear English, that was all
I needed from their voices. They were back
in that third carriage. That same interval

had passed and there we were. I tried to look
at how the carriage altered, how the staff
departed from me, but the plainest trick

prevented that, a tunnel was enough
to seal all from my sight. When we emerged
on a bright rainy day in my old life,

at Chadwick Grove, all things were rearranged.
The reek of that enactment was so strong,
like gunshot smoke, an incident that changes

now to then too suddenly for some,
for us. When I could breathe, I made a last
valediction to the ghosts now gone,

those who had been more solid than the past,
and went to find my two. Wasgood was dressed
for work, in a dark suit, pinstriped and creased,

his tie undone. He must have looked his best.
Polly was in an anorak and jeans,
brown army boots. Her brown hair was the shortest

yet, I thought and her eyes had little lines
around. One eye was uncorrected still,
looked wrong and tired. A necklace with a dolphin

she clutched and she was smoking. 'Hartisle,'
she said, and she was pointing at me. 'Christ,'
said Wasgood, 'if it ain't. I told you, Pell,

this kid is it.' 'I told you that at least
a hundred times,' said Polly. Now I sat.
'Afternoon,' she said: 'Look what you missed.

Rain, electric pylons.' 'He *is* it,'
Wasgood repeated, 'You are it, my friend,
I'm going to show you something.' 'He's a writer,'

Polly said beside me: 'lost his mind,
I'm telling you.' Woz found in his black case
a little sheaf of papers, staple-bound,

a lilac cover. *Poetry and Prose
of the Millenium. Tales of the Supernatch.*
He turned the pages till he found the place

and passed me it. *The Man Who Can Not Age.*
By Crawford Ronson. 'I told him,' Polly said,
'you sound like in a porn film.' 'Shut up, Podge,'

said Woz, 'he's reading. Told you he's well read,
it ain't just like polite. It's a page-turner.'
The story was about me. It was short,

six pages, and I finished it: 'I'm honoured.'
He said: 'It's on the Web. It's all the times
we met.' Polly broke in: 'Like you remembered.

I had to help. It should say both our names,
Crawford and Babe Ronson.' 'Talking it,
you are, Pell. Babe's a pig. They made the films.

D'you rate the story?' Holding it, I nodded.
Wasgood took it back. 'I was the guy
who saw the light. I saw it, I beheld it!'

'What do you mean you saw – ' '*Si–lent Night,*
Lee, *Ho-ly Night!* Like you and me
we're in the fucking slammer, jailhouse, right?'

'Yes – in '91, on Christmas Eve – '
'It's *always* Christmas Eve,' he told me. 'Sure,'
said Polly, 'like you need to know that, Lee,

just ask the big authority.' 'We're there,
the pigs are singing, you and me, there's this—'
'You saw me go? You saw me disappear?'

The train now jolted forward with a hiss,
and looming over all the lights ahead
was the dark form of the mall, the shopping place.

'I'm sleeping on the floor, you're on the bed
across the cell. I wake up and it's only
light on your side and there's water, wet,

everywhere, like spray, it's in the story,
didn't you read that part? And you're like gone.
You're gone. You're gone.' 'He says you're gone,' said Polly,

standing up. Woz said: 'This cop comes in,
I swear he cacked himself, he's saying Christ!
I say don't swear. He says what's going on?

I say: "That's Lee, that was, and he's a ghost.
Ghost and a friend of mine. He don't think much
of your singing, mate." He goes and gets his boss,

you know, his super, and it's scratch, scratch,
well I never, three bags full. He's gone,
I'm telling 'em, he's parted, he's a witch.

They're staring at me and this kind of green
gel that's in the room, like minty fresh.
I said he thought he'd give the place a clean,

he's a tidy fucker, Lee. Don't mind my French.
But it was light I saw, man. Anyway,
they get me in a room. You ever mention

this *incident* to any soul, they say,
we'll have you back in here, wink of an eye.
I'm winking, man, I'm winking . . . Christmas Day

I'm out of there scot-free. I know a guy
who comes each seven years and never ages,
well, you can keep old Jesus. Know why?

I ain't seen him round lately. I'm religious,
yes, I say, but now I got belief.
And you can read about it in these pages.'

He stood, I stood with them and we got off,
walked up into the mall. It was 4.19,
as always, when the train comes to a stop.

I turned to look at it: it was the same
as any other. Nothing marked us out
as any different either. I was home,

in that I felt again the seizing fright
of people far too many and too quick,
the noise too loud for me, the light too bright,

each pink unnerving and each red an ache;
to look away impossible: above
I've made clear why. This was the night to take

my leave of the great clamour, time to wave
the matter off. The witness I was with
could love, and so could act in spite of love

to spring me from the fire. What pain in death
could top the agony of the abyss
that held my speck of life? Now every breath

was conscious, was an act of tenderness
towards the thought of life, towards the dear
intentions of it, all its pride and stress:

each one was mere rechannelling of air
into a ship that I could fill to burst,
so it would rise and ebb away from here

a giant O, a sun, a star, be lost
to view. I felt for sorrow and saw white.
Faces I sought within and I saw dust

of morning sunshine by my childhood bed.
Four years ago or forty years? Which one?
Only the words could differentiate,

though none could cause or cease that single vision
shining in me: I was going home
in my own way, to the unresting station,

the place I was before one lonely atom
shared its one idea. Doors opened wide
into my past as if like a breeze had come

from nowhere on a day. *When Edmund died*,
it whispered through the slats of an old barn
and out across a field. My heart was bright

with promise. I could cry that I was won!
That I'd been struggled *for*, and not against;
that I was gained and soon I would be given.

Quicker than I had time to see, my friends
had steered me through the mall. My only words
while this, as I recall, possessed my mind

were 'Cutters Row', and she knew where it was:
she'd checked a map the day after my last
departure. They were arguing. 'No, Woz,'

she said: 'if you came back and were *that* lost,
you'd go to Dad's whatever.' 'If I had
my whole life twice I wouldn't,' he insisted,

shepherding me over some main road
as the rain intensified. 'We'd go to Mum's.'
'Same place for him,' she said: 'Lee's mum and dad

they're radical, they live in the same home.
Except they had to move, it got all filled
with snobby arseholes. I was there, I saw them,

I know. They went to Spain, the house was sold,
that's why they moved to Nutters Row. Lee here
can find them there, not halfway round the world

like Dad.' 'Lee, man, we're taking you right there,'
Wasgood assured me and I loved him then,
and hoped he loved me too – it was required

of him, *to love you and still want you gone . . .*
My road away. What he would undergo
I had to disbelieve in now, become

indifferent, take the cold and common view
the dead might hold, the living incline to.

XXVIII

It seemed a customs point had been provided,
a border of some kind. There was a booth,
a silhouette inside. I was reminded

of holidays in France, this fist of earth
is France, this fist is Belgium! Take it home
and is it England? *Mummy, Edmund's half*

is full of mud! It's for a project, Mum.
THE CUTTERS ROW: PRIVATE COMMUNITY
a sign read on the booth, and out he came,

Father Christmas, dressed as, we could see
by his lit window, and he had a phone
without a cord but used it anyway,

then stowed it carefully. 'This bloomin' rain
is *not* so seasonal,' he said, perhaps
to us, or to himself. 'Always the same,'

he added, 'when you make a plan. The hopes
of men and mice, you know. Go all to grey.
What can I do for you three, or two, chaps

and one let's say chap-*ess*, I shouldn't say.'
Wasgood said: 'He lives here, number eight.
You won't have seen this man, he stays away,

we come here with him.' In the cold pink light
the streetlight gave he saw us closer now,
Santa, he was businesslike. 'You're not

expected, least of all down on my trusty
clipboard,' he confirmed, and had produced
from nowhere: 'I've a, let me see, Blake party

arriving Boxing, then there's Dr West
and *Ms* C. Lea next week—' '*His* name is Lea,'
Polly snapped, 'he's got no time to waste

with what's arriving.' Santa bristled. 'I
doubt he has, in the great scheme. I hope
one may conduct oneselves with dignity,

pertaining to the season.' 'Call 'em up,'
said Wasgood, 'Number eight.' This dialogue
I know for sure: I saw the moving lips,

I saw the faces pinched against the fog
as dusk was coming down, I heard each voice,
I heard the voices rustle in the smoke

and felt them freeze in air. I was of ice
out by the booth. All movement was preserved
for diggers in some future in this place:

they'd find me here, they will, they do, they have.
You've seen the pictures: mummified I am,
was buried with the bits of what I love

and time could spare. The Father Christmas man
was silhouetted phoning in his booth.
Polly and Wasgood traded names for him

and rolled a little cigarette. They both
would look at me. Woz said if we got in
they'd wait for me outside. I watched the moths

above, about the orange light. The rain
was stopping now and everything that moved
was cold. I didn't move, though I stood soon

beside a home and must have done. 'They left
a light on,' Polly said. A bungalow
had coloured lights along the door. 'They saved

some brandy, Lee, let's hope, or you won't go,'
Wasgood was joking but he tailed away,
and his sister said: 'There's someone at that window,

Lee,' and I already saw. 'It's me,'
I said and in the next of what seem frames
I'm looking back at Woz from a bright doorway

opening behind me. On the stones
of the short path, the stone trapezium way,
three shadows come and still themselves like stems

after the rain. The middle of the three
is shortest: dark, with focused edges. Hairs
are picked out on his shadow-head, it's me;

on either side are looming larger figures,
giants grey and blurry, but they reach
to gain his sharpness, they get smaller, blacker,

then all three fade and grow. One would see each
become enormous and seem anything.
By then was I in an old world of touch

and I first melted to a babbling spring
beside the heat of voices, then I froze
the life of what I touched, so where it sang

it could be stone, stone carving for my frieze.
In a bright hall I sat, then in the room
they sat in, with the fire, the Christmas tree.

'It's wonderful,' I commented between them,
my words a valley both could lean towards
from their soft chairs, to hear the little stream

still running in the hush. 'All golds and reds
this year,' I said, and nodded. 'Red and gold,'
my mother said, 'that's right. It was your dad's – '

He signalled her. It wasn't me that held
her eyes, I saw, it was the photographs
around, behind me, all of me, the world's

last look at me, a shrine to the belief
that I was gone. It was my mother's eyes
that shattered though, made fractions of her breath

and widows of her hands: 'It's still the face
of who he was,' she reasoned to the floor,
then stared again at me. 'I have these days,'

she told me, then was calm and golden-haired,
grew calm, was mild and steady by the fire.
My dad was grey, strong-looking still, he poured

red wine for me and something clear for her,
then sat back heavily and from the side
found spectacles and placed them on: 'I'm here

for once when family pays a call,' he said,
sipping his whisky. 'Meaning of it all,
Christmas, that thing. Spirit. Family. Blood.

Blood all right. Deaf and blind, you'd tell.
Deaf and blind you'd swear it is.' 'It's him,'
my mother sang, one tone, but he said 'Well,'

and down that elongated word there came
a light to him, late in the syllable,
a small decisive point he could call home

and settle for. 'We miss him. Always will,'
my father told my mother. Equably
I saw where he was safe and could hold still:

I was his grandson and would have to be,
was all I could be now, could make do with:
was more than being no one, being me,

the shade uncredited, the catch of breath.
Between us in the room there grew that whole
generation, flashed the birth and death

of Edmund Lea, left charred in its bright trail
survivors of it, peoples by its scorch
brought closer who had never met. The smile

with which my father greeted my sad speech
was a bridge we built together, both for her.
'My name is Arthur Lea. I was not in touch

because I travel, go by here and there,
have never stopped for long. My father died,
my father died. That would be fourteen years

ago tonight, of a rare type of blood,
nobody had, to give him.' 'Christmas Eve
of '84, I knew,' my mother said,

'he came to me.' 'Your grandmother believes
in certain possibilities I don't
at all rule out, I know we lived past lives,

is one I share for starters. What she meant
is, she imagined seeing him that night.'
'I did, I did imagine that. He went,

he had to. Cally says I was quite white
for weeks. I got my lucky silver strand,
now all I've got are them.' In the warm light

it all looked gold to me. 'Seven years went,
there was a letter. Tom said, didn't you,
it couldn't be. He said he'd come again,

tonight.' My father said: 'How could he, though?
We have the next best thing. We have a room
we never use, you could—' 'No I have to go,'

I howled but in a mutter. 'Had to come,
have to go. I wanted you to hear,
only some words he said I might pass on

if ever I got back. He loved you dearly,
always, missed you more than he had words
to make, and, in his travels he was happy,

was cared for, in the – Californian – woods
with a lady, beautiful, his girl – my mother –
Clarissa, always dancing, with the birds

singing in the morning, near the river.'
My father poured more wine. 'That's quite a scene,'
he said: 'He was a puzzlement, your father,

and will remain a puzzlement.' 'Your son,'
my mother told him softly, 'so will he.'
'We never said he's died, we said he's gone,

didn't we? Yes, we said he's gone away
and well he might, at seventeen, his choice,
freely acted on, we used to say,

freely followed. Boys, we used to, boys,
we used to say!' He laughed till there was quiet.
'But we never said he's died, and now he has,'

he added, 'and it's good to know, it's right,
it's godly, one might say, if one was, well—'
'Godly,' said my mum. 'Godly's the word,'

he finished, and he offered me a smile
as if he begged me take it, and I did,
so when it went he shut his eyes. 'Thy will . . .

be done and all, amen.' 'Edmund is dead,'
I heard my mother state: 'I have my days,'
she added to me. 'Arthur's here,' I said,

'admiring all these decorations.' 'Yes,'
she caught my eye, 'he used to be the one
for all the colour schemes. Our Christmas tree's

our annual tribute. When the carving's done
we never eat the crackling. If you stayed—'
she countered quickly, 'but you must get on,

I know it's true. It could be set aside
for next time!' 'I insist it is,' my face
responded, 'in his honour, my old dad,

I insist it's laid aside.' My father rose,
restored somehow, he beamed and said: 'It's grand
to have another grandson! If you please,

excuse your old granddaddy!' When he'd gone,
my mother sat alone, with her long life.
She thought a bit, then smiled. 'My wandering son,'

she spoke across the space to me: 'The grave's
no resting place.' 'This is my resting place,'
I answered, 'only I'm required to leave.'

'Tom can't see you. In his world your face
should be his own. In mine it's as you are,
it's this.' I stirred and said in a thick voice:

'My name is Arthur Lea—' 'We've had brisk weather,'
she cried, then: 'Don't try telling me. You can't.
It's been enough to know you're off forever,

without you gone again.' 'My father went
against his will, and so do I.' 'Dear love,'
was what she said, 'dumb angel, I'll be found

here or nowhere, won't I? In my grave
or in my dreams with you, and as it goes
how different are they? What does the one have

the other doesn't? Visits, I suppose.
That costs the dream the game, late in the game.'
She stared. 'I'm fixing you. You're one of those,

the pictures now. You'll sit there just the same
until I've gone. You'll sit there after that.
I'm choosing you a frame, a copper frame

I always think with you. I'm placing it,
and an engraving, any names you pick,
there'll be no argument. It's caught the light,

my Eddie, pride and joy. And now Tom's back.'
I stood when he came in. He'd wrapped a gift.
'A diary of your father's, it goes blank,

you look, on Christmas Day, the day he left.'
I took it from him. 'Something you can use!'
In the bathroom a blue towel, damp and soft,

smelt of shaving and I lost my eyes
to that a while. I set tubes in a row.
I saw myself. I made lines on my face

by pressing, pinching skin. I let them go,
then I was smooth again and death to know.

XXIX

Farewells were over quickly. In the game
we played there was no cause to linger. Soon
I'd write to them, I'd come again: next time

I'd bring them presents too. I crossed the room,
a bird over the ocean, and embraced
where I'd belonged. 'You know it's all the same,'

my mother said in private to the ghost
she needed me to be: 'When you were born
you were beyond belief, there in your nest.

You came from where the life is. Once at dawn
I just, I shrugged, to have you there.' 'Now now,'
my father cried: 'My turn!' and in the hall,

then on the porch, he hugged me. 'Better go,
or else I'll wind you!' An ungainly boy
was up the path. My father grinned: 'Oh-ho,

two grandsons in a night!' Younger than me,
he seemed, he was my sister's son all right:
he had her sort of cheekbones. 'I can't stay,

Tom, I got the mix for Jabbo's. Mate,'
the boy said as I started walking, 'that's—
I know his face, it's him from the website,

what's his name.' My father's puzzled words
I couldn't hear, kept going – looking back
I saw the two of them like palace guards,

matched for height, stock-still. The porch went black
and they were moving shadows, then obscured.
A car was coming. Headlights pierced the dark

and stopped two figures walking on the road.
Police were with them by the time I was,
and asking them their business there. 'The old,'

said Polly. Wasgood said: 'I want a house
round here, I'm the prospective buyer.' 'Right,'
said the policeman, 'and I'm Michael Mouse.

Been on the chocolate walnuts, have we, mate?'
I said we were together. We were free
to leave The Cutters Row: up to the gate

the car crawled by beside, then sped away
into the orange mist. We got no word
from Santa Claus, blue-lit by his TV,

not even when we called to him, and Wasgood
wondered 'where my fucking presents are,
you wrist-artist!' We pelted down the road

like children till we had to crouch for air.
My breath was coming back when it came back
for one thing only and it didn't care

what else I said. 'The station.' 'Ten o'clock,'
Wasgood showed me. 'Man, you got all night
to be around. We'll hit the Virgin Oak

and we can talk, and you can set me straight
what I been getting wrong.' They let me in
only because they knew him there. We stood

squashed in against the wall. I looked in vain
for anyone familiar in the smoke,
saw only Polly rowing with some man,

and nowhere near the bar yet. 'That's her bloke,'
her brother said, 'he's pitiful, he skis,
he's loaded, it's just sex with him. I'm like

you put a foot wrong, man, and I'll have these
on skewers. Lee, I got to ask you stuff,
now she's not here. I love my sis', but she's,

she ain't too quick, I'm saying. I've enough
to go on now, I know, I'm in on you,
Lee, you know it's you I'm thinking of

in all my fiction, man. What's up with you,
what's up with you? How is it, this? You're gone,
you're gone no matter what, like you *got* to,

but every bleedin' seven, man, it's done,
that calculation, seven years fly by,
it's Christmas Eve, I'm on that Hartisle train

and you show up. The same. Then Christmas Day
and walls of flamin' Jericho's no hope
to keep you here. I love that. Gone away,

it's just how good that is, it burns me up
how I'm right on your tail! You shake my hand
and feel it burn, I'm right? I am, one step,

one step behind you, son. Get thee behind . . .
it's me you mean. There's some eternal flame,
Olympic's what I'm saying, being burned

for you, old mate, or hallowed be thy name,
whatever. Where'd you go to, where'd you go?
You're on my mind out there, and I become

your writer here, your pensman, Lee, you know?
I'm keeping you in mind, in the world's mind,
or else who will?' 'Nobody will, it's true,'

I murmured, certain of the scheme I'd planned
and nearly ready. 'You're the only soul
who knows me, Wasgood, who can understand

what's happened to me. Once I met an angel.
He tried to help me but the curse was strong,
the cure beyond us. You're my one disciple,

the one man I can speak to, and the one
to keep my secret.' It was all he held
for once, as if he'd seen a man take wing –

He hugged himself as if it had turned cold.
I breathed. *Two rivers lead from out the fire.*
The first is to be known and to be killed

by he who knows. To find a soul out there
who knows and loves you, yet desires your death,
still wants you gone. This is the first: Despair.'

– 250 –

He shifted closer, I could breathe his breath
of mint on cigarettes. 'You're rhymin', man,
you're rhymin', always something to rhyme with,'

he pondered: 'you and me, we rhyme, there's one
is always there, that's me, the other rhyme
is you, you come and go – take us alone

we don't do shit, we walk, we're just the same
as all these folks, we're pitiful, but see,
you rhyme us and we *mean*, we make a name,

we're in the frame, we're on our game, we're Lee,
we're me, we're what it is and was and will be,
see, I got it too . . .' 'There's a second way,

Hope, I do not have the strength—' 'See Lee,
I got the strength, you're down? well I'm in town,
I make your sound—' '*Don't have the strength to try,*

nor to repeat to you—' 'I ain't no clown,
I move around, one bound, I cover ground,
I set the pace, I'm going to win that—' '*Now*

I've suffered long enough. I've reached the end,
Wasgood, it's goodbye.' He gripped my arm,
I shook him off and ducked away behind

some tables and was leaving. 'For it's time,'
I spoke ahead, 'high time I left this earth
to its own Silent Night.' 'That isn't him,'

I heard somebody say. 'Somebody's death
can't stand it here,' I heard myself retort
over my shoulder, and I beat a path

out of the Virgin Oak and down the street.
I waited, saw the door swing, heard his cry
of 'Lee!' and then I heard his running feet

as back I led him for my reason why,
towards where the sky glowed with the crane-lamps
of the huge mall. 'I last saw Edmund Lea

last Christmas,' now I sang, 'one lonely glimpse
as I was passing by' – I was myself
panting to the rhythm of dull thumps

I made in running – 'his demeanour grave,
I gave a wave, I couldn't save him, why?
he was already falling from his life,

he had already packed and said goodbye
to *Ma*, to *Pa*, the Leas, yea, to the Leas,
grand people, and to Polly and her *guy*,

who's pitiful and loaded and he skis,
skis down the world in love and is the man
inheriting all that I choose to lose,

I choose no more to use. I leave to him
the sun that rises up, the ones that sink
I'm taking with me, got a place for them –

be grateful when I'm gone, for I don't think
your days will ever end. I also leave
unending countries and a sea of drink,

just shy of thirty years' unneeded love,
a train in mint condition and a town
that won't stop growing outwards. May you thrive

in time, I've quite sworn off it, and I'm gone,
within the hour *auf widdershins*, bye-bye,
remember me to women and to men,

but keep me from the thing by whose decree
I bore this curse, and let me go – a human.
Last whine and testament of Edmund Lea,'

I said aloud in a deserted haven.
Gallery West. I waited there for Wasgood:
he'd seen me come this way. The only person

else was someone who had stood and staggered,
flopped back on his bench. The things he had
were plastic bags with him, he looked exhausted

and I went no nearer. The Gallery was sprayed
with a grey-green material like marble
but not it, it was high up, it was weird

to look down on the various shopping levels
there below so quiet now. I saw
Wasgood on one look up. I saw angels

painted on the ceiling. 'It was here,'
I said the instant that I recognised
the place I'd come to. Quillers Lane was here.

This space they'd made (for what?) for Gallery West,
had once been that high bridge over the track.
There Creek had fallen, Cole, and now I noticed

a fire-door in a corner and a catwalk
out towards a roof. I wore the smile
of the caught murderer in a murder book.

Now Wasgood pounded up the last stairwell
and halted, gasping. 'Do you love me, man,'
I whispered to myself. 'Had to leave Pell,'

he coughed the speech, 'wanted to say so long,
she did, I said it's *au revoir*, I'm like,
I'm with the guy, I'm with him, thick and thin,

I'm by his side, and he can dodge like fuck,
I ain't about to call it. Where'd you go,
where'd you go to, Lee?' 'I go to work,'

I told him as we sat, 'I'm made to go.'
'You're forced to go?' 'I'm forced, for many sins.'
'Oh, man, I know it.' 'Sins I can't tell you.'

'That's like a major insult to your friend,
Lee, you got to think of me like now
I'm older, man, I'm more than your right hand,

I'm like your guide on earth, man, and I know
exactly what you done.' 'No you don't know.
You know I killed a man, but you don't know

what else I did.' 'You ought to know there's no
sins so bad—' 'One sin was against you.
You and your sister, thirty years ago.

I'm irredeemable.' 'I'll stand for you,
Lee, there ain't much as it comes and goes
can't get you mercy in the Woz world view.'

'Is that the truth?' I muttered and I rose.
'It's mine and you can have it, Lee,' he tried,
his tone uncertain now, 'it can be yours,

whatever, what's the nature of your deed?'
I edged from him towards the fire door.
I knew he'd kill me when I said the words

I planned to, but I had to get to there,
had to have gained the parapet. 'My friend,'
I played for time, 'it happened in the year

of 1968.' 'I was young then,'
he nodded, 'I was fit and fine.' 'You were,
it's true, I knew you, Woz.' 'You knew me then,

I know that well, because you can't be older,
because you took the hex.' He stared hard.
'No one did shit to us when we were younger,

'cept my dad.' 'How can you blame your dad?'
I cried my punchline out, 'it was your mother
loved a boy of fifteen – name of Edmund.'

This lie delivered, I was haring over
patterned carpet to the weighted door,
thumping it open to the wind and weather,

slithering out along the ledge and there
I waited for him, facing the night air.

XXX

When nothing moved as if he hadn't heard,
I breathed my weight into the sky, sat tight,
then turned to see him. He was where he stood,

gazing out at me. Had he heard right?
perhaps he wondered but he moved his hands
calmly about him and produced a light,

a cigarette, a flame, smoke. Behind
now rose the form of that bag-laden soul
I'd noticed on the bench. Wasgood turned

to meet the gesticulating figure, pale,
bearded, thin. They spoke. I couldn't hear
a sound except the streets and the soft drizzle

hitting the plastic sheeting. I hung there
above the world, impatient to take flight –
and neither man was watching me. The pair

were arguing as if about to fight!
The vagabond made boxing gestures, Woz
was tensing, with his hands held by his sides,

one smoking, one still held a match. The voice
I heard was of the homeless man, so loud
it reached me, but its sound was meaningless

and Woz had had enough. With just a stride
he met and took the legs from underneath
his challenger, who threw his arms out wide

and toppled like a clown to a mimed death.
Wasgood kicked him and without a look
walked off towards the stairs. I saw him breathe

his final smoke and off behind him flick
the fag-end. It smoked thinly. When it stopped,
the vagabond sat up and rubbed his back.

He shook his head and carefully stood up.
My man was gone, my plan had failed. I stared
at seven years. My heart uncoiled, cried *Jump!* –

my head knew it was hopeless. I would start
this seven years in wilderness, alone.
My botched escape would cost me. My one night

I'd end with no one but a homeless one,
the loser with the lost. 'That's very fair,'
I mentioned calmly in the steady rain,

'that's quite appropriate of you up there,
we're very grateful.' What I meant as hiss
felt dizzyingly honest, bright and clear.

'Very fair,' I said. 'I get my wish.'
The slashed and dirty sky was all I saw
when suddenly a scuffle was a crash,

the fire door opened and the tramp was there.
'You been the middle of my seaside dream,
young gent,' his fingers playing in the air

a lost piano. 'Candyfloss, ice-cream,
young gentleman, you been. I lost my girl
and don't know where and don't know where she been,

and don't know who. I trot about the world,
time to time, I cart a Christian soul,
happens, wasn't always, I was held

away and now I'm home and I'm consoled,
and you're who. You're who.' 'I'm who, who what?'
'You took her, he's her son, now I been told,

my seaside dream, it's Wozzie there, he's it,
her son, I loved her, didn't I?' 'Loved who?'
'Wozzie's mother, back in '68,

Grace and me, Grace was the world, and you,
you say you *did* her, I just heard you say,
you told him how you *did* her, and I knew

from in my seaside dream how any day
I'd know it all, when all the candyfloss
gets eaten and it's just three licks away:

lick, and lick, and lick, and here's what was.'
'His mother was your love?' 'A Christian soul
I cart along, was born again's the phrase,

and *it* ain't any small thing, any small
component of it to be of a mind
to kill you, but it says it's time to kill

when it's gone time for all the rest.' 'My friend,
two-rivers-lead-from-out-the-fire-the-first-
is-to-be-known-and-to-be-killed-by-he-

who-knows-to-find—' I spluttered out the rest:
it only had to reach his ears, this man
who'd come from nowhere when all hope was lost,

who could deliver me, fulfil my plan,
release me from the endlessness – 'Despair,'
I finished, 'it's the way of. Yes, my friend,

I wanted Grace, I *had* her and I *did* her,
we lay down on the beach and how we loved!
It makes me hard to think of it, the shudder!

Back it comes – somebody's always left,
you sad old nutcase, somebody's abandoned,
left to watch the years sail by, to drift,

to dream the old regrets. It just so happened
you were him, and sad that you're so feeble
you couldn't hurt me, which is why you haven't

even tried.' He stood there in the drizzle,
rubbed his neck. He was ten feet away.
I climbed on to the railing. 'Best be careful,'

I called into the sky, 'It's Christmas Day
tomorrow, wouldn't want to fall!' He stirred,
slowly, carefully, he picked his way

along the fire escape. 'My Shepherd Lord . . .'
he growled, 'but I can't stop myself, I hate,
with righteous hate I do, I'm of the world,

and this boy was my ruin. It's my fate
to cast him to Thy care!' I shut my eyes
and lifted both my hands out into night,

balanced there intoning my goodbyes
to all I knew, shins aching at the rail,
and waited for the pressure that would prise

this pebble from the earth. 'It's time to kill,'
the vagabond was breathing at my ear,
'for time's the only thing there is to kill,

get it?' Air committed to the air
for the last time, I felt his clutching hand
and leaned into his force. 'How green you are,'

his voice said from another time. His hand
had dragged me back and I had both my own
to grasp the rail and grip so I could stand.

'I told myself I can't believe how green
he's getting in his youth.' He pulled the beard
away in one and couldn't keep the grin

from spreading cheek to cheek. 'I've never heard
a likelier story. Banged the mother, sure.
He spins them, he'll believe in them, I thought,

hook, line and sink the Bismarck. Put it there,
companion of the track.' He wiped his hand
of rain and held it out to me. 'I'm here,

Edmund, it's okay. You'll understand,
no path from out the fire tonight. I'm dirt,
but so it is. The clue is in the sound:

despair, *despair*, no ending there, the word's
a rope-and-pulley and it moves the train,
that dear train. How is the train? Regards

to him in the old bar, and to the fireman
who skips across the corn, oh, and the old
girl with the red tulip. Who'd imagine

that wasn't Hell at all? There's a whole world
worse than it and here I am alone,
depreciating in it.' 'You were killed,

Cole,' I said, now squatting in the rain,
my spine against the railing. 'You're a ghost.'
'I must be if you say so, as you've shown

such brilliance tonight. You could do worse
than shake my hand, old lad.' Which all the time
hung there for me. It lowered and mine rose

to touch it and could not, but in a dream
passed through it. It was solid, though, was bright,
was not transparent as a horror film

but was hard-edged as mine and oddly bright,
went through again, the edges giving way,
and I grew ill, his hand was real and bright –

but surfaceless, untouching. With a cry
I jerked away but Cole, turning his back,
reached for the railing, leant against the sky

and spewed his guts; they milled into the dark.
'The only thing,' his croaky voice said next,
'is if we touch, the spirits make us sick,

and hell, you know, is mopping up the mess
forever.' When I joined him at the rail
I vomited grey water. 'Less despair,'

he said quite cheerfully, 'on earth. In Hell
more mopping up for me.' I looked at him.
There was this eerie brightness about Cole,

it lit him from elsewhere. 'So you've become
what exactly?' 'What? A station person.
I know my station, Edmund. It's my home.

I'm only here. I watch the men and women
come and go. I touch them and it's, well,
fetch the sawdust bucket. I'm just someone

no one knows. There's you, but what with all
your travels, Edmund, why, you're never here.
I was your predecessor, and I swell

with pride as you alight again. I feared
I'd lose you what with this excitable
young coloured fellow hearing all your weird

fantasies of love, but he's no fool,
alas, like you are. And you really are,
Edmund. You're the stupidest immortal

ever to be honoured so. You ever
think what you've been given? Look at you.
Seventeen, mysterious dark stranger

until the end of time. What do you do?
Head for the exit.' 'So did you.' 'I did.
There isn't one.' 'But you were told of two,

two ways, a way of hope.' 'I never heard
which way it's pointing. Maybe it's the past.
So why don't you try standing on your head

and walking backwards? Maybe get so fast
the housewives turn to girls and the good times
rewind and play again. Or else get pissed

and that transpires. Does do in my dreams.
Did do in my dreams. Get on the train
and take it all. There's stuff'll make it seem

to push along like billy-o. This sign,'
and he was scribbling on an envelope –
'don't worry, this won't make you sick, it's clean,

it's from your book – this sign you carry up
into the drinking-carriage, give it him
who's always there, he'll see you right, the chap,

the years'll jump to it, the months will seem
like weeks, the weeks like days, and you'll be back,
fresh, fit as when you woke up seventeen,

ready for the future. That's our work,
old lad, we two twin tunnellers in time.
Think of a child who's bedridden, who's sick.

To cheer him up, imagine, his old mum,
she gives two gifts. Of course he busts the one
and keeps it in a box. That's me, struck dumb,

some old schooltime recorder. That day's gone
when air blew in or out! But, Edmund, you
by contrast are the loved one in his hands,

the favoured one, there's nothing he won't do
with you and that imagination. Friend,
you're some machine, and what he sets you to

is to observe the future, be on hand
to see for him what happens. What he gets
is a demented lad at pains to end

everything. You're nuts. You own the rights
to anything. I had them, so I know
what losing them feels like and, well, it hurts,

it takes a hundred years to learn. And oh,
there's nothing else I'm taught here. Nothing's learned.
Nothing's revealed to one who works alone.

But you. You have eternity, old friend.
You travel forward, and the ones you love?
The day you met them they were left behind.

Who wouldn't lose them for the gift you have?
These are the last years anyone will care
who Edmund was or why on Christmas Eve

they waited for him. *Damned for evermore*?
Well, I'll be damned. Welcome to evermore.'

7 *Demundo*

For seven years, Edmund takes his mentor's advice and finds hallucinatory comfort in the wilderness. He is still confused when he reaches Hartisle on CHRISTMAS EVE, 2005.

Polly wants to forget about Edmund, but to Wasgood he has become a messianic figure. Edmund is unable to say much, so Wasgood leads him through the altered streets to a dark, exclusive club. He is introduced to various faces from the past, twelve in number, all of whom believe in his supernatural state or knew him earlier in life. Among them is Clare's daughter Laura, now Wasgood's girlfriend; Kyle, Edmund's nephew; and Russ, his childhood friend. Their leader, Nelson, a rock millionaire, has arranged a Night of Celebration at his mansion, when Edmund will explain What He Is, and the Twelve will film his disappearance and prove the miracle to the world . . .

XXXI

'That You are good: somewhere there is a place
our deeds are reckoned with. That You are not:
You reckon with them idly, over years

You hear atonement and, unmoved by it,
You alter nothing but its tone of voice.
That You are good: the dousing of the light

so sleep can come. That You are not: the force
that hoods my senses till the afternoon,
denies to me the leap of the seen sunrise.

That You are kind: the splendour of the train
these fine millennial days; that You are cruel:
You set the question but You knot the tongues

of those around me, You unleash a babble,
tweaking it by day like torturers
might think of doing, finding it's no trouble

to tease the pliant skin. That You are wise:
You know love to be futile, You know shame
is shrugged from the old world, and only lies

have reassured: *I am not him, I am
his son, I am no one*. That You are mad:
You shot me from the light but took no aim

at anything. That You and I were made
by the same hand: the red eye of the sun
that is both Yours and mine when I have cried

to see the night come on, the night come down
on no familiar sight. That You and I
were forged in different factories: how long

I suffer so – to make me yearn to die
I can't forgive. Thus You and I are one:
You can't forgive. The victim of my crime

himself is punished and in deeper gloom,
immobilised and in an isolation
that makes mine seem society. My doom

is arbitrary: some untested poison
cracked its beaker, sloshed into my life,
and modified all matter to dimensions

of a benighted physics. Is enough
discovered now? That You are hearing this:
the sun is sinking as I drink the stuff

that helps me glide unfeeling over days.
That You are not: I look and the red clouds
are all there was. No rainbow for a promise,

nothing for one. Only my learned words
dream of a home and make me think a space
stays white for them.' The stuff was in small wads

in paper, it was powder and its taste
depended on the time of day: I watched
it plummet fizzling and disintegrate

in my clear glass. 'To set before a witch,'
I grinned at Happy Hour. When it was nothing
I drank it. I woke up on a black beach

in the wrong coat. I walked. Before too long
I saw the train arriving at the dunes.
The recent past forgotten, I'd get on,

have more. Now there were passengers sometimes,
men of the ages seen out there, their faces
occupied as if some waking dream

were preying on them. Now, with orange roses
on her frock, a lady came for once
into the carriage, sweetest of surprises,

sitting there, looking out, her hands
smoothing a new notebook. I was shocked
and said so in my language. Curving lines

she drew, ignoring me. I said she looked
more beautiful than ever could be said,
and she replied in nonsense as she worked.

Inspector Stick came in, of course, he would,
with his great ticket-stamper. I stood up
as always to repel him. When I had

I sat down, brushed that triumph off my lap,
and looked to see her looking at me. 'Here,'
I said, and tore the corner off a tab,

'refreshment on your journey?' In her hair
she wore black ribbon and her hair was brown;
she made no motion or a sign in answer.

I woke in the blue ruins of a town
in foul rain on a hillside. What emerged
in smoke and silence from a huge hay barn

was the black train with the red roof. I touched
the face of a tall girl against the window
one summer evening in a mountain range

where every mountain quietened in shadow.
My fingers met such softness I recoiled,
queasy. 'I will love you till tomorrow,'

I granted and was on her. She was held
until she wasn't there and I came to,
elsewhere, empty, sickened, sorry, dulled:

nothing retained, no memory, no view.
As I describe it is as it survived:
bare outline of a face, rind, residue

of appetite. I was a thirst that thrived
on slaking of itself. I was the thing
that lay in wait, warned-of if not believed.

Now nothing, I could be – do – anything.
I was on no one's ledger, I no longer
felt my fate was alterable, I hung,

swaying, conscious, as a bestial hunger
shorn of body could observe its beast
with scorn or pity, unattached, unhindered.

I made my two hands meet about the waist
of a thin lady in entirely black,
from long ago somehow. In a cold mist

one winter there came two; the air was slick
with iciness, two thousand either three
or four the year. I giggled, I'd lost track,

I told them and they smiled identically.
One other was infected by a sigh
beside the blue peculiar long sea

some sunny era I spent lying by.
All men I stared at till they looked away.
They couldn't touch me and they didn't try.

Naked I strode out on a cloudy day
in June, July, who knows, the air was warm.
I heard, for the first time, a music play,

music play. Where it was coming from
was anybody's guess. This was a place
of little trees in rows, always around them

flowers planted by some phantom grace
departed now. A single melody
was all it was, tin-bright, at a brisk pace,

five notes at most and in a minor key,
but gradually it slowed, unevenly
was winding down. That's what it seemed to be,

coiled, and then unspooling like a toy,
a clockwork treasure. For a spell it ceased.
Then it began, and closer now, close by.

In vain I looked for children whose it was,
or anybody close. Yet this event
would not have been among the ones I chose

to have by heart, committed – there were moments
stranger, more alarming – were it not
for the fact that it recurred, not only once

but often, that same tune. My lines apart,
what I composed about my history
and memorised until it formed inside –

no sight or sound or figure till that day
had ever, in the world beyond the train,
appeared a second time. That melody,

I heard it deep in woods, on the parched plain
without a shrub in sight. It was my jewel,
I said aloud to people, 'She's my moon.

She goes with me, she's saying the sun is cruel
to keep me here, she follows me and hides.
She says if I'm a fool then she's a fool,

and if I hope she hopes, and if hope fades
I'll hear her and keep hoping. She's disguised,'
I said to a small woman in sunshades.

'The moment that she shines she's recognised,
the sun will put her out. But he can't see
the music play! He can't hear with his eyes,

and I know well he's deaf as deaf can be!'
When she seemed deaf to me as well, I moved
and knelt down on the floor between us. 'Me,'

I spoke, 'I am the reason you arrived.
I'm why you waited at the place you waited,
I'm why you caught this train and I am why

you sit there. Here's damnation as created
by Edmund Lea. To you my words are mere
loss – as yours to mine, if you were tempted

to hazard words. You could be hiding fear.
You could be hiding love.' I shuffled up
towards her. 'But you're here because I'm here,

you're a cast image, you're a shadow-shape,
were sent to punish me. Which makes me care
scarcely at all what action I might take

about your being here with me, my poor
shade-eyed little temptress.' In one lens
I leered at her, was licking in the other,

my skin so devil-smooth – how my two grins
each nudged the other wider! Then both smiles
were driven off. She freed her hidden hands

and lifted off the glasses: her eyeballs
reflected nothing. She was the first ghost
to speak for many weeks, in yawning vowels

and gaps for consonants, and all got lost
with how she wouldn't move her scarf, her mouth
was smothered by it. I felt vaguely blessed

that she'd responded. *Eman, teleruth,*
she said, *eterna carta sikofin
isentri ager.* I could sketch her breath,

the carriage was so cold that afternoon,
but what I thought I saw was the ghost skin
of language I could write, I could write down,

could even try to understand: *Eman,
teleruth, eterna carta* – charts?
eternal maps of what's beyond the train?

I sped from the small woman, to some seats
I often used for writing, in first class,
and set to work excitedly, with sheets

of paper curling from my pen so fast
I didn't see them curl into the path
of the same woman, setting free at last

her mouth to speak: 'I said: *to tell the truth
you're turning into quite a sick old thing
this century, aintcha?*' Through a pall of breath

I watched her and her brother, in a long
ankle-length black coat, bring to my side
hot tea and a sealed cake, and I saw beyond

the window lights were passing by, a road
with trucks and cars, the rain was coming down
and wipers wiping, and I cried and cried

to see them there, to lose my lucky train,
my realm, my sphere, my cell. They were so grown,
he looked so edgy and she looked so drained.

I watched her as she slouched and wittered on:
'Lee said I was a shadow, I was like
his image, he can screw himself for one,

however terminal he is. He's whacked,
is what's the matter, Woz, it's all too much.
He's terminal and if you want the facts

he always was. He may be the white witch
in your mad world, but on my street he's this
disappearing shadow, like, an image

every seven years, it's just a sickness
in his skin. So that, here's where the ways
are parting. Lee, you and your crony, Woz,

you're going to spend the fag-end of today
in some old hole with all his scary mates
who think you're something special now, while I,

well I wide-berth your town, which is the pits
like even more than earlier, because
I've stuff to do that's real, no shadow-shit,

no image-shit, no moon-shit, and because
there's people are depending on me, Lee,
people who need a hand. I'm, you ask Woz,

you ask him. This is Hartisle, you're free.
When no one gives a monkey's, think of me.'

XXXII

My hands were at my sides out there. I chose
to hold them thus, the sound of that dream *gare*
was stifled, loud, as if I'd plugged my ears

and with that dam turned rivers to a roar.
The woman stayed behind on what appeared
to be a rush-hour train. We came from there,

decisive through the people, with my guide
dark-coated, close, escorting. I had times
and errors to explain, goals to confide

to faces looming up and by. *My dreams*,
I notified along a candled alley,
consist of frozen images and names,

or labels if you like ... When no reply
forthcame it hit me I had said no words,
had not deployed them and was now not ready.

A car was moving by us, at our speed,
speeding and slowing with us, but indoors
it seemed to be, and I informed my guide

by use of signals and his own name, 'Woz,'
which went from me, was fluttered out, a fledgling
in tried streaming air. By faster cars

we next proceeded and the night was falling
clearer now; I said so and my hands
each found the other and my mind a calling:

Here's where the ways are parting. 'You have friends,'
I heard him say. Towards a crown of blue
illuminations along Christmas lines

we were advancing and 'This place is new,'
I was assured and passed on to the next,
who overtook us and 'No need to know,'

my guide believed. There was a starry *X*
in tiny bulbs above us, not in blue
for long but red, then a black lightless *X*,

then white again. Below it the word YOU
was fixed in pink and changed to YOU ARE HERE
as we arrived beside what seemed a queue

of men and women by an open door.
This queue we passed. I pressed against my guide
in velvet dark, confused a while, then 'Sir,'

somebody called me, 'Sir,' as we were led
by figures to a little cell. The noise
so deafening had entered to my head

as hush, as if a coin had flipped. *Oh yes*,
I nodded to some questions. *Not at all*,
I shook for others. In that cosy place,

by tiles of purple light we stayed a spell,
my guide and I: 'A friend of forty years,'
he called himself, and when he pushed a bell

beside the table two short drinks appeared,
a girl with compliments who went away;
another asked if he might have a word,

then Wasgood, my old guide, was saying 'Hey,
she got her place to go to and fair's fair's
my attitude. She got a station, Polly,

she stops at, got to tend to them affairs
she has and I don't blame her. Always tell her,
every Christmas, if that guy of hers

is on my line I'm having him, no favour.
He's roadkill's what I'm saying and she's always,
Leave it, Woz, whatever, like *whatever's*

the thing to solve it, Ed! Like all the brothers
anywhere, your sister she hit zero?
You're telling her *whatever*? Maybe others,

others might say that, I ain't no hero,
I ain't no saint except how I was touched
by your affliction. I'll be here tomorrow

testifying that, I won't have budged
from where I'm at. The news you got to bring
I'll be the one still bringing in. Be rich

in not a golden sense but like a thing
that's needed. When you've travelled to your place,
I'll be your voice. You're here now, seventeen,

I got you in, they know me, it's my voice
has done that, you're *here* now, this place is all
you need now, for this one night it's the boys

like old times, Woz and Eddie, all's well
with Woz and Eddie, mortal and unmortal
duo you can call us, seeing double

life and death, you copy? The same bottle
we're supping from, the dead man and the, look,
god, I won't go there, some think an angel,

the way it seems. Same bottle, though, same block.
Mortal richness, Edmund, is key here,
the mortal deal. We read from the same book,

except, to use the book as metaphor-
type aspect, I'm like scrolling to the end,
bang, whodunit, well I never! Yeah,

know what I mean, and you, you stay behind
on page whatever, reading like *in further*,
finding more, and always, always found,

staring at it. Me, I'm the page-turner.'
I saw food was in front of me, some meat
I didn't know, and chips, a tasty supper

it seemed I had half-eaten in red light.
This little cell we had for Wasgood's words
was crazy-panelled, and behind the slats

were silhouettes of people. Did they need
help from us, I frowned, and was ignored
as if there were no people, but they stood

and waited there regardless, like the shade
around where we were picnicking. 'You know,'
Wasgood was saying, 'ever get that, Ed?

that moment when you get the green for go,
you know, like red-and-amber even, green,
and something's got to happen, and it's oh,

maybe I'll wait a while . . . It's like a game
you play with heaven, if you mind me naming
heaven – I been near, I got no qualm

in naming it – you let the thing you're dreaming
hang there and not happen yet, in case
you lose it when it happens, then it's something

sliding from you. Yeah, but what it is
has got its own, like, timing. Ed, my friend,
I got a second angel for this space,

I name her that, and the New Rose of England
also I been calling her, it's like
Di never died, that never even happened,

they're saying now, some quarters . . . I mean, look,
who knows what really transpires? There's me,
holding back the tide, though, when the book

won't let me stop here, but I'm done with envy,
Edmund, I have love, and there's three jewels
without which you got nothing and of them three

the greatest one is love.' One of the girls
who'd been a silhouette behind the wall
now sat here, tilting forward, beautiful,

and drank from what he drank. She had a smile
that knew I knew she had been waiting there
for what he'd called that moment, so the smile

was mine as well. Wasgood was kissing her
while she was looking straight at me: her eyes
were seeking something, they were keen and clear

and finding it went misty. 'No surprise
you're you. I knew you might be.' This I thought
at first I *gave* to her to say – her voice

was what I would have chosen. How they met,
Wasgood was saying, 'is a story too,'
as if the girl herself were one. She sat

and shrugged as he said, 'Somebody I knew
went out with Laura, said she said her mum
had known this kid at school who'd died: you.'

He pointed, and she said, 'Exhibit One'
and sipped her drink. 'But hadn't died,' said Woz,
'had vanished. Twenty years pass, twenty-one,

he surfaces and looks the way he was,
and talks the way he did, I'm saying nothing,
I mean, to Laura's man, but I say, Raz,

(that's who she's seeing), let's go out, do something,
surf the clubs.' 'And I'm the something done,'
the girl called Laura said. 'And so I'm checking,

clandestine if you like,' Wasgood went on,
'I know a guy can fit that like a glove,
that tale you tell, *identikit*. This man

you mention, does he come on Christmas Eve?'
'And *I* say,' Laura said, 'if I'd been stiff
for twenty years I'd come on Christmas Eve.

He stared at her, then me, let out a laugh.
Laura sighed: 'I told the man you came
in 1991, with your pet Goth.'

'Turns out it's my kid sister!' 'What's her name.
Pal. Pally. Something, anyway.
Something canine. Rover. But you came,

and when you left my mum began to cry,
annoyingly, since we were all awake
till four. Then Wasgood asked was your name Lea?

and that was our first date. We spent the week
debating whether you were superhuman
or, in my humble view, some sort of freak.

And here we are.' The drinks came. 'Where's my lemon?'
she asked. 'Oh well. You know my mother. Clare.
She's got this dog called Dog. She's seeing someone.

They're gone all winter, down in the timeshare.
Out on the putting green at dawn, it's mental.
I would have gone somewhere but I stayed here.'

'For you,' said Woz, 'the magus, the marvel.'
He had a flimsy paper in his hand
and then in mine: my picture in the middle

and tiny writing printed all around
in what they said was English but to me
was soot on snow with fences in the ground.

I saw my name in there. '*For EDMUND LEA*
is from a Place we like to call the Know,'
Wasgood read, '*the Place that holds the Key.*

I didn't write this bit, this is all new.
It's just a chatroom thing. There's no one there
but this guy Morfeus.' There waited two

behind the panels now and here they were,
a woman in a cap and a tall girl
with gazing eyes and plaits in her fair hair.

Five of us were cramped inside the cell
above which it was flashing SECRECY
in high white neon bolted to the wall.

The woman in the cap was nearest me
and said her father was a friend of mine
in the old days: 'You knew him, Gareth Cholsey,

he talked about you, said you was the man,
you had it in you. He's out fishing now,
in this, you know, in this, the worse the rain

the better. But he don't believe in you,
you coming back, he says it's what I'm on.
He says they did some stuff, but they all knew

what stuff it was, the kids these days – I mean,
he's one of *those* – in *my* day, in *my* day,
he goes and he's all out there on his own

in pouring rain, with worms, his flask of tea
I done him, and his hat, and I say, Gaz,
you're welcome to your day.' Her name was Chrissie,

she grinned and had gold teeth. 'Hey listen, Woz,'
said Laura, 'ever feel the need to spend
the morning on the river, now you passed

the big four-o?' The women laughed, my friend
sat back and swiped his finger past his throat:
'Don't need the rain,' he said, to make an end.

The other girl said nothing as we sat,
just stirred her drink and looked in it. 'You're safe,'
said Woz, 'while you're with me. It's understood

I have the access, as I'm who you gave
the inside information to. Except
there's others have to meet you. They'll arrive

at given times, according to exact
provisions made, in sessions. Mean time,
Edmund, my old friend, you just sit back

and bring us word of where you're coming from.
As we been waiting seven years for word,
and like to think we make a kind of home

you can still call. It's been mixed times we've had
since you last lighted up the neighbourhood.'

XXXIII

The silence that was me, and had been me
since I had reached still ground, must then have swelled
and burst its bank and been the Southern Sea

for all of them, as now the cell seemed filled
with that green water so their claws of hands
in twos along the table had to hold

for dear life to our sinking raft. The sounds
of help, the shoot of light from high above,
they fought the general pressure, but we drowned

together there at peace, marked out a grave
and muddled on as spirits. When all breath
was finally exhaled and the life over,

the women rose I had been falling with,
and swam behind a wreck, excepting her
I beckoned to, selecting her like Death

in cartoon form. 'He wants you to stay here,'
my guide pronounced. I nodded, visibly,
but she was gone, as if I too weren't there,

like her; she wasn't there, a quality
of having left the place that we two shared,
though you could see a charcoal sketch of me

still nodding if you looked. But she had stared
so long at me. A finger I would lift,
and add two more to mean her friends. I had

four, I counted Wasgood, I was left
with one hand and a thumb for any more
who drifted down by there. The light was soft

and yellowy when a new smiling pair
descended on us, either side of Woz.
A man who smoked dried out the atmosphere,

and so I surfaced to my visitors.
The one who smoked became the one who talked,
a man who sat, and said 'I'm ravenous,'

then lit his thin cigar. His suit was black,
his shirt was white, done up but collarless,
there was no tie; his face was narrow, marked.

'I've not set eyes on you in fourteen years,
young customer, but I can sign a voucher
I saw a face that has your soul, and here's

our breaking of the ice, *voilà*.' A picture,
reversed for me to see: a line of lads
beside a puddled field – and with his finger

being the lightning bolt he touched the heads
of three of them: 'Master Michael Nelson.
My father. Master something Mohin, his,'

and he nodded to the other, who said: 'Moon,
you would have known him as,' and the third bolt
hit me, half-hidden, wincing in the rain,

a wood for background. 'That young man is called
Edmund Lea.' He smoked again. 'The spit,
some say. The man, some say. Not of this world,

say others. What I say is there's a slot,
I call it, there's a gap to go for, sir,
a gathering towards, a grouping at,

a buzz, a thermal, like a thirsting-for,
we all have names for what it is.' 'Belief,'
his dark companion termed it, 'Either/or,'

said Nelson, in two little darts of breath,
'We're ruling nothing out and nothing in
at this stage. There's a certain surge of myth,

that goes unsaid, the Zeitgeist type of scene
from Y2K, the fallout, that's a doubt
without a shadow. We know what we mean

when we say thanks to this man whom without
you would have been pure rumour,' (he meant Woz,
who grinned and nodded). 'He's the man who got

a group of us communicating, he's
the catalystic man in obviously
a sense of it that's modern, post-religious,

it's him who keeps the lighthouse. He's the eye
that opens, he's the tongue that tells, it's us
who do the dirty work of thinking why

with all of this, and in pure human race
terms what does it mean. What my – what our –
Association feels is it's unwise

to leave you to the vagaries, and/or
downsides of a choppy sea, this time
of omens and predictions, where before

it's pretty sorted. Look, they've found your name
at points in history will form a shape
that can't be accidental. Falls the same

on every chart, it just keeps coming up.
Debate I leave to others; I'm the man
who writes the cheques, who raiseth up the tab,

so to speak. Through no fault of my own,
the OPM is mine. It's Meadow here
interprets. What I'm saying, my old son,

is, you have friends.' 'I really made that clear,
Mr Nelson,' Wasgood ventured, 'Edmund knows
he's got mates on his side.' 'It's for my father,

bless him,' Nelson said: 'your pal, he was,
Demundo's what he called you, actually.'
'Mr Nelson's father passed away,' said Woz,

'Peace rest his soul, last year.' 'In January,'
said Nelson, 'guy was God-squad to the end.
I couldn't make him listen. Like I'd say,

there's signs, Dad, I'd tell him his old friend
has come back from the dead, apparently,
it's probable. He didn't understand,

he said it was false gods, I ought to pray.
I said – but not to him – you're on, I'll pray.
If He (capital H, like Him on High)

can keep the oldster breathing till his birthday,
fine, I'll be the man with the two hands
glued together and the bloody knees,

and does he? Nada. No more little bargains.
We're growing, sir, old son, we're moving on,
we're past the old beliefs, all the old legends,

they're *passé*, been there, done that, sang the song,
it's retro, if you like. It's a new world,
with new demands – that word, *millennium*,

for Christ's sake, that's conceptual, it holds
enormous new potentials, so to speak,
those zeroes are a symbol. We've new goals,

there's been a revolution if you like,
a faith in what we're feeling. If we feel –
yes, a man's been chosen to come back,

to come back never ageing – if we're all
agreed, or like we mostly are, what's true,
then that's what we believe, our principle,

and dissing us is a fascistic view.
The future's we, we clock what's in our hearts
is where we're at, is what we're moving to.

Bit of a speech, I know, but these are words
from on the edge, I nurtured them, they flew.'
A tube of ashes toppled from his hands

as his cigar was lifting. 'What we do,'
he said, though by this time the light was out,
'is also meditational *re* you –

why you appear, how you appear, and what
in terms of how we live you represent,
an urban myth, a test or a clean slate?

And plus we can protect you. Top point,
we have to, as there's lunatics out there,
superfluous to say. What *we* don't want

is real disorder. The man Wasgood here,
he knows what time you make your presence felt,
what place it is, he's on the when and where,

his secret . . . That's his right and it's pure gold,
he's someone I applaud for that, that choice.
And where we've come to very few were told.

Some known to you, some not – The Girls and Boys
I call them, but of motley ages. Lea,
there's twelve of us, *apostles* I might use

in not a Christian, more a Zenlike way,
apologies to Dad, it's just . . . to form,
to place a ring around you, like a sea,

keep you from all the recent sort of harm
is what's the feeling.' 'You're a soul in pain,'
said Meadow, 'who requires a zone of calm,

a quiet wayside. On whatever plane
you make your home, we hope to be that port,
that haven.' 'That you'll tell us where you've been,

and how that came to be, we're in no doubt,'
said Nelson, grinning. 'Barely worth your while
to come here saying nothing!' 'It's his right,'

said Meadow gently, 'to keep personal
what he can't say.' 'I hear you,' Nelson said,
'and value that. I only say we're all

awaiting, in our way, in our own mode,
for what he can divulge. To disappear
with not one revelation being made

in any shape nor form, to leave us here
not one the wiser, would, it's me implying,
be of a nature saddening and/or,

borderline bad faith. Is all I'm saying,
and in full knowledge that this man, this soul,
is now, with every fibre of that being,

preparing to be heard.' Into the cell
the water rose again. I saw the two
both agitated by its speed and swell,

that doused the flame in levelling of blue
and made them gasp again. This time my hearing
closed to them, and soon the ones I knew,

the women – Laura – sat among the living.
Bouquets of people followed, like a show
of blooms someone was feverishly matching:

two sat with Nelson, three then sat with Meadow,
Wasgood perched on a gold stool. I chose
to speak to them next time the light was yellow,

but when that colour came I shut my eyes
and I imagined walking in the morning
with Laura or with any one of these

in sunlight to a mate's. The sun is shining
out impossibly in the burst east
was what I pictured all the livelong evening,

while these arrays of people trembled past,
becoming known as I became a stranger.
A girl with curly hair and a black vest

had seen me once she said when she was younger,
'and just a baby really, but my dad,
he said you were like *this*.' Her name was Gemma,

her father's name was Nick, I tried a nod.
It seemed a benediction, and she bowed
then seemed embarrassed to and quickly stood,

explaining suddenly: 'This is the crowd
they listen to, it's cool. I didn't ask
to hang with them, I don't do what's allowed,

and you and me we share – the right to risk
is what it is! I need you and don't care
who knows it, least of all my half a sister.'

She glanced at Laura once and through her hair,
she ploughed her hands. One in torn jeans appeared,
bashful and excited. 'No one here

but me is blood-related,' he declared,
extending out his hand to me. 'Behold,'
he faltered when I didn't move, 'my dear

uncle.' To the rest he said, 'his old
nephew, Kyle. And no one of our clan,
apart from me, believes in the new world

he represents!' Of this bizarre young man
I almost asked a question, but the fire
would roast me if he answered, and the rain

that fell inside me I'd long settled for.
In front of me were girls of my old age,
seventeen, a slim bewitching pair

that Nelson only said were 'Out of reach
of mortals, they are here because they're here,'
and, smiling all the time, the girls got each

a hand of mine and kissed it. Then the air
too kissed it, and they said a word in French
that I'd forgotten. Someone old was there,

a man with a large face, in middle age,
whom Nelson told to hurry, and who beamed:
'They talk about you on my world wide page!'

And 'Dodge,' somebody said, and it was him,
still beaming when they helped him from the room.

XXXIV

I rode in a long car. I had my hands
made into fists to signify two fives
of people who were with me as my friends,

and one eye shut but I was short of twelve
until I recognised across from me,
opposite (we'd space enough to have

an opposite, and drinks and a TV
somehow inside that car) another face
from times I'd been alone: his hair was grey

at either side, I saw and his old voice
was weather-beaten but it said the same
as everyone. 'Retiring to the house,'

he said. A lad inside me said his name,
Russ, and it did seem so. 'The old gang,'
the grey man said. 'Back in the old routine,'

he added, and two doors were opening
apart into a dimly-lit long hall,
with photographs and candles all along

on either side, not in a car at all,
I noted. I was being led. Eyes closed,
we sat when I had counted twelve. A girl

on either side was near me, and I eased
each hand into their pairs of hands. 'Like toast,'
said one. The other slapped her, said 'Like ice

is what it's like.' They held me at the waist,
then when I looked had gone. In my deep chair
the girl called Gemma in a silk black vest

was stroking me. The older men were there,
perched on either arm of a settee
with no one on it. Someone's camera

was passed between them and repeatedly
it flashed too late to blink. The man called Meadow
drew enormous curtains I could see

the night behind until he did. 'Tomorrow,'
a girl was saying, and I turned to see
the highest Christmas Tree by a black window,

Meadow drew the curtains on. 'Today,'
the same voice said, and this the blonde-haired girl
who hadn't spoken earlier. 'Today?'

she wondered; she was lifting from a pile
of shapes in tissue round the tree, with Laura
standing near her, clapping. The man Kyle,

hands awkwardly beside him, seemed forever
nervous by whatever door was there,
and in a different room there was a supper

some were eating. We passed by that door,
myself and Gemma, she was taking me
with someone's blessing down a corridor

and then another. 'Are you fond of me?'
she queried when she sat me down. The room
was small and full of clothes, and on my knee

she sat herself. 'You have to steal the moment,'
she believed. When other ones were there
she moved her legs together: 'Not to blame,'

she told them. Later: 'Do you hold me dear?'
she whispered in the hall. 'You're holding out,'
said Nelson as he guided me to where –

I counted them myself – eleven sat,
and he made twelve and left the deepest chair
for me to take. I plummeted in it

and gazed across the rugs at a great fire,
so amicably beckoning. The words
began with Nelson and from here and there

went back and forth to more or less applause,
but in my mind they were wood-gatherings
assembled for the fire and that was this,

my stack of silence, my unuttering.
That ate all things and Nelson had to speak
to keep the fire burning. There were things

that needed answers! was a shriek, a spark
that spat from out. And I across the room
was contemplating someone, with the look

she gave me given back. She said her name
was Syra when we passed, perhaps before,
before the silence that it all became.

Elicia was the other: all her hair
was twisted into strands and both these girls
I picture smoking on a bed somewhere,

I picture disagreeing, using pillows,
the heaving breath of the bare slender two
when that was settled, tracing of the hollows,

shifting of cloud cover, and the view
between them out of an uncurtained window
of a cold slivered moon we said was blue

on close inspection. There was time with Meadow,
a leather couch, a low glass table, wine,
beer, whisky, vodka: 'anything you want to,'

he was insisting, 'anything is fine.'
That he knew nothing of my real life,
my friends and travels on the wondrous train,

was clear, but I might sample mortal stuff,
I did allow myself. 'It's what we've lived,'
he tried again, '*without* for long enough,

Edmund. *Miracle*. That you've been saved
for something, that means everything to us,
that time itself might . . . When my father left,

and when he left he did that for always,
when I was nine years old – the world and I,
we two stopped moving. We've been face to face

since then, as if I feel no time passed by
since he was here, and seeing you appear
as he'd have known you – with no reason why –

it somehow moves me past that – stone – I've clear
sight across a valley. All of us,
our little tribe, our reasons to be here

you'll not find two the same – but you've the face
of one recovered, even, from a wreck,
the wreck of it, perhaps it cost your voice

to speak to it, and there's no need to talk,
and he, I'd tell him that, I'd tell old Moon
you'd know him as, only to have him back,

no need to speak at all. It sounds insane
but you might tell him if the place you are
is where he is, could you? Tell the old man

it's late, time to stop playing on the square!
Homework to do, bath time tonight, you know,
might jog his mind. But, keep returning here,

Edmund Lea, and find me. I'm just Meadow
to everyone, I'll keep the candle lit
whatever winds are – I'll be at that window.'

Equipment was appearing: blinding lights
and cameras and connectors of all kinds
in coils across the floors. The hall was bright

with mirrors as we waited, and my hands
were dipped in something blue to make a print.
Gemma washed them after. 'Your two friends

are lost without you,' she was adamant,
and so were others who were helping out.
'Hey Ed, we should have had you in the band!'

The old two men were drinking where they sat,
and Nelson stood beside us and said, 'Here,
the gay old corner: here's what it's about,

the good old days, get this,' and Kyle was there,
aiming a microphone into the space.
'Edmund auditioned for our band, The Hunger,'

Dodge Mendis said: 'formed in the seventies.'
'Say your name,' said Nelson. 'The – The Hunger.'
'Yours, you twat.' 'Formed in the seventies,'

said Russ, and Dodge was frowning: 'In December,
1969, was historically,
the first beginning. I can well remember

that classic line-up, Russ. Originally,
it's Stanley Burke on vocals, Russ on bass,
Gary Cholsey on the skins, and me,

Roger Mendis, was on rhythm, plus
Moon on lead. That's that first classic line-up.
Our manager was Michael Nelson. Whose

esteemed son, who's standing there – ' 'Shut up.'
' – Protects our business interests.' 'Oh bag that,'
said Nelson. 'Do the Edmund stuff – no, cut,

we'll do it later, look, it's knocking midnight.'
'Today our band has been renamed The Whoosh.'
'He's not recording, man.' Time up to that

is fragments I could place to form a dish,
all fissured with the cracks, but time beyond
is particles of loss no man would wish

to set together, fearing what he'd find.
Wasgood is leaning on the bannisters
and drinking from a bottle. 'It's a blend,'

he says. 'It isn't mine, it's mine and hers,
Laura's. I'm in trouble. She and I,
we are the closest ever friends of yours,

I safely and, do say as I survey
this scene . . . You know, it's me who knows the path,
from out the fire . . . It's nothing that I'd say

ever, to another, that home truth
you said, not even to my lover, Laura,
the one I love. About the way of death,

the way of life, or stuff you said whenever,
because you're in *accord with mystery*,
Edmund, and it's not my *place*, to wonder,

not about what's said and done, you see,
is it?' he concludes. It's when he mentions
Laura I don't know if she'd already,

by that time, by then, drawing the curtains,
thrown the young girls out, or had they left
before? From a black skirt white underthings

she bustled down and shrugged away enough
somehow to spring me out into her hand,
to make me what she wanted to now have,

to move below her while her wet hair rained
into my face until I gripped and came,
and she was staring through me to the end,

until she saw me. 'World enough and time,'
was all she said, and rolled herself away.
Before or after Woz? Encountering him

unsteady in the corridor? 'Your day,
my day.' They are assembled in the room
to film themselves and film me go away

into the place I go. I look for him,
Wasgood, my old friend and see he's there,
grinning at me with the welcome grin

of one oblivious, and I seem to care
as I remember. I see all the girls
about the place and it perfects the air

to see them smile. I envy the four walls
that each will see them when no curtain here
can hold the sky back from its meal of colours,

and I can feel my enemy, his copper
ice in my own pocket, the sour coins
he deals to me, the red-eye, the decliner.

That all around me is a site of bones
is not worth writing: writing will itself
defy it, fleshing out its broken lines

for all it's worth. They formed a ring, the twelve,
when I was close to sleep. I heard the rain's
sublime disinterest starting to dissolve

whatever would remain. I saw my hands
begin to rise, ten fingers outward, those
and these still seeing eyes, somehow to send

a word to the sad twelve – to shield my eyes
was all I thought my hands and eyes could do.
But that was wrong – I'd have friends recognise

the sight of them was dear; besides, no view
could frighten me. I made my hands embrace
in prayer and glanced above – *I can't see you,*

I whispered so that no one heard – and last
my palms were upward-facing and my sight
was on each person till each realised.

And then my eyelids, with inhuman might,
began to roll the screens across. I heard
the hum of filming and a voice too sweet

to keep me conscious – *Angel, leave a word* –
then I was waking and my face could feel
a rash of air, iron smell, and I beheld

a flock of birds fly up and turn, then wheel,
dark on the sky, white on a passing field.

XXXV

Once on an ocean distance in the day
I saw a ship, distinct on the hard line
as a lone nail in wood. It sailed away,

and once I woke in moonlight, when the moon
lit up the mud-clouds lofting by, enough
to see a stump of lighthouse. Once the moon

was lucent and unthreatened; once a wave
stood up and broke on us and the carriage floor
was washed with salt a moment. I could pave

the way from here to anywhere you are
with all that happened once where the black train
was made to go, a hundred times as far.

The hand I write this in, the hand that's seen
to break the surface of a sea of grey
one day that promised nothing, and is gone,

can move its fingers and will feel the sky
between them. What could raise into the sight
of sun and moon these fingers? Memory

of what repeated in the world outside:
what Time remade – what came again. I woke
as I had always woken, young, restored,

with eighteen pounds and finding with a shock
the bracelet gone, the only thing I'd bought
for Christmas Day! – and everything came back,

mid-afternoon, the view, and the first thoughts
of all the far from home. I'd walk the train,
between the wiped-down tables, the bar shut,

into first-class, where every day, again,
I'd bring my work to if it felt like time.
I'd use the washroom there, rinse, and return

refreshed through the four standard cars, first mine,
then one for exercises, one I'd pile
with work in old mail cartons, then the one

I might just hack to pieces in a while.
No deed was mine that couldn't be undone.
The Driver glanced back with what seemed a smile.

I smiled at him, could smile all afternoon,
the truth be told, but once I also smiled
a smile as different in its origin

from his as were my wishes from his world:
for the melody came back, the little clasp
of notes, the little cluster that I'd heard

the year before, before my night of hope
had come and gone. The train was slowing, crept
on cloudy upland: on a nearby hilltop

mills were turning, nine of them in strict
maniacal big circles. Otherwise
the place was still, or otherwise except

the sun made clouds a moment or their shadows
striding up the dale. So I stepped down,
enchanted by the tune again, my eyes

no less infused with hope for having found
not once a source for that lone melody.
And so I set off up the rising ground

to where I thought it was. The half a day
I was allotted darkened to my mind
too quickly. I was brushing a new way

through bushes, with the sunset low behind
and gone in cloud, when suddenly between
two trees a wide field opened up, farmland

beyond it. It was grassy and uneven,
but broad enough to take the last of light
and even have its grey recall the green

it was perhaps ten minutes back. My sight
was dimming, to be sure, but far across,
before the edge where it would get too late

clearly to tell – at least until, of course,
the train crept into view with all its lights
alight – something was standing in the grass.

I started out and held as many thoughts
as I took breaths, so often did it seem
a different figure I was bound towards.

Again the music, at the pace of dream.
Was it a person or a sign of one?
It was a lullaby, and that word came

with a first star when all the warmth had gone.
The wind rose as I went. I soon felt sure
the thing was nothing and the music some

phenomenon, some solace I'd yearned for
unknowing, which my poor neglected brain
had hauled up like a child demanding care.

I nodded and the music came again.
I heard a breath behind me and turned round
to hear myself start breathing. In the faint

withdrawing light I halted, heard the wind
for company, and I could wait no more.
I ran towards the form at the field's end

and slowed on seeing it was a small chair,
a baby's pushchair, in which sat a child.
He was wrapped up against the evening air,

and in his hands in little mitts he held
a box that played a song. No one was there
but this, I knew that when I loudly called,

clearly, loudly asked was someone here?
and it grew dark and he began to cry.
A question, something wanted or some more,

or someone, I had no idea – that I
knew nothing that could help was very clear.
I knelt down by him and I asked him why,

not knowing why I tried to and quite sure
it couldn't matter really. It grew worse,
his face in rage, the tears and the cold air

that chilled them on his cheek, the furious force
of his unhappy breath that made of me
an infantile dissolving helplessness –

'But it's your world,' I sobbed, 'you know the way!'
He hushed at seeing this and with his hand
began the music box. The melody

restored my sense. I cast my eyes around
in search of light. The moon was in a stream
of ragged racing clouds it lit. I turned

the pushchair so it faced the way I came,
and started off across the grass. This proved
impossible, the wheels would clog and jam

with stone and soil beneath. Aghast, I heaved
the thing into my arms, the child and chair,
and tramped towards the silhouetted trees.

An awkward burden on the flattest floor,
but over dark untended earth a joke:
twice I stumbled, swearing, and before

we reached the field-edge I had pulled my back
with this unasked-for labour. He, of course,
was crying all the time, and that same music,

so swiftly spun from lullaby to curse,
he never, in the throes of grief or rage,
neglected to restart. It served for bliss

to lower the thing to ground beside a ditch
and curve my spine the other way. The night
was here, it was relieving of the watch

a day whose bright informative report
it didn't care to hear, so I could tell
no way from any other. Now I thought,

letting the infant cry till I could feel
no meaning in it. Then I said aloud:
'I cannot aid a thing that is not real.

You are not real. You are a thing that's made
according to a law that I no longer
care to credit. I have blindly rode

to all intents and purposes for over
forty years. I cannot take with me
a thing I don't believe in. There's no mother

anywhere whose dearest you might be.
All this is netherworld, its size too great
for one to ever reach another. I,

Edmund, neither born nor dead in it,
assure you it is no part of Creation.'
I stooped beside the baby, who was quiet.

His eyes had closed and when I looked were open,
closing, he was sleeping. With a nod
addressed to what I'd said, I stood again

and started walking. 'You are not of God,'
I said. The wind was blowing hard. 'I am,
or was, a godly soul,' I then averred

in some confusion. For the first, last time
I looked behind me at the little chair
against the hedge, the faintest of outlines,

and kept on walking: 'There is nothing there
that is my life,' I said. I looked again,
it would have vanished to one unaware,

but knowledge of it lent it a faint gleam
of light on its pale handles. To the wind
I turned, deserting and disowning him.

Beyond me, something turned this stone around.
Retraced me on the air. Lifting the child
I didn't wake him and I left behind

the pushchair. He woke up some half a mile
into the dark and screamed to find I'd ditched
his music box. I walked another mile

to find the place again and only did
by the moon's having slipped her guard of cloud.
I carried him, for he was what I had,

though I was tiring and I knew this deed
would end as all, in sleep, the train in light,
the child a curious thing I might decide

to kid the crew about. The moon had set,
the dark was total and I felt my way,
or fell my way into a hole, and stayed,

the baby sleeping by me restlessly,
and I waited for the ending. Forty years
without a sunrise, since a morning sky,

yet cold in utter blindness and through tears
of anger and despair I could believe
there was an east in which might still appear

the land outlined, then grey with dawn arriving.
Sleep, reluctant, empathetic friend,
a weary victor reaching the horizon,

would try to slow his steps, he was that kind,
but nothing was his rival. So it was:
I slept, and was departed, and returned

alone and unrewarded for these hours.
It was, again, as if it never was,
the night's excursion. The succeeding years

were pitted with that melody, like stars
in an uncharted corner of all space,
somewhere so unconsidered that no eyes

could tolerate the blackness and would close
in search of light to go by. Me it saw,
astronomer it was, emitting trace

I made, and I would set out anywhere
I heard it, thought I did, or couldn't have,
because its faint recurrence was a flaw,

the flaw that lit my world. I couldn't leave
what thorough darknesses it wound me to
until the pushchair, noticed like a grave,

appeared again beside some blue hedgerow.
But it never did, and without lamp or thought
I sat down many nights. The tune would go,

persistent, intermittent, and then out.
 – That's all the story of the only sound
that somehow pushed between the bars of light

immuring me, that vanished but returned.
I chuckled over drinks that given choice
of saving and deserting to the wind

that little child, I'd made the rightful choice,
and earned the right to – *What. Make it again?*
I had the barman growl, *some kind of choice,*

and I'd go quiet at my reprimand.
It's not as if the world has changed, he smiled,
and totted up. I say the only *sound*

that came again, because, once in an old
stone dugout by a mist-defended sea,
I found a filthy envelope was scrawled

with writing, yellow, torn and tinder-dry,
and I would see a sailor in the snack-bar
finish, seal, and shyly fold away

that letter two years later. 'Missing her?'
I giggled, reaching for my ice-cold lager.

8 *Still to Want You Gone*

CHRISTMAS EVE, *2012*. Edmund is met on the train by Wasgood in disguise, who says that many people are hunting for him, including devotees of Nelson, who has turned the idea of Edmund into a supremacist cult. They jump from the train. A van picks them up, but the driver delivers them to Laura Kendall and her two friends, who have other plans for Edmund. They visit the house of the Poet, who is now fifty. At Laura's, the three women suggest a promising path to redemption. When the Nelsonites come looking for their 'Messiah', Edmund and Wasgood escape across the fields towards the railway station, and Wasgood remembers an age-old rhyme . . .

XXXVI

The seventh year was hills seen from afar,
the mistiest of blue, its weeks and days
all estimates. A keenness in the air

I took for autumn in a pinewood place
we glided through forever, and the frost
I called *No-temper*. I required ice

on every pane and from myself a mist
at every breath before *Descender* came,
and then my joke was 'under train-arrest'

until the day arrived and my one time
was watched for like a comet. I was wrong
by a good month, and in a mournful gloom

by then, when in composing of a song,
a song intended for my music play,
I crossed a word out and a light went on

beside a pond out there. It was late day
in Hertfordshire, West Europe, and some boys
were playing by a goal: the ground was dry,

the weather clear and wintry. As I rose
to weep against the window: I say *weep*,
it's all it was, habitual response

I let be like a sneeze until it stopped.
For I could see the Christmas light displays
that fondly and elaborately wrapped

what seemed whole streets and buildings of this place,
this, something Grove, the name was gone. A valley
swung below, all houses and estates

I'd never known, a silver dome that surely
never was before, then tunnels, one,
the light, another. In my seven-yearly

hopefulness I stood, swayed, holding on
as if an old, old man to every headrest,
every seat, and made my way along

to where I might find company. The dust
that made me sneeze was coming from the room
I had for washing. It was being used,

to my annoyance, nor was the aroma
dust at all but cigarette, of all
forsaken things. I sat down in the corner

nearest it, in an accustomed cell,
only to hear the user slide the doors
and slam into first-class. Unusual

for Polly, if it was her, but it was.
I saw a combed head with a fur-lined hood
arranged around it. I inhaled the air's

impression of her, breathed again and said,
before I was in view: 'Good afternoon.'
She seemed to sigh, and leant a little forward,

slowly craned her head around. 'The teen,'
was what she said, 'rebel without a ticket.'
I sat across from her, and she went on:

'Have mine, it's on to Creslet, you can take it.
Skip that dive of yours. I never set
a toe there. But it's yours, you have to like it,

maybe. Do you smell a cigarette?
Must be you. You can't smoke in this train,
Edmund Lea, you can't smoke on this date

is all the news I have.' She sighed. Her tone
was softer by the sound, but somewhere gone
was some bright energy. There seemed a yawn

set to arrest each motion or opinion,
and she wore plain brown things. As ever, all
I wanted was to hear her speak, a person

other than me make one syllable
I understood, to anchor my adrift
and sinking heart. 'How are the—the old people?'

'Them? When I last looked we had some left.
We set some places for them, on a whim,
and played some carols, wrote a Christmas list

and there they are, all sitting there. That's them.
They're what I'm on my way to. People are,
Edmund Lea, it's only you who's on some

detour.' 'How's your brother?' 'How's my brother?
I don't know. The same.' She passed her hand
across her face, it shut her eyes. 'Or rather,'

she blinked them and looked out, '*the living end*
is what my people say, I mean my clients,
my customers, my punters. I've this friend

they beat up in your town. She had these comments
down her tee-shirt, and a Man U cap.
That's a bad combination down at Gladlands,

Edmund Lea. She got herself cut up,
Tanja, which is sad, considering how
she only just arrived on the old doorstep,

you know, UK, seeing as her country's now
made out of landmines. The old garden man,
he saw her staggering home. We don't blame you

for how the place is hanging. You're the teen,
you don't know better.' 'Did your brother, Woz,
tell you he was with these – twelve – I mean

who want to help me—' 'Someone said he was,'
she said, unpeeling chewing gum. 'That bloke
he used to know turned out a right old menace.'

'Who?' '*You* know him. Mr Nelson. Sick,
it all came out about him. Not too nice.'
'What came out about him?' 'What the fuck,'

she snapped and chewed ferociously: 'Goodbyes
all round, for God's sake, look at me, you teen,
you fuck-up, I'm in charge of the goodbyes,

I make them out of paint and plasticine,
and then I get them with the glitter can,
and you should see the walls of our canteen!'

I stared out at the still blue afternoon.
We passed some rail equipment. I was set
to ask again, she seemed to have calmed down,

when came a screech and force of stop – upset
us both from where we sat, fell us against
each other to find balance, which we did,

and saw we had no station, just a fence,
a field of bleak allotments. 'Tows Hill,'
I said aloud. 'Ba-*naa*,' she said: 'two points.'

She sighed and sat right back; she looked so small
in her giant parka. 'This is where we say
the same in all the languages, old pal.'

She stared at me, relaxed and looked away.
'Kids, they never get it.' There was noise
back down the train and I was asking why

and what I ought to say when a curt voice
was in our carriage: 'Edmund, man, that's that.
I pulled the cord.' His collar round his face,

his big clear spectacles and woollen hat
were meant to hide him, but he moved like Woz,
deliberate and bulky. 'He's like that,'

said Polly, 'I forgot. He's in the biz.
It's all a movie to him.' 'You okay?
I got to ask,' said Woz, 'as you're my sis',

and it's the season.' 'Sod that, it's Monday.
Let's celebrate,' she said. He stared at me.
'You made it, man, oh man, I'm apt to cry,

I'm apt to, but we're jumping, Mr Lea,
we're jumping ship.' He sniffed. 'You've had a smoke,
you fuckwit, Podge.' 'I'm guilty, I'm guilty.

They made me do it. Here's those angry blokes
you ordered.' Two men – none I'd ever seen –
were striding up the carriages. 'No joke,'

said Woz, and gripped my shoulder. 'Major scene,
Edmund, at the mall, and the gig's off.'
He pulled me by the elbow and we ran.

I saw his sister struggle up and move
to be some obstacle, I glanced ahead
as Wasgood forced a door with a smart heave

on the deserted side. 'Jump out,' he said,
and star of forty suicides I leapt
wholeheartedly towards the gravel road

alongside. Then he did it, and we crept
bowed down along the train, until a space
appeared in the black brambles. Through we dropped

to a rough wooded track. And I kept pace,
with nothing else to keep, until at last
'Lights of the passing cars,' I said, my voice

bell-like, peculiar, in the sweet mist
of what I called *before*. 'Not bad for one,'
Wasgood was panting, 'one not in his first

flush of youth, you know. I'm forty-seven,
man,' he said. We walked beside the road.
'You're seventeen. You're ten years old and seven,

I've thirty years on you. I've got one load
of stuff to tell you, taken with all stuff
you might tell me. You lost it in the head,

we figured, back in '05, had enough,
we figured. I was one who knew you'd turn,
man, I'd known you since the age of five,

five, man, amazing, strange but true. We learn
co-ordinates from you. But you could sit
and be attentive, man, at seventeen,

could hear my voice. It's not like I've a kid
who's going to. And Pell won't even, like,
save herself. *She's* lost it in the head,

X times you, you could have brought her back.
She fought the big one, man, and only won.
She only won, my sis, she only took

the bastard, Edmund, Pell, she took him on.
Gave the big C the big E, whack! And shit,
I catch her on the smoke. My sister, man,

although we parted of the ways, that's that.
Now look, the gig's gone rotten.' We had reached
a busy junction so alive with heat

the daylight went without a word. I watched
the thinnest cloud remember and forget
its histories, rid finally its edge

of rust and blood. We passed a bench, and sat.
I counted cars. I used to. There were cars
that looked like they were racing, but inside

whole families looked out. 'Black wins the race,'
I noted, 'silver second, silver third.'
'They're desperate for word, in any case,'

said Wasgood: 'Word is key, *word* is the word,
the buzzword, man. It split the thing in three,
the thing we had before. I'm a fourth part,

not even mentioned and that gets to me,
Edmund, when I'm only *He you chose
to be your witness*. Gave it the big E,

my sister, she's the other one, but she's
too out of it, too slack. She's not a player.
And no one is if I'm not, no one is,

a player, like me . . . Nobody seems to care
who I am, only you. It's me and you,
in fact, in my world view who make a pair,

who really could bring word, could break on through
to something there. You pass to me the sights
you see between these times, and what you do,

and what it means, and we're within our rights
to phrase it for the market, and that thing,
you know, is really blown. I mean the outlets,

Edmund Lea, the dub-dub-dub is king,
I'm telling you, the outlets. Where's the guy,'
he said, now on his feet and muttering,

'I'll do him if he's shafted me. This guy,
knows nothing, just a driver. Copped a load
for doing this – I said it's Christmas time,

it's triple – and the zombie's only late,
would you believe? We're driving to a house
that's in no database, my friend, it's white,

it's unrecorded, think of it. Just us,
you and me, the only joint that's left
where you can breathe, where you got living space,

the rest is out of hand.' Just then he waved,
and a white van was slowing in its lane,
just past the roundabout. 'Should be relieved,'

he told me, and I said to him: 'My town,
Hartisle, please.' 'I love you like a friend,
Edmund Lea,' he said with a sad frown,

'but this ain't a fucking taxi.' Then he turned
to meet the van. When we were both inside,
he touched the driver's arm with his gloved hand,

and we were off. 'Sit back, enjoy the ride,'
he grinned at me. His eyes were red and wide.

XXXVII

I did enjoy the ride. Or I enjoyed
the peace of it, unchanging music soft
inside the van. I looked out of my side

at traffic moving slowly till it stopped,
in tinsel-chains of scarlet light or white,
but we went smoothly parallel. He kept

smiling at me, Was, as if he might
ask me more, but all I might reply
was how as we proceeded not one sight

reminded me of home. Uncannily
he did provide the question to which that
was a true answer and he nodded sagely,

'That's the flipside, that's the back of it,'
he said, more to the driver. 'What's a flipside?'
the driver wondered and they both shut up.

It is peculiar how these things collide.
The very second that I knew we went
along a street in Hartisle, the east side

I'd never really known – that very moment
Wasgood turned both ways in every sign
of agitation. 'What we said, you haven't

carried out,' he told the driver: 'Dean,
Dean, this isn't Washfield, it's the Slope,
you prick, I said express, *express*. Oh man,'

he nudged me, saying this: 'We've mission-creep
is what we've got here. Dean!' We stopped at lights.
And I was right beside those, as I hoped,

three colours I could taste they were so bright.
Woz tried the door his side, but with these eyes
I saw the locks sink everywhere. 'Oh great,'

said Woz, 'a Christmas traitor in the house.
That's fucking A, that is.' 'Oh back off, money,'
the driver said, 'I make a personal choice

that is my right and you're complaining. Really,
you're such a throwback, sir.' 'Well . . . point made,'
Woz conceded; 'Someone come in early?'

'Early birds,' the man agreed, 'in stealth mode.'
'Fuck 'em.' 'Well, I wish, but we did business.'
'What they offer, Dean?' 'Basis of yuletide?

Seven-ex your shit. And don't say Christmas,
not in here, I'm of an eastern mindset.'
Wasgood found a phone in his black trousers,

without a wire. He tapped it. 'Have they answered?'
the driver asked and nobody replied,
anywhere. 'Edmund, we've been pincered,'

Woz told me, 'by your lady friends. A slight
change of layout. What's the B, my man?'
he asked of Dean, and Dean said: 'I won't bite.

That's bony, sir. No threat, though, and you're in,
she says, if you want in.' 'My lady friends,'
I murmured after. 'You're two lucky men,'

said Dean, as we were slowing round a bend
then right into a narrow lane. 'The mean,'
he added, 'justifies. And here's an end

on site.' Three figures waited down the lane.
Two climbed into the front, but the third figure
slid in next to us. 'We're doing fine,'

said Wasgood, 'nothing hidden, and no anger,
it's out to dry, you businesswomen.' 'Good,'
the women said. 'Hello, you,' said Laura,

'next to me. We're in the neighbourhood,
my dear, we thought we'd take you out to tea.
Wasgood's got the jelly.' 'You're dead,'

said Woz, 'you little star.' 'It wasn't me,'
said Laura, 'I blame Alice. Christmas Eve
and here we are as squashed as squash can be.'

In front, a woman taking off her gloves
was smiling kindly at me: 'Christmas Day
will dawn for you, dear.' 'Point of fact, my love,'

Dean intervened, 'it's Monday.' 'Edmund Lea,'
another said, her hair in bunches – Gemma –
'there's been a book about you. I can say

I know that person, also in the summer
there's going to be a Special, and that person
the Special's on I know. And I can say more

not in present company.' 'The passion,'
Laura chuckled, 'the sheer thrill and spill
of Gem's imagination.' 'That's you wishing,'

Gemma said, 'you hanging at the well,'
and more besides. The soft-eyed woman, Alice,
I recognised. I warmed to her wide smile,

how she relaxed and how she mentioned Christmas,
which made the driver clear his throat, the way
she rolled her eyes to hear how the half-sisters

lazily went at it. 'Landfall, money,'
said Dean, but this to Laura, for it seemed
money stood for anyone nearby,

and now we'd stopped. Gemma looked: 'Hyde End.
That isn't it.' 'It's down it,' Laura sighed:
'We'll walk the rest. Dean can stay behind

and powerchat with Wasgood.' 'Are you high?'
said Wasgood: 'I'm with Edmund. Want me gone,
you make me gone, feel free. Plus homicide

to your portfolio.' 'Fair enough. Come on.'
The women waited as I struggled out
with Woz behind me to a wooded lane,

very dark, a single amber road-light
all there was, some starlight, no moon.
'No moon,' I mentioned to them. By my side

the women walked. 'I saw you. I was nine,'
Alice said: 'You know how many years
that means?' Woz drew up: 'That's twenty-one,

when we were in our primes.' 'That's what it is.
You were bewildered. You were in our house
one Christmas Eve. I saw you on the stairs,

they made a great production of it, how
this prodigal returned. It was the way
you looked about you, pretty much like now.

My mum was sorry all of Christmas Day
about how they'd behaved. She said our house
was yours in the old days. That stayed with me,

your thinking it still *was* yours – I suppose
I pitied you, romantically. The cat
they got me that year didn't take your place.

You stayed with me, a thing not to forget.'
'Me too,' said Wasgood, 'never dawns a day
without me thinking: Edmund, where's he at?'

Laura laughed at that. For now our way
was down another lane, with every house
set back, all Christmas-lit. 'I was just sorry,'

said Alice, 'that our home, our only place,
had failed you. And I know Mum sent you off
into the night to find your new address,

but I believed that might not be enough.
Enough to have performed. What made me sure
was that I felt new absences of love

around the house. I'd not felt those before.
This little heart was dripping with it, though.
Dreamlife began. You were the wanderer,

whom only love could save.' 'The answer's no,'
said Gemma shortly without catching up.
Alice shrugged. 'Of course nobody knew

what happened to you. Then your name came up
some drinking evening in the dreaded Virgin
before the Travellers burned it down.' 'Good job,'

said Gemma. Laura went on: 'Alan Nelson,
Man with a Plan. King Arthur fantasies.
Albionism. Martyrdom, resurrection.'

Gemma was lagging back. 'I need a piss,
is what I need. I hope this guy won't mind
if that's my first request.' 'There were rumours, lies,'

said Alice, 'pieced together, and old friends.
Nelson pooled us all. Remember that?
That house? There comes a time to make amends,

Edmund, and that's what's to come.' 'That's it,'
said Wasgood, hand upon my shoulder, 'now's
the time for forking over. We there yet?'

No answer, but far off a well-lit house
was last of all. The path towards it twined
illuminated down through the tall trees,

and so we filed along, Laura in front,
then Alice, Woz and I, then Gemma last,
singing words, explaining what they meant.

We seemed revisitant from evenings past,
here for a reason and I thought aloud
what might one time have brought us on our quest:

'carol songs.' They wondered what I'd said
a moment, then decided and were keen,
discussing what they knew, and 'Silent Night'

they settled on. We had arrived by then
at a bright, decorated porch, and Alice,
hushing them, stepped to the door alone

and started sweetly in her voice. The others
joined, the women both harmonious,
Wasgood trying high notes first, then silence,

then low ones that he couldn't hide, a bass
that brought one silhouette, and then two more
to hear the carol end *in heavenly peace* . . .

Three ladies stood back from the opening door.
They looked like one discovered in three shades
of light: each one a while possessed in her

the bearing of another. Something shared
itself along the beauty of their eyes:
its present, past, and future rose and flickered

in one look. We were not recognised
by what it was, and two of them were gone,
barefooted up the stairs as if surprised

in waking, so the third inquired alone:
'Aren't there more verses?' 'Nothing that we know,'
said Gemma shortly. 'Oh. Some other song?

These days they come and sing a line or two,
then break your windows if they can't retire
with a small fortune. That's what we've come to.'

Alice said: 'We're actually not here
for any money, it's—' 'It's for the song?'
the lady wondered. 'That's, I mean, bizarre.

That's brilliant. That's really a great thing
you're doing. Songs for nothing. That could sweep
the country, like a movement. Go on then.'

A glance went back and forth around the group,
and Alice ventured: 'When we, last July,
he said, I mean, your husband, we could stop,

if we were passing. I was in the play,
I played – it doesn't matter, but he said,
if we were passing with the, with this boy,

we ought to stop.' 'On Christmas Eve?' 'Well not,
or yes.' 'And what, and sing?' 'Oh no, just stop.'
'Just stop and what? Show him this boy? He did?

You did?' A white-haired man was on the step,
he held a wreath of fairy lights. 'Ah, carols!'
he celebrated. 'No, it's a moving shop,'

his wife rejoined: 'they come and talk in riddles,
but you don't have to pay. It's all laid on.
They need to show a boy, though. Shit, the kettle.

We're mulling wine,' she told us and was gone.
The man was beaming at us. Alice said:
'Sir, I was in your play, you know.' 'Which one?'

'The fiftieth.' 'The fiftieth. Was it good?
Are there fifty?' 'No, the birthday one.'
'The birthday one?' 'Your fiftieth, in the garden.'

'Have there been fifty in the garden?' 'Glen . . .'
I said to him, and, grinning, he said, 'Close.
Get it? No, too young.' I said again:

'Glen, it's Edmund Lea.' 'Of course it is,'
he smiled and shook my hand, 'Of course, that time,
you know, in the, that festival, fine place,

wasn't it . . . Heigh-ho.' 'Look, man, it's him!'
Wasgood said fiercely. Laura shut him up.
Then said: 'Excuse us coming to your home,

at Christmas Eve, appearing on your doorstep,
warbling like we do, but you know this boy.
That's what you said to Alice.' 'In the workshop,'

Alice said, 'the theatre one? The story?
You said about the Dutchman, that one day
you'd write about him, and *I* said I really

knew a man like that, called Edmund Lea.
Well, here he is, in, in – reality.'

XXXVIII

The husband put aside his ring of lights
and with them his broad smile. He blinked his eyes
as if in readiness for these new sights

and seemed to lean out into the night's breeze,
his life's own figurehead. I had no doubt
by now why we had come, or who he was,

and felt a warmth inside, that I could wait
all night for him to know me. I was here,
by that kind woman's action reunited

with one who knew me well. But in his stare
I saw no recognition yet. 'I did,'
he started, 'say that, yes, and you were there,

you say?' 'You said you met a boy who said
he was in Hell, one Christmas, on the train.'
'The workshop, yes. I did say that. Indeed . . .

We were discussing things that come again.
Stories that can't die, like the Third Child,
the Giant-Killer.' 'And the Flying Dutchman.

You taught, because of sin he sails the world
forever. This poor boy sails in a train.'
'And isn't Dutch,' said Wasgood, 'but he killed.

That was a sin.' 'Still is, I heard,' said Glen.
He looked at me again. 'Well, Alice. Look.
It was a splendid summer, work was done,

times were had. Good chapter in my book.
But this is Christmas Eve, and now our garden's
resting, yes? And Santa's hard at work,

and Robin Redbreast is, and all his cousins
send him cards from Rio—' 'You know how
the story ends,' said Alice, 'that the Dutchman's

saved, he finds redemption.' 'Is that true?'
I asked him to the shock of all who stood there.
'Is there a thing to do that I can do?'

Glen swayed and straightened. Laura pressed him: 'Is there?
For us he's not a tale or myth. We each
believe in him. Poor Woz is like his brother,

aren't you, chicken? We're not asking much.
Just what you know about it, and it sounds
as if that won't take long, a quarter-page

in what you call a chapter. We're his friends.
We suffer, for he's suffering.' Glen sighed,
then shrugged: 'Well. Consider your demands

caved into. For a time.' He stood aside
and let us in in single file. 'Straight through,'
we heard him say. We walked into a bright

and comforting back room, with the walls blue,
two couches, and a fireplace with a fire.
A slender screen hung down, a changing view

of sand and ocean breakers. Everywhere
were pictures and framed photographs of them,
him, a lawn, a cobbled street, a funfair.

'We've Life, and then we've Art,' so he began,
when we were quiet on the couches. 'These
are separate. It's true I met a man,

and many years ago, once in my twenties.
Last century, that is, in a past life,
and yes, he did tell numerous tall stories

when we were stuck somewhere. It was enough
for leaves to fall, in those days, all the trains
would grind to total standstill. What you'd have

was private, uncontrolled, yet rival lines,
each running—' 'Glen,' said Alice: 'Don't you see
that soul in front of you?' Glen drank his wine

and looked again: 'It can't be. It can't be.
I wish, you know. But that lad would be old.
I wish I could believe what I can see,

I—really. But, you keep that world. My world
tonight's preparing stuffing and mulled wine.
It's a good world, believe me, good as gold.

I'll get you some.' He rose, it was a frown
across the face that left us. 'Look, his books,'
said Gemma, by the bookcase: 'all by him,

but all the same. A load more in a box.'
'Leave things, Gemma,' said her sister. 'You,'
Wasgood said to Laura: 'new old tricks.

I get it now, you're *saving* him.' 'Well, *duh*.
You're quick.' 'And have you asked him if he *wants*
to be like us? They ask you that yet? Nah,

I bet they didn't. Want you in their pants
is what they want.' 'Oh, shut it, Woz,' said Gemma:
'You ain't picked for this squad.' 'The choice is Edmund's

all the way,' said Laura. 'Live forever,
till everything you know is gone, or else . . .
take the path this poet knows.' 'This tosser,

he knows jack. It doesn't kick, it's false
to him, it's just all books to him – look here,
books, books, by him, by someone else,

by someone else again, it's all unclear
who's true and who's all lying. Look at you,
saviours, guardian angels, sitting there,

like three closed books. I choose not to read you.
You think you know his mind and what he wants.
He's an *Immortal Man*. You think he'd choose

to be with you for life, like three great-aunts,
when he could skate right through the end of time,
do anything, take anyone? Great-aunts,

you three, and soon you won't be even then.
I witnessed him, was with him, I know Lea,
know what he's thinking and I think the same.

Let's get the fuck out, Ed, or you and me
we'll both be for the boneyard.' I sat still,
only aware. The women watched to see

what action I would take, till Woz said, 'Well,
looks like they got to you,' and he sat down.
Glen re-emerged, with glasses and a bowl

he set on the low table. 'That's mulled wine.
It's got bits in it. And it's also hot.
Traditional. Doubtless you all drink plain

macrobionic water as you're what,
twelve years old.' He served himself then us.
Everybody drank. Woz muttered, 'Shit,'

but asked for more. Then Gemma sighed and rose,
and left the room. 'Sorry about her,'
said Laura: 'she's like that.' 'Well I'm like this,'

said Glen, and sipped and added nothing more.
Girls' voices in the kitchen we heard,
the graceful lady's voice, and Gemma there:

surprise, then conversation. 'But I did,'
said Glen quite suddenly, 'I do remember.
And yes, you do resemble . . . though you would:

my *mind* suggests to me he was your father.
A weird inheritance. And for that sake,
that coinciding – though I know this feller's

going to wake tomorrow with a sack
of presents like the rest of us – I will,
Alice, tell you – matter – from a book . . .

The Flying Dutchman, being doomed to sail
forever round the world, is given one
potential path to freedom. If a girl—'

That was too much – I stood: 'My Setting Sun
is blind to that, is blind to love, is deaf
to all repentance, does not give a damn

what course I take. Mine's an abandoned life,
I came for nothing!' Wasgood added: 'See,
the wildest chase, you bitches, see!' 'Enough,'

Glen stood and said: 'My hospitality
I'd rather you not take for any sense
of anything but that I think you're crazy.

That or stoned. You know, don't push it, Alice.
Call me out of touch but Christmas Eve . . .
some manners!' Alice pressed: 'If the Dutchman marries,

he's free, you said.' 'If someone pledges love,
he's free,' said Glen, 'a virgin, though, a maid.
If a virgin pledges love. Unto the grave.

With which I wish you luck. And, God speed.'
Alice and Laura led me from the room,
Wasgood right behind, and we acquired

Gemma somehow and were gone from him,
my erstwhile Poet-Angel. I looked round,
expected some last word, some knowing gleam

of recognition, empathy, but found
no more than a sad smile he had until
his family reappeared. Quickly he turned

to the delight and fuss of their bright hall,
and someone gently closed the door. We strode
away, back up the path and up the hill,

the women talking all the while. Wasgood,
right beside me, muttered, 'There's a scheme.
There's more to come. They're dangerous, they're mad.

It's like with Nelson: many went with him.
Worshipping some king from never-never.
He had a race thing going, know what I mean?

Sons of Albion, you know, King Arthur.
That you were English, man, that you were like,
ours, but meaning *theirs*, snow-white. Some paper

splashed it all. The specials searched his attic.
He had a nail-bomb. See what I've been doing?
I'm looking out for you, and then this chick,

this chick of mine, once was and no hard feeling,
all good things must, you know, she has this crazed
notion they can save you, but it's nothing,

man, that poet talking, what a waste!
Hooking up some virgin . . .' Dean was there,
reading by the white van. 'Newscast,'

he hissed, stubbing a cig. 'We got crowd here.
Behind me, in the bushes.' 'Well, drive fast,
might be a useful strategy,' said Laura.

'Drive fast and you know where.' He did drive fast.
We rocked about the seats, and Laura's hand
was on my hand, and Woz had closed his fist

about the other one. 'You heard the man,'
said Laura, 'there's a path.' Her other hand
came up around, and leather on my cheek

was pulling me towards her, where I found
her mouth on mine, her lips, her tongue, her teeth,
one eye observing and the lash inclined,

then the unearthing sweetness of her breath.
The other women whispered. All the while
Wasgood gripped my other hand. 'A path,'

Laura repeated, drew back with a smile,
and rose-and-fell my hand with her dark glove.
'An exit light, my darling, out of Hell,

and into life, on Christmas Day, and love,
can you imagine?' Dean said out aloud:
'I think we're clear, I jigged 'em at the Grove.

Or is that them? It is them. There's crowd,
money, we got extras.' Laura turned:
'I don't see anyone.' 'That's why I'm paid

and you sit back there swabbing your young friend.
I'm saying, we got extras.' 'Lose them, Dean.'
'A quality idea.' He screeched and slammed

the van about this city that had been
my town but was beyond my knowing. Home
was where I next could see my breath as steam,

and that was in another quiet lane,
this time with red-brick houses near the road.
Laura signed her name somewhere for Dean,

who looked at it. 'Sniff that, money. Blood.'
The van drove off and five of us were dropped
on the cold street. 'Coming in, Wasgood?'

Laura hugged him: 'Long time since you stopped
at mine for coffee, isn't it?' 'I state,'
he told her thickly, 'long time since I hoped

for anything but hardship.' 'So a treat,'
said Laura, 'I remember how you like it.'
We went into this quiet house and sat

in a dark tidy kitchen. 'A rare visit,'
Laura said, 'for both of you.' 'That you?'
said Gemma, staring at a pencil portrait

taped to the fridge door. 'No, Gem, it's you.'
'Heck, I'm ugly.' Alice cut some bread
to make some toast. 'What are you going to do?'

Wasgood asked of anyone. I stared
past him at where a woman by the door
was in a nightgown, scratching her grey head,

talking about tomorrow. 'Early, dear,
worm-fashion. So. I'm going to disappear.'

XXXIX

As I was staring, they were showing me
in albums on that table, of all things
some pictures of a girl in infancy:

her? Clare Kendall – with the names for wings,
some life of air and feathers through the dark
came beating: here a young girl colouring,

there laughing by a sandpit in a park;
here she rides her bike with stabilisers,
there without them; there she's raised a stick

to point at us. Obligatory princess;
horseback hatted child. Another page,
a decorated name in felt: CALISTA'S

10th, a clown, a table by a hedge,
and there they were, the three of them, alone:
Clare, Laura, her – Calista – on a beach

but out of season, sheltering in rain.
I lifted over the broad gleaming page
and next was an unsorted pile. 'That's Spain,'

said Laura. 'Gem, you're in these.' 'For a change,'
said Gemma, as she came to see. 'I'm new,'
she told me, 'I'm in favour now. We lunch,

we shop together. If our mothers knew,
the scrap would be primetime.' 'We tell no lie,'
said Laura: 'Edmund. When we last saw you,

we weren't too smart. You know about this guy,
Nelson. You might call him charismatic.'
'Laura thought so,' Gemma said. 'Okay,

we didn't know, but that night it was drastic,
deranged. No one agreed on what we saw.
We sat there when the dawn came up, in panic,

truly, gawping at this empty chair.
I thought you came to me and said a word
I'd understand one day – nobody there

saw that.' 'I saw the walls blow out, they did,'
said Gemma, 'then melt back and you were gone.'
'I thought a long time we were all outside,'

said Alice, 'cold, and there was nothing wrong,
or strange, that you would simply rise and leave.'
'*I* saw flames,' said Wasgood, 'and you sang,

sang eye to eye with me.' 'And the whole twelve,'
said Laura, 'went to pieces, really split.
Those little sluts he wanted you to have,

he gave them names himself—' 'The cool one's dead,'
said Gemma, 'heroin.' 'The mad one's dead,'
said Woz, 'the cool one's dating Candy Ward.'

'Bull*shit*, the mad one's dating Candy Ward,
Woz, I saw them at it on the Net.'
'You're off your face, the loopy blonde one's dead,

and it was Gs, not H.' 'The blonde one's *not*
the mad one, she's the cool one,' Gemma said.
'And it ain't real blonde, though, but you're right,

she's dead.' They nodded. Woz said: 'Suicide.'
'Come *on!*' cried Gemma. Laura shut them up.
'Chrissie, though, she's rich, she has it made.

She rode the thermal, right at the wave-top,
spring two-thousand-six she went online
with a cosmetic range. *If Time Could Stop*

it started as, then it was called *Your Time,*
with these school-leavers manning terminals,
so every punter thinks she has a team

that's working on her look.' 'And on her files,'
said Gemma, 'her portfolio, her dates,
all her compatibilities. What else,

her doomsday clock.' 'She had her cybershit
together,' Laura chuckled, 'while that surfer,
what's his name, your nephew, Kyle? He lost it.

Meadow, he went travelling forever.
Dozgood? No one knows.' 'No, people know,'
said Woz, 'they just don't care. It doesn't matter.

Ed and I we go back years ago,
and I'm entrusted, in a way beyond
all other trust, so. Do what you may do,

businesswomen, you're all left behind.'
They talked and argued. I was going to ask
about the whereabouts of two old friends,

but nothing came. Then I was going to risk
an older question, but I had no heart
to try, and Laura's palm was on my wrist:

'Over these last seven years, or last—
three years really, Alice, Gem and I,
we started seeing each other. We all lost

part of what we had: they leave, they die,
careers, hopes and husbands, all the same,
all of them males. We thought we'd meet, we'd try

to think about what happened to us. Time,
and that's a male as well, was working hard
to keep us moving, keep us in a line,

but we found space to sit. We all agreed
we did believe in you. We disagreed
why each of us believed you should be freed,

but we all knew you must be. That the world,
we – couldn't have you falling from us so,
we couldn't bear it. You seemed like a child

that God disowned, that Time would, like, forego,
which thing to us was hellish, though we're not
Christians – she's Zen, I'm, I don't know,

agnostic, she's—Al?' 'Pantheistic.' 'That,
but Time means something to us. So we said,
we would not worship, would not celebrate

or make a symbol of you, like they did,
the Nelsonites, the Meadowish, we'd say:
he can be saved, be brought from his – this wood,

and life could travel on.' I caught her eye.
I nodded slowly and she squeezed my hand.
I felt the toast crumbs. I was tiring, 'My—

time is coming,' I pronounced. She yawned.
'Our hearts can't bear it, finally, Edmund.
Our world can't bear – a thing that has no end.

Then Alice said that writer knew a legend,
and that he'd met you. And it's up to him
to hide it from himself that that did happen,

but now we know what *he* knows.' In a room
above I heard a muffled cry. 'It may,
I know, we know, be nothing. It may seem

strange to you to be redeemed that way,
a virgin's love, it's not of our own time,
but Time is broken, Time has been passed by,

and what we're living could be tale, or dream,
falls open to all things. So there she is,'
she sighed, and took a single picture frame

down gently from the wall. 'In seven years
Calista will be seventeen, the age
you always were. I want her to be yours.

We three are all her mothers, so she's rich
in love and care. She's bright and kind. She'll be –
like Mum – a beauty, but you know that much,

because you liked her once. You'll have us three
for in-laws, but that's that on the downside,
Edmund, isn't it? And you'll be free.'

I looked at the framed picture. 'As a bride,'
I said, though it was scarce a croak that came.
The women nodded slowly. 'As I said,'

said Wasgood quietly, 'there'd come a game.
This is the game.' The girl was on a swing.
The album opened out for me again

but this time *Clare* at seven, seventeen,
twenty, thirty-one, and I sat back,
drew my hands to me. 'She's her again,'

I ruminated, and they gave a shriek
of thinking so. 'It's true!' said Laura. 'See,
they skipped a generation – beauty, freak,

beauty – don't have kids! No, look at me.'
She knelt before and held my hands: 'My girl
is kind and bright and decent and carefree,

and awful and a mess, and beautiful,
and everything out there there is to love.
I want her to be yours. I know you well.

We three can strive, with all the strength we have,
to make her love you when you come again.
We'll meet you where you want on Christmas Eve,

we'll all be there, two thousand and nineteen.
Now I sound monstrous, Edmund, but we know
it can't be forced, and if she can't be won,

we won't be there. And we will let you go,
understand, forever, on your way.
But we're . . . we're hopeful. Not so long ago

we *were* those teenage girls, and we can see
exactly how we might have once been, well,
induced in a direction. So we'll say

you're to be feared, shunned.' 'No, you're the Devil,'
Gemma cried, 'you smoke and you do horse.'
'Oh please,' said Alice. Wasgood had been still,

his sleepy breathing lengthening each pause
in what was said, but now he'd say his piece.
'I am the only person who there is

who knows, who has been told what is the place
and time to which this person comes. He's told
the information strictly for my eyes

only, to me only of the world,
and no one else. Not even my old sister,
his only other friend, who as a child

he did protect. So . . . if he wants Calista,
and all that life you think he wants like that,
like growing old and sick, and maybe after

years of pain and suffering and dread,
dying, being, say, gone forever, gone,
to come back never, brain-dead, body-dead,

and no returns, we used to say, a man
there was, who isn't now, like you'll all be,
if that's now the desirable new gain,

then he will have to tell you – and not me,
because I won't – exactly when he comes
and where he comes to. If he does, so be,

hallelujah, you and your e-chums
can make your lovely wedding with, I quote,
Death himself. But if, as it may seem

indeed to him, he'd rather not just yet
surrender what he is, *Immortal Man,*
he'll keep that information rather quiet,

and you can meet him with your bridal train,
but he may be elsewhere, with his old friend,
his man who's always kept his word with him:

namely me. It's you to call it, Edmund.'
And so it seemed, by the dire drowning hush
that rose around. Here, pictures in my hands,

the little girl, as if to make a wish
the world could work on. There, the burdened man
who called out from so far away in age.

'Between,' I said, I tasted it, 'between . . .
Fleur Manor and a stop called something Grove,
I find myself upon a certain train

that reaches Hartisle Station, platform five,
at 4.19, p.m., late afternoon.
Will, seven years tonight, on Christmas Eve.'

Wasgood turned, and Laura sighed: 'Dear one,
we'll be there if it's in our power to be.'
Alice smiled: 'We will. May it pass soon.'

Gemma winked an eye, then suddenly
light shone against the curtains and at once
the doorbell rang. 'Car headlights—' 'It can't be—'

and Laura looked a moment. 'Time he went,'
Gemma was urging. Woz had pulled me out
into the hall, 'The Nelsonites, they're mental,

I'm telling you, and this old face don't fit,'
he stared and said. The women cut the lights
and followed us; I glimpsed a silhouette

outside the door and 'Kill the landing lights,'
someone was hissing, and a little girl
was looking down and wrapped in yellow sheets,

asking Laura, '*Mum?*' 'Nothing at all!'
her mother whispered, and then right by me:
'Go, though, go now, we'll spin them some old tale,

you hop the gardens – Woz, you know the way,
you take him—' 'He's with me—' The bell again,
then constantly, and Gemma waved, 'Goodbye,

vanish – jeezus!' We unlocked and ran,
the two of us, out to the starlit garden.

XL

We steeplechased to shelter from the last
occasional torch beam; we took our breath
in someone's shed. 'I haven't got you lost,'

Wasgood was panting: 'Better to find it with,'
he grinned and meant the back of his own hand;
gloved, I noticed now. 'I mean this path,

this stuff I know like that! I'm still her friend,
Laura Kendall, though we fight like two,
we fight like two long-term. There was a boyfriend,

had no idea the ways I used to use.
That was her mother's place. She must have figured
her gaff was on a target list. The dues

where they're deserved, three ladies, man, I'm knackered.
The threesome had it figured out.' We walked
in darkness on a sidestreet. 'Thank you, Wasgood,'

I said to him, 'for helping me. I looked
to find you and your sister, every time
I came again. I paused to hear you talk

together, through the tunnel on my train.
I'm going to be set free.' 'Reckon I know.
Next time, in seven years, at four-nineteen,

I'm hearing you, it's being let – that's so,
I see that and I'm up for you, my friend,
I'm up with it, I am accustomed to,

and am on message.' There was a soft wind
unsettling the trees. 'If it's the path,'
he muttered as if made to by the wind,

'it's only in a myth, and it ain't myth
that brings you here, and takes you off. It's blood,
it's blood for blood, an eye for, or a tooth,

a giving back in kind. Two rivers lead,
Edmund, from the fire. The way of hope,
you've said you've not the strength, if that's indeed

the way of hope, that river. It's the step
nobody took, perhaps, the walk on water?
Love of a virgin girl: that's what coughs up

for him you've killed? Love of Laura's daughter.
Calista. Got her ice-cream in the park,
when she was what, had to inquire what flavour,

cinnamon, you know, her mum's at work,
Caliss. She'll be a beauty, though. That girl,
she'll fall for you. The threesome set to work,

there's nothing's out of range. To know a soul
out there who knows and loves you, but that's what,
the other river, U-turn into Hell,

if memory still serves, and I'm exempt,
being as how I don't – look at the blue
that's coming out of – being as how I don't

know you, man, or love you, do I? No,
so I couldn't be that service to you, he,
and the desire that's necessary, no,

I couldn't do you that. Do you know me?
No. And love me? Well, who ever knows
what lies what way.' The road grew narrow, stony,

weedy, wound away from the dark houses,
and surely I could hear for once a river,
as if the word released it. 'Know what this is,

Edmund? It's yourself. I'm being clever,
don't you mind. This is the river Lea,
or some of it. It's really not a river,

is it? And I saw the Ordnance Survey:
non-represented. Never shows it here,
this tributary stream. It's only really

a little trickle now.' I saw it there,
a murky shallow blackness in a ditch
between two playing fields, and I knew where

at last I was. I saw the cold high H
of rugby posts, and this was once my school,
Valley End, this was the rugby pitch,

though where our buildings should have been, a whole
housing complex, orderly and dark,
slept silently. 'If Pele scores a goal,'

I said to my companion, as we walked
between the pitches and the stream. 'One-nil,'
he nodded. To the east the railway track,

the land gone missing, dipped to its bright level,
and our thin river turned into a road
somehow, went underneath it like a fearful

animal. I had to wait. Wasgood
was hanging back, as if a boyhood whim
had got him, wouldn't let him go. 'Wasgood,'

I called through the cold air: 'We'll have a home,
Calista and I. I see you coming up,
I see you always welcome.' 'Always welcome,'

he was concurring: 'Edmund, on your doorstep,
help the old man in, his favourite teas
you offer him in an old china teacup;

leave him fingers crossed with seven numbers,
seven's been the bonus ball these million
billion times, Michelle. Press on regardless,

Barry, I'll take six again. That's brilliant,
that is, my, Michelle, my belle.' The grass
was wet with dew. Beside a hedge I went,

some yards from where he was, or he last was,
as it was dark enough to hide him. Breath
was all that picked him out, the deeper sighs

he made, for he was tiring. A lit path
was just a quarter-mile ahead, it seemed
to lead to where the station mall was wreathed

in misty violet light. There I was aimed,
for like some time so long ago the cold
had nothing else for me: its bitter wind

was herding me from what had been my world
into what had to be. I heard his voice
and saw his figure on the rugby field

call from across: 'you tired out these eyes,
Edmund, and this dumb heart you dismayed.
Truth is, it takes a ruin to recognise

what never would have ended. He was made,
the man you killed, to point you to the sky.
There's pride in being that. I got my pride,

Edmund, now, my pride's for telling why
we have to do the deed we do, it clears
the cloud from off the stars, and I am he

that loves you, am that suffered soul out here
that wants you gone,' and he drew out a knife,
and said, 'I am the way of your Despair,'

and rose it up while I was trying to laugh,
and dug it in my side and brought it out,
staring at me. Saying 'Quite enough,'

I started moving nimbly for the light,
nimbly, I believed, across the grass,
putting yards behind me, with my side

jutting out, it felt, and here he was,
just behind me and he jumped so far
I fell with him, and he was fighting, Woz,

fighting me, his hand was in my hair,
his breath was at my throat. 'Lea river flow,'
he cried, 'and you go free!' But my hand there

took something slashing skin off, and although
I was now streaming every kind of ice
from every chilly hole in me, somehow

I didn't want this and I tore from this,
and swung a hand that hit him, so he stooped –
'You're dead and gone—' We ran a second race –

pounding along a metal track – I tripped
or nearly on a rod, and ran, and heard
it whack his shins, the cursing. Now I seeped

full scarlet blood along the way, my blood,
'My blood,' I uttered; he was after me,
Wasgood, I was better to him dead;

he knew the words. 'I have the strength to try
the way of hope,' I thought, but I cried out
at something flapping in my side. The way

was straight as wire: the far light was the street
beside the station and my legs could still
achieve it if they only could, the light

was all my thought, the light through the wire well
I fell along, the fences, and the rest
was building site – I saw the shining rail,

I saw green lamp and red, and smelt at last
the oil of what expected me, the train,
my poor black carriages where I exist,

and staggered through a hall towards the line,
falling finally down on a cold floor
too far from it to be. I knelt in pain

and waited and was dizzy. He was near,
a coughing I could hear across the wide
and empty chamber. Blood was everywhere,

mapping the clean ocean floor. He cried,
'Can't, it turns out, can't, the truth be told,
outrun the old man any more, outplayed,

England, it's one-nil, and it's the gold,
gold strips of the Brazilians, and silver,
second place for Lea in the new world,

the silver salver. No one can remember
anyone that's second – it's the gold
that stays with you, that's got your name forever

on the books. That something won't grow old:
victory. One for one's seven brides,
one's seven children when they're all assembled.'

Now he was very close, and his last strides
arrived at the far curl of my red sea,
unstoppable new limb of mine. 'Your deeds

are each forgiven,' Wasgood said, 'You die
forgiven and go peacefully at last,
amid the noise and waste. Your memory

will guide me through my odyssey, my quest,
in the immortal world to which I now
do turn my stepping feet. What thing was lost

is also found, what thing would die will now
exist immortal—' I was on one knee,
and raising it to move when he, somehow,

altered and crouched down: 'Help, Edmund Lea,
done to death!' And others said so too,
as if there were some. 'It's a tourniquet,'

somebody said about my arm, 'Not too—
that's it,' somebody said about my side,
and I was lying flat, with a smooth blue

blanket at my chin, and had not died,
was on the move, was airborne and back down
in a bright light and I could hear Wasgood:

'I thought I'd find him here, I'd been round town
searching, but no luck, and then, I mean,
this, I mean, that person must be found . . .'

He faded and they heightened to a drone
of voices, and I turned and saw a smile
from a fat girl who said, 'He ain't that one,

he never come, my mate was at the mall
and no one's come.' I may have said: 'Enough
is suffered,' and did say: 'It was a girl

who stabbed me, but she did it all for love,
and is long-gone, and you will never find her.'
A tube was through my nose. A plastic glove

was stroking me. I saw out of a window
nurses gathered and a Christmas tree
across a room. 'Already *is* tomorrow,'

someone said in answer. Soon they left me,
and I should try to sleep was good advice,
and tried to, but I thought of him who loved me

and wanted me to die; I saw his face
in my mind's eye, and thought about his sister,
my friends and enemies and witnesses.

A solitary voice spoke in a whisper,
words I couldn't understand. I asked
for Happy Hour, I said he'd have the answer,

then someone placed a white bowl on a desk,
and two of them were whispering, then none.
I felt the plastic ribbon on my wrist,

the cool of the clean sheets, the flash of pain
in any movement. 'All of this will heal,'
I said to someone, and it felt as plain

a truth as I had ever spoken: 'heal
and be forgotten.' I seemed in the care
of someone tall, who nodded for a while,

then lowered softly to the straight-backed chair
to watch me closely till I wasn't there.

9 *The Candle Palace*

CHRISTMAS EVE, *2019*. Once more the Train returns Edmund to familiar surroundings. Polly reappears, on her way to buy Christmas decorations for her retirement home. As the train approaches Hartisle station, they see that thousands have gathered in expectation of Edmund's miraculous return. In the centre of the crowd stands his young betrothed, Calista, who is about to redeem him from his unending journey . . .

XLI

He sold cards at the counter, Happy Hour,
he always had, blue-backed in cellophane
beside the cakes and blocks of writing paper,

called 'Regal' cards. I would explain a game
I couldn't seem to lose. He'd scratch his head
and move his chips across, then choose a game

and we'd be even. Many travellers played;
games simple, hard, involving, boring, strange;
some over quick, some ploughed on through the night,

or on until I slid my final change
across the table and collapsed to sleep.
One time we'd been a week in a dry range

of craggy mountains, slowing to a stop
for hours of quiet. Then we played like fiends,
the sun on our red hands. The oddest chap

for many months was with us, in those lands
to wear a suit and waistcoat, tie his tie
to join our game! He only comes to mind

because it was that summer, one July
(these seven years I never lost the date,
not once) when something new began in me,

my favourite game of all. That man, the Suit,
spoke in a tongue melodious and clear,
and in its use and pause, its dark and light,

I started to imagine I could hear
McLeod, my English teacher. Many years
I'd fastened to the voice of Happy Hour

those sounds I needed others to express,
but I began to sense in any speech,
however alien to my own, the stress

and nuance of real figures. I grew rich
on this dear finding. Everyone who came,
brief travellers welcome always in our carriage,

I made a memory of, I drew from time
long gone the echo that could make them whole,
and lit each afternoon and night with them.

What I discussed with them only a fool
would wonder – what to do, how to exist
when I was free, how to reclaim the world.

A boy with an old rucksack, who had crossed
a field of nettles to be on our train,
his voice was singsong and it went too fast,

so he was Russ, he'd be, at seventeen,
'Russ Parrish,' I anointed him. *Good thing,*
he pointed at me, *I'm the very man*

you want to talk to. Time for anything,
you know now, Edmund, take it from the one
who's always gone the freedom route. You're young,

that's to the good, and what you say you've done
is you've been in a case of alien
abduction, man, that's what. And what you've seen,

and what they told you in their, you know, den,
you're going to tell the world, but only if,
and that's our trump-card, only if all men,

that's all Mankind, and *Women's-kind, all Life,*
is like, they gather somewhere, in a park,
no a whole nation, say, if it's large enough,

to hear your five demands. And then, you talk.
'What do I say? What are they?' The next spring
a lady was Aunt Frances when she spoke.

I would have laughed but she was frightening
to me, she always was. She would have died
some fifty years ago. *For there's not long,*

you know, my lad, the world is on the slide
to pure O-blivi-on. What you have seen,
you owe it to salvation to describe

as Hell itself, the vault of the obscene,
inferno of all garbage, all this stuff
you see, that 'woman' in that 'magazine',

you saw her chained forever by the mouth
to a great rabid hound, you must divulge;
you saw Rick Jagger with his fiery breath,

and 'homosexuals' in the malebolge,
doing, my lips are sealed, but something else
forever, and free people being purged

of – what they are; you must relate these tales
at once, for you have seen what lies ahead.
That lady must have nattered thirty miles,

but I was wrong to foist my ages-dead
aunt on her: she gestured to the bar
when dusk arrived and drank me off my head

on excellent malt whisky. I tried Clare
from time to time, but no one had her quite.
Stan Burke I had. I even heard my sister

nagging me at dinner time one night
as an old feeble man. *It's all a lie,*
you'll have to say, a wrong to be put right.

You were mistaken. When you went away
you made a lifestyle choice, and what you chose
has wasted all your life. 'The butterfly,'

I had to tell her, him, to his old face,
'that will outlive you was just given wings.'
Eventually, one winter night of course,

my Dad was calling through the dinner things
across the buffet car. *It is a source,*
when all is said and done, of pride; it brings

pride as well as pain to me, to us.
That you were chosen, Eddie. Bear in mind
there's always someone wishing it would please

be otherwise. Poor mug who begs the wind,
Please blow some other blighter off, but ours,
just breeze him home. It happened though, and happened

only to our Eddie. Whom you chose,
Lord. You see? we got there in our day,
Eddie, to the Lord. We took the byways

to and fro, for sure, but we found the Way,
His Motorway! We make good time. Being chosen,
Eddie, show the wisdom of our Way,

and tell the world you saw the Keys of Heaven,
the Keys of Heaven, son, and what they were
was faith and hope and charity and – action,

son, and fun, and tolerance, and care,
for this and that, you know, that it was true,
regardless, Eddie, what you saw out there,

that it came true as written. They ask you,
you say that, just do that, we never asked
that much of you – when we still had a chance to!

It wasn't long. Nothing lovely lasts,
son. You make a difference to the game,
you play me through, I'll run. I'll run so fast

they'll think I'm you! They'll tell themselves: see him?
The father. It's not worth much, but I spent
the last three years at work on a great scheme,

to tell that tale, tell what the journey meant,
make it require some good of us, of all,
discover light in its environment,

tear lessons down in paper from its wall,
blackboard or chalkboard, plaster, stone, or sky,
tear lessons from in strips and bring that pile

home to the world. But that same memory
that would allow the smoke of what I suffered
to form into this verse seemed to deny

the meanings I constructed. What was left
of lessons learned each time I woke again
were squiggles on the page, a scent, a drift,

to be seen, heard, inhaled and sooner gone.
What you can read is all the narrative
considered fit by my declining sun,

still glinting like a brass plate on a grave
a living eye goes past. For once, it set
as I was smiling, eve of Christmas Eve,

and, draining one last glass of a warm red,
I waved to Happy Hour and turned away,
as I believed, forever. And my bed,

the royal bed, we called it, sighed *a day*
and folded me in sleep. When I awoke
I strode the length of my dear enemy

for the last time and, with the burning ache
of my impatience, battered on the glass
for streetlight to appear. 'And I will make

a friend of Wasgood, offer him forgiveness,'
was my resolve. 'He didn't know his mind,
and hope his sister's well, I'm sure she is,

angry as ever.' All night it had rained,
but now pale lemon sunlight glittered down
through cloud and I addressed it as a friend:

'You saw me and you took me, and now soon
I leave you. For I now have learned the way
to freedom and I swear, this afternoon,

I shall be loved by she whose love for me
redeems me from your spite. And Christmas Day
will dawn on us, together, joyfully.

And for those gone from me I pray. I pray
beyond you, setting sun, into the dark,
into the past and future, joyfully.'

And then I waited for the spell to break,
my hands detaching slightly from the prayer,
to show that little cave of hope, that crack

into the world you know. Then I was there,
and breathed a breath so deep the next you take
is warm with some of it, whatever air

presents itself. Fleur Manor and Fleur Park –
created, dirty, peopled, lit, outliving –
cars on the far motorway, the smoke

from fortunate small houses, lost in heaven,
cold expanses, cycle-paths, a lake,
loud coloured signs, amazing, meaning nothing

all the day, somebody's home from work,
the sprinkled Christmas light, 'It's Christmas Eve,'
a high street flashing past in a bright streak

of light and shops, that must be something Grove,
I said in this dim unassuming space
of any old commuter train, 'Arrive,'

I said and savoured – language in a place
where it could *mean*! I said at last the word
I'd held from saying, as a thing of bliss

too much to bear: *Calista*, I prepared
to say and said it, whom for seven years
had life in my imagination, shared

life with me, restored life, and a tear
began in both these eyes at that: that soon
out there in that cold heaven, that *elsewhere*,

bold in the face of the declining sun –
now crimson as a father set against
each wish of his one child – I would become

entire, I would be dearly recompensed
by love and beauty for the price I paid.
She was the one whom life would offer once

to keep forever, mercy of a bride,
fountain of light in my deserted soul,
the dream beyond the riddle, the new life.

I saw the grand old houses on the hill
go by, a chain of lamps, a foggy street
already night – and then, into the tunnel,

myself reflected, staring, as the lights
came on throughout the train, myself arose
towards the first-class carriage: empty seats,

empty seats, except one taken place,
the end, where a small woman in a dark
enormous duffelcoat opened her eyes.

She had been sleeping, had the draining look
of one too quickly woken. I sat down,
across from her. She saw she had a book,

and stared as if it just appeared. 'Your town,'
she muttered as she closed the book, 'Hartisle,
have to get out at. And it's soon, it's when,

it's soon.' 'It *is* soon, Polly, in a while.'
She turned the book. 'The things they say these days.'
I nodded, sadly: 'What's in . . . in Hartisle,

these days?' She looked out, shielding her dark eyes.
'Work,' she said, 'a work-related errand.'
She gazed across the rooftops: 'Otherwise,

see me for dust, that place. The humble servant
of twenty senior citizens. Do I seem
a figure of authority now, Edmund?'

She didn't look the same. 'You look the same.'
'We do to them,' she said. 'We do to them.'

XLII

She struggled from her pocket a short list
she had, and from another a white pen
with a monkey riding it. She tried with this,

her whole hand shaking till it got a line,
and then sat, poised to write things: 'Classy, hey,'
she said, 'my pen.' 'Things not to be forgotten?'

I ventured and she nodded. 'But maybe,'
I said, 'an elephant, then you'd remember!'
'Then I'd remember. My, would I. The monkey

knows that. And I've had him since the summer.
That's long to not have lost him.' 'Are you well,
Polly, then?' 'Oh yes, and what fine weather

we've had, these few past centuries. I'm well.
I always am, I'm – Adidas of Sparta,
today I am. Ignore the capital,

fight the province, draw them off. A slaughter,
see them fall, and heal, heal, it's nightfall
now, pour every cell with the pure water,

bye-bye Greeks, bye-bye. Polly *prevails*.'
She underlined some item, caught my eye
and looked away. 'It's – battle for the cells,

the sequel, Edmund. I'm as clear as day,
you want the truth, but every day I'm told,
you know, fight on. Fight with the cavalry,

use of the bow, Prince Edward with the old
artillery, you keep them on the move,
barbarians, you chase them through the cold,

let loose your arrows, up, like high above,
then down and wipe those pagans off the map.
There there. Sectionable but still alive,

and in, you know, the forces. What's this stop?'
The train was wrenching to a halt between
the tunnel and Tows Hill. She had cheered up,

and shut her book now. 'Nurse on the new team
said this would change my life, but look at this.'
She showed me where the bookmark was, a green

ticket for a fairground ride. 'It has –
let's see, twelve pages left to do that in.
No way.' She zipped her bag. 'And how is Woz,'

I thought it time to ask: 'I'm wondering when
he'll push me out, commando-style.' 'Well, not,
probably,' she said. She drew a line

between two items. 'Both those things I'll get
at K-Star, anyway. But no he died,
Edmund, as it happens, though. That's quite

some time ago, I mean, I mean a wide
stretch of time, enough, well, not enough
to make it better, really. But he died,

I can't do battle with it. Best you have
is to forget a while, and you caught me,
you know, at that old business. We're alive,

we do that.' I looked down. 'I'm very sorry.'
'Reminding me? Don't be. I mean, it's Christmas,
they put a wreath round us, they make it pretty

heavy really, Edmund. SUPERSAVERS.
Where is this? Let's go in there, you and me,
save some super stuff. Or they save us,

it could be, I don't know.' 'We're on our way,'
I said; the train jogged forward half a yard.
'I'm very sorry, Polly.' 'Well, don't be,

I guess I say. Is what's, you know, required.
Don't be. You didn't do it. It don't take
Sherlock Holmes to – don't take Scotland Yard!

He drank, you know, that's all. And stuff he took.
He worked where you could get it, so he got it,
Meyer Prodax, but he got the sack.

It's ancient news, you know. Like you might find it
carved on something. But – it's carved in here,
there's that. He just got full of, you know, habit.

They took his licence but he didn't care.
Boy swiped a fucking Merc, never by half,
and pranged it, and he's gone, the ending's there,

that's it. And that was, well, in earth-years, five
years ago. Like Di, though, with the Merc,
not bad. He loved old Di. Said she's alive

somewhere. Well, she is now. Piece of work,
my brother, piece of work, and God, I mean,
we'd drifted way apart. It's like a shock,

again, each, every time, again, not pain
even, just a shock like from a wire.
I'd like to think it passes, but the signs

suggest it don't – it doesn't. See me there,
correcting errors. That's because tomorrow
I'm going to be Napoleon: the fire,

you have to concentrate your fire! Plus also,
what, the breach is made, the enemy
broken at a joint or something. No,

I'll look it up.' 'You home for Christmas Day?'
'What? Home's where I work. Kill both birds.
In Creslet. S.C.Centre. Come and stay,

I'd offer, you can help with the old biddies,
tell them what their crackers say, all that,
pour their sherry, mop it up. Help Phyllis,

flirt with Tanja, she's about – she's great,
Tanja, but you'll go – I know, don't smile,
you'll go.' I sat back. I could see the lights

along the track, the roof of the big mall,
and cranes ahead, like building cranes. 'Oh yes,'
said Polly, 'there's that crew. In fact they're all

gathering, you know, your little mess,
your little hopeful gang. There were these shows,
about all cults and stuff, how you can use

these hologrammatic videos? There's these
people do it: I've seen film of men
who seem to disappear, it's just not news

so much as when it started. Then again,
you got your followers.' 'I know that's true,'
I told her, 'and I'm staying here – staying on.'

'You're staying on?' 'There was a path to go,
the Dutchman said, there was a path of Hope;
he failed, he tried Despair, for which he's now

a ghost around the station, he's—' 'Of hope?
Whole lives go by, old son, and now you say
the path of hope. What an inspiring step.

What do you do? Hail Marys? Do you pray?
That cracks it, does it?' 'No, in fact. I marry.'
'You marry? Are you high?' 'I do, today,

to someone waiting, up there, waiting for me.'
'Is where you go to Cyberparx?' 'What's that?'
'My God. Last man alive.' 'I'm leaving, Polly,

I know it absolutely. Up ahead,
there stands a girl I know, she's seventeen,
she's waited for me, she has been prepared

to love me. I was cursed by the cursed man
I killed, and he had killed to be so cursed.
I've understood all things. To live again,

to live in Time, like you, only the purest
love can help me: only by that faith
can I return, and only—' 'By the purest?

By a *virgin*?' 'Yes. It's not a myth.
It's the redemption of my sin.' 'You say,
but *seventeen*, in *Hartisle*? That's a path

not too well-trodden. That's one quiet alley,
I'm telling you.' She sniffed. 'We're nearly there.
Going to have to say goodbye to Polly –

I mean *Aunt* Polly. May not, anywhere,
meet, you know, oh shut up. It *may* be,
may well be you stay and have your pure

unusual like, local girl . . . It may,
but if you don't, though, and you're gone again,
that's seven years, old son, way way away,

and fingers crossed, and I may find someone,
you know . . . I did, he lost me though, he did,
somewhere back. I'm stopping in your town,

for once, there's nowhere else. It's Christmas Hut
or make the streamers out of string these days,
these Supersaver times. Big crowd ahead,

lots of little elves for you. Surprise!
or not. I'll get out quickly, clear the way,
prepare ye, it, you know.' She rubbed her eyes

and got her things together. I could see
as we were slowing, there were many there,
set back behind a rope. Slowly, slowly,

my eyes began to scan the faces, sure
to find the ones I knew, but not at once –
first let them find me. We were still too far

for either recognition, and my hands
were taken by my old companion. 'Look,'
said Polly, and her hands were old, 'last chance

to give you this.' I thought she meant her book,
but what she said meant nothing. 'Every time
we met I meant to, it's a giving back,

Edmund, not a gift. When we got home,
you see, when we got home, me and my brother,
when we were kids and ran away that time,

the time we saw you, trying to find our mother's,
'cos when our dad blew up, I was, like, two.
So don't ask me, but Wasgood said you gave us

this, it stopped me blubbing, I was two!
You know, Mum always said it kept me safe,
'cos we were out there in the cold with you,

that time, we were all night, frightened the life,
poor Mum! She said it was my lucky charm,
my rainbow-bracelet, but it's just cheap stuff,

Edmund, and it's kept me out of harm,
you know, but it's still yours. It's long ago,
but things are, now.' She rolled it from her arm

and held it out. I took it. I said no,
but she dug both her hands inside her coat
and backed away. 'Napoleon's going to go,

this time,' she said, 'first to the last lifeboat.'
The train had reached the platform. I could see
the crowd up close, but not a face, not yet,

a home for me. Polly I wished goodbye,
and heard her go, but saw her figure waiting
out by the far door glance back at me,

then dip away. Others were disembarking,
unsure of why a crowd was gathered, turning
curiously to see what they were watching,

pausing a moment there and learning nothing,
shyly grinning, or just pressing on,
towards where K-STAR CITY XMAS SHOPPING

changed to green for them in giant neon.
But those who'd come for me stayed there for me.
There were about two hundred, women, men,

children, mostly women, though. A lady
held a card that said MY TIME HAS COME,
one said I KNEW YOU, one said DREAM OF ME.

Some men were swaying in unison, and one
knelt down to pray. I was searching every face
for somebody I knew, had ever known,

but sought in vain. I had stayed where I was,
near my aisle seat, and stooped not to be seen
till I was ready. From this crouching place

I noticed Polly stepping through the scene,
a little figure passing by the crowd,
pausing, looking in her bag. She seemed

concerned and stopped there, taking something out,
her piece of paper and her monkey pen
perhaps, then she was shoved against a gate,

and gone. The crowd was jostling with the men
supposed to hold them back, and those who'd left
the train were being questioned by children,

while on the cranes and gantries up aloft
great cameramen swung here and there, their beaks
in search of what, of me. Police arrived

in cordial mood with mistletoe, and cakes
were offered round on trays. Now seemed to form
a kind of swathe that led from the railtracks

into the mall, it was policed by them,
the crowd behind. It was a plan, a scheme,
and as a welcome for a man come home,

lacked only the red carpet. Here it came,
unrolling through the dust like a dry tongue
in need of water. 'Give the boy some time,'

I heard a voice cry out, and one by one
they quietened, some talking, two, one, none.

XLIII

The train was emptied of its innocent
and now bystanding passengers; alone
I crouched down in the aisle. My vantage-point

was perfect: out of sight of anyone,
I'd everyone in mine. Would she be there?
I doubted for the first time, looked down

in fear into the dust of my own threadbare
carriage-carpet – she had gone her way,
Calista, unimpressed. *I'm well aware*

he's that miraculous, I had her say,
but I don't want him. When I looked again –
as if that sagging of my hopes, that sigh,

had jogged her from the dream – she stood alone,
Calista, darkly beautiful, dressed all
in grey and scarlet. I could feel within

my throat contract, my heart grow heavy, full,
as if that joy would slow me to its pace
forever, she'd be close, be claspable,

eyes wide and watchful, pale bewitching face,
her hair long, glossy, brown. Then right behind
I recognised them all: I saw their eyes

come out like stars, as soon as two were found
two more appeared, and all appeared to see
from long ago. It was as if my mind

had rendered what it dreamed: the memory
of my first love was in the eyes of both,
she there, grown old, and she so soon to be –

the moment that I stepped on that red path,
that river from the fire and into hope –
my bride and my salvation. I let breath

so very softly go, longer to keep
those dear ones still, still waiting, as if breath
might put the candles out. I thought of sleep –

so long my only friend whose friend was death –
how he could take me back, how he had still
some seconds to reclaim me from the path,

entice me back, embarrassed that his Hell
had hurt me so – that I could think to leave!
I stared out at that beautiful young girl,

and thought of firelight, and to have a wife,
and walk out on cold days that very Christmas,
across ice-fields in love, to live a life

forever so, be one of two young lovers,
begin a life together – and with her!
My heart beat fast to look at her, Calista,

whose hand was rising into her rich hair,
drawing it back, whose coat was red and grey,
who had been told of me and who stood there

waiting for me. In her soft dark eye
my life could start again. Her fragile hands
had force enough to make new memory

out of still air; her arms were where all lines
that carried me could rest. I do not know
how long – just seconds, only giant seconds –

I waited to stand up, to walk, to go,
to step down to the platform, still the age
I was at Christmas fifty years ago;

how long I thought I'd wait until I touched
the face of my desire, how long would pass
before we were alone . . . It was a page

I wouldn't turn, which turned into a voice
that said I couldn't. Then it turned itself.
The air it troubled and the merest breeze

began in me, a sigh – cards on a shelf
at Christmas would withstand it and then fall –
but it grew stronger and I needed breath

to sigh it; it was more than sigh, a bold
possession by the air, my ribs and chest
were heaving with the force, and I exhaled

so deeply I was weakened by the gust,
too weak to stand in any case. I rose,
and slumped against the seats, and realised,

and now the water washed into the space
the wind had made and I was made of tears.
I had no other element, my face

was streaming, and a sea that seven years
times seven years was not enough to sail
had swept my hopes away. It was not here,

it was not here, my home – was not in Hell –
but neither in her soft and wishful face,
nor in her house, her dreams, or her dear people –

I was not home and this was not the place.
I waited longer in a pose I thought
to mean I was in agonies of choice,

but I was not, and knew it, and would wait
only for the doors to close, and still
my words were chattering against my deed:

'Oh, let them shut, forget it, after all,
it's only seven years since you saw home,
and she was your one chance, that angel-girl

was yours for life, the table in the room
you share the meal you made together, grass
she treads across to you in summertime,

the sheets you fold, the heat of her embrace
for every night you are on earth, the same
beginnings, the same memories, all this,

but never mind, I say, win some, lose some,
let shut the magic doors and wave goodbye
for good to all of it.' Whatever time

it took, I took until, with a fresh sigh
they made, not I, the doors slid shut again,
and the train jolted, stopped, and to a cry

I made, not them, a grinding noise began
and we began to move. I couldn't look
behind me when I had to, when we'd gone

so far that every eye was too far back
to see me. She was closed round by the crowd
and some were shouting; one dropped to the track

and started running, but they disappeared,
one by one, because the line was curved.
Then all the rest, because I turned my head.

'Well, I was dead, and now I'm disbelieved,'
I said in the warm quiet. I was tired,
aching with the 'incident,' I laughed

to term it; I would weep soon like a child,
I knew for sure. Instead I just felt sick,
sick with the understanding that a world

began now, whether good or ill, its work.
I said, then thought again, then said again,
though hearing it aloud made it opaque,

unfathomably mad: 'I'm on the train.
To have remained aboard it was my choice.
The town where I was loved, had lived, was born,

I leave behind. I didn't leave this place
that is my curse. Whether or not that girl
would marry me, whether or not that grace

would free me – both forever go. Hartisle
is history to me, for I stayed on,
I kept my seat, and what was not my will

proved stronger than my hope. Now I am gone
for all time from the home I knew. I break
my heart to do so, but—' Pure horror then –

a face appeared outside, a figure knocked
as he was running, clinging, that bare face
I knew but not its wild ecstatic look,

he seemed so keen to tell me, Cole, his voice
was loud but could no more get through the glass
than his thin hands – the fingers were all claws,

so old, I had not seen how old he was,
and as he stumbled off they were white twigs,
his fingers, fell to bits, and all he was

spread out or littered by the rails. My legs
were aching now as if I'd broken both.
In pain I placed my hands on my wet cheeks

and found them dry, though hot; I lost my breath
in merely reaching up to gain a seat,
and must have bit my tongue, for my whole mouth

was throbbing. I sat up, my belt was tight,
I loosened it, and to my vague disgust
had wet my lap, so it would seem. Outside

another town went by; its name was lost
to memory, and when the train slowed down
to reach its station, through a sudden mist

was lost to sight as well. There was an N,
a W, then we were off again,
and children going past, a railwayman

who stared while he went past the window-pane,
until his head was almost facing back,
so much I caught his eye. I said, 'I'm fine,'

and swept my trouser-legs, but I felt sick,
however many times I said, 'There, there,
you're going to be okay,' and it said PARK,

the sign beside me when we stopped somewhere,
something DY, then PARK. 'New Lady Park,'
I said aloud now, 'that's the place we are.

Cold out in the park, out by the lake,
the small lagoon beside the roundabouts,'
I said, and all was for my stomach's sake.

I looked out at a garland of tree lights
that decorated here. 'That's very sweet,'
I thought aloud, 'like coloured satellites,

Venus, Moon, Mars. Mars is a planet,'
I said, 'and chocolate bar,' and then was sick
as I had ever been. Someone had seen that,

from further up the carriage, said, 'Now look,'
and went away again. That was a mess,
but it had been too quick, come on too quick,

and I'd no bag to hold. I got my breath,
finally, stood up, went on my way
to where would be a bathroom, not a bath,

a basin, just a tap, then awfully
my chest was hurting, and I sat back down
to sit quite still until it stopped, or I

could live with it, I could. 'I'm on the line.'
I heard my voice sound strange and low. 'The thing
to do is not to sleep,' I said. My spine

now felt as if unwinding like a spring
from in my back; my pessimistic heart
gave up and tried again, could get it going,

shrugged that it might, shrugged that it might not,
it wasn't its own business. Something kicked
about my kidneys and I bent at that,

then repositioned slowly. As I creaked
so gradually to upright with my arm
my guide, 'the way of hope,' somebody croaked,

my voice, my mouth filled up with some thin cream
I spat away; my eyelids now began
to weigh on me, the eyes had barely room

to see myself, but there in the bleak pane
was Edmund Lea, a wild man in a flood,
a man in flesh, an old – a new *old* man . . .

'I'm ill,' I said, 'it's medical first aid
I need.' Nobody was about at all.
I thought the place would smell, but not too bad,

strangely. There was nobody to tell
a single thing to. I unclenched my hands.
Deep breaths I now embarked on, I inhaled

haltingly, I waited, ascertained
what was uncomfortable before I sighed
the warm air out. I said: 'I'm on the mend,'

and, but for throbs and flashes in my head,
the worst was now receding. There was still
the warm and coldness of my legs, inside

and bitter taste of spew, but, all in all,
I felt I could get by despite the pain,
get moving when we got there. 'I'm quite well,'

I told the man who saw me stepping down
into the cold night air at the next stop.
He talked of me, not to me, 'That's the one,

he's made a mess of 7B.' 'What's up?'
'He's made a mess of 7B.' 'What kind?'
'Who gives a fuck?' The fellow raised his cap

as I was passing, 'Thanks a bundle, friend.
Merry bastard Christmas.' 'Eh? You're here,'
they answered my one query in the wind.

I asked a couple passing by quite near
if this was Creslet but they didn't hear.

XLIV

The air was cold and had a slicing wind
it wielded like an expert. I had thought
my coat and things enough, but now they seemed

shrunken on me as I felt my weight
along the dusky lane. My 'accident'
had made it worse: where I'd been warm and wet

I now felt chilly, hurting, and I went
quite delicately, sparing my sore thighs
from the persistent rub and rash. My hands

I turned and saw and turned and saw: my eyes
were runny at the sight, but not with tears
as I remembered them. I felt my face

was fallen to my lower lip, my ears
were buzzing with the engine I had left,
yet I was thankful that the worst distress

of that last ride had faded. My chest heaved
and held a steadied heart, my head was clear,
the nausea less, and every breath I breathed

was calming and restorative. The air
was kindly for the moments when the wind
suspended its assault. I smelt the air,

but, learning little, cocked my head and listened.
At the sound of music, I turned all the way
around to seek the source. 'It's a brass band,'

I said, and limping on, began to see
the cheerful light of a commercial street,
shops open, neon signs, glad, Christmassy,

I made my way there. 'That could be the high street,'
I said. Two girls were passing and they giggled,
as if I was quite wrong in my belief,

and I would have to ask. 'I'm not a local,'
I said as I was turning. Anyhow
both girls had disappeared. An older couple

slowed as they approached me. 'Tell me how,'
I started, 'would I reach the Creslet Centre?'
He grinned and passed by: 'Soldier, you're there now,'

he offered as they went. 'And you ask Santa
get you some new slacks!' the lady called.
Then looking back at me across his shoulder,

she shouted 'Happy Holiday!' I strolled
with confidence beside the busy lane,
and passed so many faces, young and old,

I had a world to choose from when I came
to ask my only question, and the cold
was less among the people. I spent time

looking in the windows, which were filled
with goods and gifts. I felt in my right pocket,
and took out notes and pennies, which I held

and counted for a while. 'Eighteen, I make it,
eighteen pounds in all.' THE CANDLE PALACE
was nearest to me, and I went inside it,

stopping by a sign for STOCKING FILLERS,
and lifting up to sniff an orange candle
labelled *Honey*. Then I tried some others,

a blue one, and a swirl of blues and purples
labelled *Celtic Midnight*. All that seemed
distinctive were the names and colours: *Maple,*

Myrtle, Lime, October, Fennel, Cream.
I weighed them in my hands, my poor old hands.
I put them back and two assistants came

to help me, but they must have changed their minds
because they said it's time to go now. 'Those,'
I wondered, 'smell of nothing.' 'That depends,'

a young boy with a beard replied: 'on who's
doin' the sniffin', mate.' Against a wall
outside I rested. 'Better kick the booze,

eh, matey? Got to learn some self-control.'
The two assistants went inside. The band
began again, along the lane, a carol,

it was; I downed my head towards the wind
and went in its direction. Children singing
'Silent Night' together sounded grand,

and everybody thought so. Bells were ringing
afterwards, but tiny bells on sticks;
a boy held out a basket. 'Sir, something?

Earthquake Relief?' 'Gotta be joking, Becks,
you can't do that. We should be subbin' *him*.'
Another boy asked: 'Been in any earthquakes?'

'No, none at all.' 'Forget it, don't mind them,
you're free to go.' I saw across the road
a little shop called VILLAGE SHOPPE, its name

in amber neon. On a plinth outside
was Jesus with green fairy-lights. I crossed
and joined the queue. The statue if you paid

would tell *Your Personal Future Chart*, which cost
ten pounds a person. I had changed my mind
before a lady took me by the wrist

and led me from the line. 'Not here, my friend,'
she beamed. 'Yes,' I replied, 'I'd rather know
nothing at all these days.' She dropped my hand

quite suddenly, to see me in the glow
the statue made. 'You need a bit of help,
perhaps,' she pondered. 'Any place to go?'

'Oh yes,' I said, 'the Centre.' 'What's up,'
a man was asking. In the same green light
I saw they were in Roman kind of get-up,

togas, sandals, odd this chilly night.
'He needs the Centre? Is there one?' 'Uh-huh.
On Bateman Street. You take the third–fourth right,'

he pointed up the hill, 'and then you're where,
St Madeline's, and then it's the first left,
Bateman Street and then ask someone there.'

'Aren't you cold?' I asked him, and he laughed.
'I'm fucking freezing.' 'Not in front of him,'
the lady said, and I could feel her soft

fingers on my skin, 'he's not to blame,'
then I was pointed in the way to go,
and off I went, repeating like a rhyme

the names of places. It was evening now,
the darker realm of quiet lanes, where great
hedges hid the gardens. Albion Row

was the first right, I noted; 'The *fourth* right,'
I said, and hurried on beneath the trees.
A clump of earth had fallen by my foot,

I noticed, from above. I raised my eyes
and saw it couldn't have. The second right
was Bellevue Row, and I increased the pace,

because someone behind me, out of sight,
was throwing soil at me, and did again,
a spray of earth that missed by a few feet,

a muffled question and this time a stone
that fell and rolled before it hit my shoe,
as I was crossing Compton Row, the turn

before the fourth. He'd wondered if I knew,
the voice, this was the 'Traveller-free Zone,'
and was I leaving. I was trying to,

I did say as I saw a bigger stone
so nearly get me that I felt the breath
it made, before it bounced with a dead clang

against a sign. 'Don't want to catch your death,'
the voice called out, and now I turned to see
a hatted figure yards along the path,

already turning homeward, done with me.
The fourth right was Drake Row, and I turned there,
exhausted by the chase. The frozen sky

was pale enough to show a thin church spire,
to which I made my way. It was indeed
St Madeline's: I stopped and heard a choir

all practising inside. 'They're very good,'
I told the smiling man who hurried by,
'they're right on key.' I went back to the road,

and found a left turn after quite some way:
the sign said Bateman Street. I almost touched
the metal with my forehead till my eye

was absolutely sure. I straightened, stretched,
and set off once again. Along that road,
about ten minutes' walk along, I reached

a larger house than any, white and broad,
set back with shrubs and a brief lawn in front.
There was a sign I went to, and it read:

HERTSREACH: SENIOR CITIZEN LIFE CENTRE.
MANAGER S. WOODMAN. There were lights
in windows, not too many, but in winter

any lights seem friendly. By some seats
some people stood, a little group. A girl
in overalls was offering cigarettes,

and older men all standing by the wall
were listening to her story. 'Please,' I called,
as I approached them, somewhat limping still

with that discomfort, suddenly too cold
with slowing down, 'I wonder . . .' 'Don't you move,'
the girl said, 'it's the best joke in the world,'

and all the men were nodding. 'Man alive,'
she told me, reaching me: 'You ain't equipped.'
A red-haired lady came and with a wave

all sorts of things were going on. We stepped
together into warmth of a wide kitchen,
such heat as made me close my eyes. I kept

my two eyes tightly shut as a young person
helped me from my filthy things and found
warm woollen things instead. 'You smoke a Benson,'

I told her, with my eyes still shut. 'Last count,'
she answered, 'I ain't quit.' When I was warm,
I open my tired eyes and looked around

at where I was. We were in a long room,
a long, bright, decorated room. We sat,
some four of us, the girl, the two of them

who'd helped me in, they shared a double seat,
and I had my own armchair at the end
of a long wooden table partly set

for many people dining. 'Who's your friend,'
a voice asked from across the room. 'Slow down,'
the girl replied, 'he's coming into land,

know what I mean. I'm Simic, this is Brown,
this is Chang,' she said, 'that council twat,
he wants us to wear name-tags, so we're now

known only by our surnames . . . Suck on that.
My name is Tanja, last I heard. What's yours?'
'Edmund.' 'Good. Bravo. That's a good start.

How's Edmund's soup developing there, Dawes?'
'His soup's defrosting, Simic.' 'Get it on,
this man is hungry, aren't you, Edmund.' 'Please,'

I said, 'I am, I'm looking for a woman,
name of Polly.' 'Polly what?' said Chang.
'I don't know, actually. I think this person

works with older people.' 'No such thing,'
said Chang. The other wagged a finger, 'Shame . . .'
'Shut up,' said Tanja, 'Go and wipe something.'

They didn't move. 'And have you got a surname,
Edmund?' Tanja wondered. 'Yes, I have.
It's Lea, just like the river. Just the same.'

'We'll have to take your word for that one, love.
Dawes, where the flaming soup? You want this man
to make it to the morning?' 'Cheese and chive,'

the man who brought it said. I raised the spoon,
and didn't set it down till the white bowl
was showing horses and a hunting scene.

Tanja watched me. 'Seemed to go down well,'
she said to Dawes, who cleared away the things.
'At least it hasn't come back yet.' 'It will,'

one of the others giggled. 'Susan thinks
he's trying to kill the patients off,' said Tanja:
'That's tomorrow's starter.' 'In their drinks,'

said Chang, 'is how he does.' A voice somewhere
wondered, where *is* Susan? 'Hartisle,'
said Dawes, wiping the table, 'gone down there,

get them bubble things.' 'Baubles, Bill,'
said Tanja when he'd shut the door. All three
burst into laughter, and they cried until

'Okay,' said Tanja. 'Help for Mr Lea.
Does anyone know a *Polly*?' 'Reckon so,'
the voice across the room said. 'Actually,'

at which a lean grey man came into view
in a red dressing-gown, 'it's Susan's name.
Or was, when she first came here. How do you do?

Pyman. Bob, please call me. Only came
to do the hedges! Still do, when it's warm.'

XLV

'Can't do it all now, so she's got machines,
and I'm a stand-in merely, still,' said Bob,
'it keeps me off the streets, and then there's things

to do these days we didn't have, what's up
around the place. I keep abreast these days,
you know, you'd call me a connected chap.'

' "And what's new on the many webs?" he goes,'
said Tanja, 'there's no stopping him.' 'There's not,'
said Bob, 'I'll get repetitive disease,

won't I, if I don't watch myself.' 'So what,
we all got that these days,' Tanja reflected.
'Except Ed here. You need a sandwich, Ed?'

'Oh, absolutely not.' You got it covered,
excellent. You lot all out on strike,
is that it? Go and do the Christmas cupboard,

or there's no luncheon. Not you, worldwide bloke,'
she said to Pyman as he rose with them.
'You take a bloomin' day off, for Pete's sake.'

When she and I were left in the long room,
she said: 'They promise us, the council lot,
new storage space, but then we get the same

palaver every year. And they forget.
Not Bob, I mean, and the residents are fine,
but it's these youngsters, want to sit and chat.

They think it's holiday for them. I mean,
this place was built for ten or thereabouts,
and now there's twenty, plus these types. It's wine!'

she cried in answer to a distant shout.
'It's wine in there, don't touch it. Here's her car,'
she said, and we heard gravel and saw lights;

then laden with her bags inside the door,
Polly was calling down to someone: 'No,
those are for New Year. No. For New Year.

I left a note. The white box is for now.
Is that Bob there? The culprit, we've a clear –
Tanja, go and sort them. Hate that town,

that Christmas Hut is rubbish. All that's there
is tinsel.' Then she saw me. 'Which is pointless,
really. Since we have that.' 'Edmund's here,'

said Tanja: 'he feels better.' 'Candle Palace,'
I told them, 'Candle Palace.' 'Well. Next time,'
said Polly. 'Tanja, go and sort those slackers.

It's like last year, they'll drink us out of wine.'
She slumped into a chair, still in her coat.
'You had your soup then. And that scarf there's mine,

would you believe . . . Now you've an ancient right
to stay, we have a rule, if we've a space.
I said to Mrs Taplow we were tight,

and would she mind a little rest-in-peace,
so off she pops two weeks ago. Some girl's
bagged the spot mid-February. It's yours

till then.' 'If I do stay. There's still those rules.'
Polly took her coat off and sat back,
gazing at me, folding it the while.

'I think you broke those, Edmund. They look broke.'
The staff all reappeared, and residents
would step inside the room, but 'Men at work!'

the young men said: 'You want to see your presents?'
Polly had Tanja show me to a room,
a small room with a window on the distance,

lights scattered out for miles. 'That's where I'm from,'
I said. 'Same here,' she went. 'You walk forever
in that direction. Got the heating on,

Edmund, but it's slow. The switch is there
for all the lights, it works from by the bed,
and that's a bell for, bicycle repair,

you know, if need be. Mini-bar,' she said,
opening an empty chest. 'Oh well,
can always dream. I gotta go.' I stood,

the longest time, hands pressed against the chill
of the cold window and the colder night.
I heard the bedside heater knock and burble,

heard clatter from downstairs and a great shout
of laughter, heard the traffic far away.
Is it – east? I'd asked her. 'Just about,'

she'd said. I traced the word on the pink duvet,
was sitting there a while. I went downstairs
at last, found Tanja when I'd lost my way,

and she escorted me through two swing doors
into a little sitting-room. We watched
television, all her fellow workers

came and went, it was a film we watched
about some future men. They got me tea,
and then warm wine. 'Ed looks pretty bushed,'

I heard, then whispers, someone prodded me,
but I was joking. 'I'm as right as rain,'
I let them know. I drifted finally,

was shaking sleep away when Polly came,
yawning: 'Yo, clear off, it's Christmas Day,
you people. Check the kitchen, the blue room,

the system. Not you, Edmund, you can stay,
but you look tired.' I rose and said, 'I do,'
and said goodnights to all, and found my way

to my great satisfaction to my new
abode, as Tanja called it, my new dorm.
I felt so tired I even told my view

that it could wait till morning. It was warm.
I struggled in, and waited with the light
still on, and I took breaths and I stayed calm,

till finally I tugged the switch and sat
gingerly back against the pillows. 'Please,'
was all I said, and closed my eyes. *Too hot,*

both feet, was my next thought, and both my eyes
were smarting. I was where? I felt the noise
of the train all around me, no surprise –

that is my life, and nothing lovely stays,
I heard a voice say – then I saw the light
of grey and rainy sky, the stifled rays

of sun behind the clouds about to set,
and why was I in here? Was this a place
I'd come to in a walk, an empty hut

I'd reached, or brought the child to? In that case,
where was the train? This wasn't it. The sun
was peering wanly through the clouds – too late

to save the day, I grumbled. It had gone
to earth without a waking thought. I sat,
was propping myself up, I had not one

memory of the day that had done that,
dragged me to this spot. Where was my train?
It ought to be here now, it's not here yet,

I said; it always finds me. Still the sun
was visible, strange yellow that could mean
stormy clouds tomorrow. Well, go on,

I muttered to it, down with you, the train
will pick me up, and then it's time for drinks,
it's time to wash and learn the verse again,

chat with HH, see what HH thinks,
plan tomorrow, watch the last of you,
say good riddance, but it made no sense,

it made no sense, the sun was still in view,
it hung there like a medal. I felt mocked,
that it would so prolong its overdue

departure. Time, to turn the screw, had stopped,
was my conclusion. The complicit skies
would hold it there for ever. I had slept

my last, the light would lever my poor eyes
forever open to that leering sun
now stepping backwards – *and I realised,*

and, as I realised I saw the dawn,
I saw the dawn, and I remembered all.
And everywhere, and everything, was gone,

and everything, and everywhere, was still,
and from the sill I hung to see that sweet
and clouded yellow apparition sail

its light into the sky: and that slight heat,
however distant, born. Right in its eye
I looked, it was too weak and pale to hurt,

and I too felt a strengthening, and I
rose myself to stand and look out there,
survey the vast anticipating sky –

how far the sun must have to sail before
it thinks of its decline! If I could spend
the day unblinking, seeing still how far,

surely the day would be too slow to end . . .
I stood back from the light. Time finds me there,
beside the window, toast in my left hand,

biro in my right. This table here
we brought up from the cellar, my work-station.
I've got my papers and my swivel chair,

my coasters and my snaps. A rare occasion
when sunrise gets around my painted table
quicker than I do! My situation

eases slowly, this and that new trouble.
Tanja sorts things out for me. Last week
I got a passport. I don't choose to travel.

I read in Polly's car. I say I'll make
the trip to Hartisle, Polly thinks I should.
She says she'll show me round, 'though I don't rate

that place at all, you know I never did.
It's just, you have to do it.' I won't yet.
'Plenty of time,' she says. Through Creslet Wood

we walk together. One time I did read
a piece that said a crowd on Christmas Eve
had gathered 'for the raising of the dead,'

but none of it was accurate. 'Our love,'
a pictured lady said, 'exceeds one man.'
The writer said the crowds were well-behaved

and had dispersed. 'Besides,' his ending ran,
'there's Christmas to attend to!' Every week
the eldest daughter of a dying man

arrives to visit and she stays for cake.
'You're Edmund Lea,' she said with her mouth full,
'if you don't mind my saying, no mistake.

We were at school together, all in all
that's fifty years ago. You disappeared.
He disappeared, Susan. But you're well,

I see. I love this cake. I'm Janet Baird.
Janet Bow as was.' I write these things,
I add them to the old account I had

by heart the night I came, so many things.
I try hard not to shape it, it's just there,
the life I went through. As to what it means,

I leave to whom I leave it to. But here,
by sunrise you would tend to see me, last
window on the block. The sky is clear,

the page is empty, and I face the east.
When nothing comes, and nothing sometimes will,
I write to Polly. 'Entered in the lists,'

she says I have, for her. At our stone wall
the garden ends, then the allotment field,
and the wood's edge beyond, about a mile,

no more, then scattered houses, Eastholt,
Latcham, the main road. When the light fades
I'm never here, I haven't watched a sunset

lately, if you want to know. Besides,
I'm to be found with Pyman, playing chess
at that hour, in The Castle. Or sometimes

off to see some landmark. Pyman's best
for keeping up with things; he's got the news,
he always has, and he says I'm the best

for knowing nothing – teaching me to use
new micro skills, he is. It's taking weeks.
He says, 'It's out there, Lea, no time to lose!'

But there's no time like now, when the first streaks
of the cold light appear. The furthest trees
become distinct. It's Saturday that breaks

today, and all is clear across the skies.
The first ray's always warm, or to my mind
it is, that pioneer. My heavy eyes

will hold it like a rope in my weak hands,
and soon all light appears, nothing but light
is lifting from the earth, over the land,

and I will look until it starts to hurt,
stare out that light, refuse to turn away,
though all is forming in me to a word

which fades again, too bright in the bright day
for ink to cling to or for soul to say.